OXFORD MONOGRAPHS ON
SOCIAL ANTHROPOLOGY

General Editors

E. E. EVANS-PRITCHARD   B. E. B. FAGG

A. C. MAYER   D. F. POCOCK

Big Men
and
Cargo Cults

BY

GLYNN COCHRANE

M.A.(DUBLIN), D.PHIL.(OXON.)

CLARENDON PRESS · OXFORD

1970

Oxford University Press, Ely House, London W.1

GLASGOW NEW YORK TORONTO MELBOURNE WELLINGTON
CAPE TOWN SALISBURY IBADAN NAIROBI DAR ES SALAAM LUSAKA ADDIS ABABA
BOMBAY CALCUTTA MADRAS KARACHI LAHORE DACCA
KUALA LUMPUR SINGAPORE HONG KONG TOKYO

MADE AND PRINTED IN GREAT BRITAIN
BY WILLIAM CLOWES AND SONS, LIMITED
LONDON AND BECCLES

FOREWORD
by Kenelm Burridge

Writing this foreword is both privilege and pleasure. The author is a friend and colleague; the subject one in which we have a common interest. But rather than commend the book with some introductory remarks on the nature of cargo movements—Cochrane has plenty to say on this very cogently in the pages which follow—I propose something more general.

Before fieldwork became a professional requirement—scarcely three academic generations ago—anthropologists had to construct their theories on the nature of society and its institutions on the basis of evidence provided by others, mainly administrative officers and missionaries. But when, in order to obtain more specific and adequate data, and within the context of a colonialism characterized by different and competing political aims, anthropologists started to go to the field themselves, the diversity of operational interests expressed itself more acutely, and co-operation sometimes degenerated into mutual recriminations. And this although, perhaps because, the anthropologist had to rely on the personal help and hospitality of both administrative officers and missionaries. Nevertheless, even when they did not themselves become anthropologists in the professional sense, administrative officers and missionaries made many refreshing and valuable contributions to a young and developing subject. Their works stud the literature.

This theme of co-operation enlivened by divergent and competing interests needs stressing. It exists today in different forms and expressions. For even though colonialism as such is of the past, the supposed purity of scientific research is often thought to be endangered by what appear to be the implicit and suspect aims of foundations and governmental bodies whose financial support makes the research possible. Yet anthropology, especially in Britain, has never been wholly the product of academics scooping out niches for themselves in universities. It was born, and is continually secreted in, a social system and more general cultural milieu uniquely remarkable for imbuing in its members an unquenchable thirst for new knowledge. Warlike, expansive, greedy for wealth, coercive and infected with a sense of its own superiority and virtue—certainly. But also eager to find out about other cultures and civilizations, record and systematize what had been seen and heard, and bring this new knowledge into its own ambience of awareness. Explorers, adventurers, soldiers and merchants contributed: whether the knowledge gained was filed as some kind of purposeful 'intelligence', or as innocent, 'research data', the main burden of piecing together the information fell to those who, living among strange peoples, attempted to bring order, teach, study and draw inferences. Each gave shape to a discipline whose core is the revelation of man's many-tinctured awareness of the moral community. In this discipline the different purposes involved in obtaining the information may be reconciled and even justified.

Cochrane is an administrator turned anthropologist. He studied anthropology at Oxford before setting out on his first tour as an administrative officer, and it was as an administrator in the Solomon islands in Melanesia that he collected the material and formulated many of the ideas contained in these pages. The great mass of the general evidence relating to the topic on which he writes has been contributed by missionaries and administrative officers— whose primary work and interests had little in common with those which many anthropologists consider appropriate to their own image of themselves. The main source for the first part of the book is F. E. Williams, who made his investigations while he was Government Anthropologist in Papua-New Guinea, and who was always torn between what he considered the demands of his subject and its moral implications, and his duty to cooperate with the often quite different aims of the colonial administration. Williams's chief, the Governor of Papua, was Hubert Murray, a man of pragmatic approach and high principle, who regularly corresponded with his brother, Professor Gilbert Murray, in Oxford, on anthropology and the philosophy of colonial administration. Professor Murray, Ranulph Marret and Jane Harrison frequently met and collaborated. The wheel comes almost full circle, describing a process that has occurred times without number in India, Malaya, Africa and the South Seas. Like the 'big man' of whom Cochrane writes so well, he and his book figure and transcend the conflicts involved in the attempt to understand, use, or change the institutions and contingencies of a strange culture.

In the first part of the book, Cochrane reworks the material of Williams and others on the Western Elema, who live along Orokolo Bay in the Gulf Division, Papua, and the 'Vailala Madness', a

particularly startling expression of that genre of activity generally
known as 'cargo cults'. Cochrane's task is a complicated one. He
has to show the convergences and conflicts of interest as between
the Elema themselves and the aims and activities of missionaries
and administrators. He has to penetrate the different evaluations of
administrator, missionary, and anthropologist on events which
took place nearly half a century ago. He has to relate these events,
and what others thought of them, to the ways in which the Elema
might have represented them to themselves. Finally, he has to
present events and relations in such a way that, contained within a
consistent intellectual or theoretical framework, they constitute a
trans-culturally valid ontological statement.

The reader may judge for himself how well Cochrane has carried
out these tasks. Yet the merit lies not so much in the conclusion—
that the Elema had lost the means of identifying themselves, the
components of their culture, and their criteria of integrity and
greatness, to themselves and in relation to the white man—which,
with the wisdom of hindsight, might have been directly intuited,
as in the method and argument. For these, whether regarded as
substantiating an intuition, or leading to a conclusion, reveal a
certain pattern or structure of relations which are of value in any
study broadly determined by race relations, rulers and ruled, or
privileged and under-privileged. Cochrane first prepared himself
by a close study of documentary sources. Reaching certain conclusions on the basis of the documentary evidence, he tests these
conclusions against events—'Marching Rule' and the 'Doliasi
Custom movement'—in which he was personally involved either
at second-hand or directly as an administrative officer. And again
he develops the interplay between an indigenous community,
missionaries, and administrative officers. Now, however, additional
elements are drawn into the web he spins. There are European,
Chinese and half-caste traders to be reckoned with. Further,
Cochrane himself is not only a participating anthropologist, he is
'the administration' and, because the situation forces him into
offering advice, sympathy and explanation derived from his own
personal upbringing and make-up, he is also as though a missionary—attempting to show mistaken or misguided fellow human
beings a way out of their predicament.

This intense and many stranded personal involvement may seem
to deny the work its objective and scientific status. If so, all social

anthropologists are tarred with the same brush. For few would
claim an objectivity on the level of observation. Though the gathering of data may be more or less systematic, the science of the
subject is contained in the way in which observations and, more
particularly, perceptions—themselves derived from the transformational experience entailed in fieldwork—reveal a set of internally
consistent and related propositions which constitute a 'theory' or
'explanatory framework'; in the intellectual elegance and usefulness of this framework for answering questions offered by other
social ambiences remote in time or space; in the susceptibility of
the theory to criticism, refinement, or falsification. If an anthropologist were to imagine or dream his data—what piece of fieldwork is not, in part, like a dream?—then criticism would have to
go to the way in which the parts of the dream were interrelated and
contained within a revelatory logic. Inconsistencies would involve
either redreaming the dream (more detailed or better ethnography),
or reworking the theory or logic, or both. This, indeed, is the way
the subject has developed. Yet while theory guides observation
and perception, and more acute observations and perceptions
modify, or reveal new, theories, the quality and force of the dialectic is to be found in an imaginative reach towards an objective
truth in which rationalization or intellectualization is seen to
correspond with action.

It cannot be said, however, that studies of cargo movements
have, in general, been remarkable for their elegance and sociological consistency. Perhaps it is too early for that—barely two
generations of systematic investigation—perhaps the study of that
to which we ourselves are heirs, and generators, presents special
difficulties, lies too close to the bone. Yet Cochrane comes pretty
near. His explanatory logic is based on the relations between a
system of statuses on the one hand, and a system of transcendent
symbols on the other. That in which conflict is inevitable is related
to that in which conflict is overcome. Elegant enough. Revealing
too. The basic detail of the model is provided by a reformulation of
the Elema material in the light of fresh theory. Statuses and symbols emerge from an interrelation of myths, life crises, and
economic and political relations. Not simply the consequences of
economic deprivation, nor, solely, an over-enthusiastic response to
missionary teaching or particular kinds of administrative action,
the events of a cargo movement are seen to correspond with an

effort to overcome the dissonances between statuses and the symbols which guarantee their worthwhileness. Elements of racism as such shrink in importance. While wider political, economic and religious considerations clearly feed into the situation, their relevance lies in the ways they do, or do not converge in statuses whose interrelationships and means of attainment are consistently ordered as to an integrity of achievement, merit, reward and moral responsibility. A status should demonstrably satisfy that in man which aspires beyond the conflicts inevitable to having power and influence. And it does this, Cochrane says, when appropriately related to particular kinds of symbol.

What is neat about this is its usefulness as a model for studies of processes of social change as distinct from history. The historical narrative may be contained within the sociological framework; there is no need to resort to neo-evolutionism; the history and sociology become complementary rather than antagonistic. Further, no damage is done to that very necessary working assumption of an equilibrium in social affairs. For instead of being seen as a difficult anomaly, the resolution of the conflicts entailed in the processes of change, or disequilibrium, may be seen as contained within the relations implied by an old and new equilibrium. And the relations contained in the triad may be seen as functions of the relations between statuses and their guaranteeing symbols.

Having made the imaginative effort, it is only too easy to lapse into the mechanical, difficult to sustain and nurture the generative insight through the tangled mass of evidence that must be adduced. Cochrane keeps his balance. Though, because he could not live with a people for months on end, and had to communicate in Pidgin, Cochrane's ethnography is an administrator's rather than an anthropologist's, he uses it anthropologically, as evidence for what he has to say about the variety of systems which make up a social structure. In all, the analysis leads into a set of conclusions which, though specialists may dispute them for a while, will certainly carry the subject forward. More important than this perhaps, is that Cochrane seems to have undergone that transformational experience entailed in living another culture which, in continuously demanding a further penetration of the mystery of man's social condition, is the hallmark of anthropologist, missionary, and colonial administrator alike. From this same experience, it is useful to remember, come those new discoveries and visions of the nature of man whose attempts at realization permeate the events and activities of a cargo movement.

Let Cochrane now show how his administrative duties, research interests, and experience have combined to make a rare contribution.

K.O.L.B.

ACKNOWLEDGMENTS

This book has grown out of a doctoral thesis, presented at the University of Oxford in 1967. I owe a great deal to my academic supervisor at Oxford, Dr. K. O. L. Burridge, whose patient and sympathetic guidance at Oxford, and while I was in the Solomons, helped clarify my ideas. This study has drawn on his insight into these movements. To Professor Raymond Firth and Dr. D. F. Pocock I am indebted for advice and encouragement. Finally, I wish to thank the staff of the Clarendon Press for assistance in compiling the index and in drawing the maps and diagrams.

CONTENTS

LIST OF MAPS

LIST OF FIGURES

PROLOGUE

In July 1962 I was appointed an administrative officer (cadet) by the Western Pacific High Commission and in the same month assumed duty in the British Solomon Islands Protectorate. I remained in the Solomons as a Government officer for the next five years. During this period, while attached to the Department of District Administration, I served in each of the four administrative districts of the Protectorate, Malaita, eastern, western, and central districts. In my first tour of duty, which lasted from 1962 till 1964, I served as a District Officer; in my next tour of duty 1965-7, I served in the W.P.H.C. secretariat in Honiara, the capital of the Solomons, and then as District Commissioner, Eastern District.

While at Oxford University, during the academic year 1961-2, undergoing the year's administrative training for cadet entrants to the Colonial Service, I had read the diploma course in social anthropology, so that by the time I arrived in the Solomons many of the theories regarding the nature of 'cargo' cults were familiar.

Most of my service in the Solomons was spent in Malaita and eastern districts which had been strongly affected by 'Marching Rule', a set of activities, lasting from 1944 till 1952 and cognate to 'cargo' cults, which has engaged the interest of a number of anthropologists, sociologists and administrative officers.[1]

As I grew more familiar with the people, their thought, and way of life, and with the additional insight that my Government service had given me, I began to doubt whether existing theories regarding the nature of 'cargo' cults had provided a satisfactory explanation for 'Marching Rule'.

'Marching Rule' was intimately involved with the Melanesians' way of life and way of thinking; and the effects of the movement continue to influence the contemporary scene in the Solomons. Changes engendered by 'Marching Rule' have done a great deal for development in the Solomons. Large numbers of Solomon Islanders moved down from the high bush to the coast to await the coming of 'cargo'; they have remained on the coast despite the goods' failure to arrive. They are now producing cash crops, and the new villages on the coast are within easy reach of the administration.

[1] See pp. 145-158.

The local government framework, which had been in existence for some years before 'Marching Rule', without attracting much interest, was later supported by the adherents of 'Marching Rule'. It is often remarked that contemporary life in Solomon Island villages is dull and uninteresting for the people; the enthusiasm, sense of purpose, and recognition of common aims given to many areas in the Solomons by the 'Marching Rule' movement presented a totally different picture.

My examination of 'Marching Rule' did not arise simply as the result of personal interest. The kinds of information that come from sociological investigation are of great value in the formulation of administrative policy, especially since traces of 'Marching Rule' ideology are still visible in the Solomons. Attempts to provide a sound economic basis for the Solomons by stimulating copra production rely on an intimate knowledge of Melanesian incentives and disincentives to production. This in turn involves an appreciation of Melanesian notions regarding the nature of status and power.

Within this background framework of objectives I began to notice that ideas on the nature of power and status that were exhibited during 'Marching Rule' appeared to differ only in intensity from the ideas that prompted Melanesians to enter small-scale business enterprise or politics in contemporary Solomon Island society. Yet by using existing theories regarding the nature of 'cargo' cults I was unable to reach any satisfactory understanding in my attempts to grasp the significance of current developments.

Unfortunately there is little current anthropological research being undertaken in the Solomons; 'exotic' societies in Papua, New Guinea, continue to receive much more attention.

The British Solomon Islands Protectorate is a difficult territory to administer. The population of 132,000 live on hundreds of scattered islands, having no common language, and possessing few natural resources. In comparison with the pre-Second World War picture, development of Government services since the war has been impressive. Considerable emphasis has been placed on training Solomon Islanders for responsible positions.

Medical services and education were left largely to the Missions in pre-war days. At present, primary and secondary education is provided for children in Government schools staffed by trained

Education officers. These schools are situated in each of the four districts of the Protectorate. Large numbers of Solomon Islanders are sent overseas every year for tertiary or technical education. The Government's policy is to replace expatriates with suitably qualified Solomon Islanders as soon as possible.

Each of the districts now has its own hospital. These hospitals are staffed by European doctors and have operating facilities for major surgery. Dressing stations for treatment of minor illnesses and maternity clinics for expectant mothers have been established at strategic points on all the major islands. Yaws disease has been totally wiped out; a major portion of the population has been immunized against tuberculosis; and with the assistance of the World Health Organization a campaign to eradicate malaria has been mounted.

Government expenditure had risen from a pre-war annual average of £65,000–£70,000 to an annual expenditure of over £2 millions by 1966. The number of civil servants in the Protectorate had risen from a pre-war total of 350–400 to over 1,500 in 1966, the majority of whom were Solomon Islanders.

A Local Government Council was created on Malaita in 1953. Since then, similar councils have been established, covering all the islands in the Protectorate with the exception of the remote Polynesian islands of Tikopia and Anuta. These councils have, under the 1963 Local Government Ordinance, a wide variety of administrative, legislative, and financial powers; powers which are similar in scope to those possessed by a local government authority in the United Kingdom.

The ultimate local authority is the Legislative Council. The Legislative Council legislates with the 'advice and consent' of the High Commissioner and subject to the Secretary of State's power of disallowance. It was established in 1960 and during the early days of its existence members were nominated by the High Commissioner. The 1967 (Constitution) Order in Council has made provision for the direct election of fourteen Solomon Island members to the Legislative Council. An official majority is still maintained and there is, as yet, no ministerial system.

Copra remains the major export of the Protectorate although considerable progress has been made in establishing a forest industry, in geological surveying for economic deposits of minerals, and in other attempts to diversify the economy. Contemporary

copra export figures emphasize that development of the infrastructure of the economy by improving services and communications does not automatically result in increased indigenous
production.[1] The amount of copra exported in 1966 was under
25,000 tons; a figure which was slightly lower than the pre-Second
World War annual average export figure.

Solomon Islanders obtain the majority of their money from sale
of copra. When I learnt that 85 per cent of the annual total was
produced by expatriates and Solomon Islanders living in the western district it seemed probable that islands such as Malaita and
San Cristobal had small monetary incomes since they were only
producing small amounts of copra. This was surprising: many of
the theories accounting for the rise of 'Marching Rule' had suggested that the movement had arisen because Solomon Islanders had
felt a strong sense of economic deprivation. But if economic conditions had not improved, and the copra figures suggested that they
had not, then I was left with the problem of explaining why
'Marching Rule' had died away and why there had been no more
cults.

In 1962 I found that the production of copra on San Cristobal
was approximately 1,600 tons. This copra was bought on the beach
by Chinese traders who then had it shipped to Honiara, the capital
of the Protectorate. Copra was bought for cash and since Chinese
ships all carried a range of trade goods which represented the only
store many of the islanders ever saw, the Chinese expected to
recoup some of the money that was paid for copra.

The Chinese calculated that they seldom recouped more than
25–50 per cent of the money paid for copra. From statistics available in the district office it was possible to make a rough calculation
of the total amount of money paid out by the San Cristobal people
in rates, licences, etc., the only other forms of expenditure.

Results showed that (since the number of transactions in which
European money was used in day-to-day life in the villages were
minimal) substantial amounts of money were being saved. I found
that money was not only being saved but was also being buried in
the ground in the same way that traditional valuables were buried.
This pattern was being repeated on other islands because the
Commonwealth Trading Bank of Australia, the only bank in the
Protectorate, reported that due to the fact that money was not

[1] D. G. Cochrane 1968.

circulating they continually had to import large amounts of notes and specie.[1]

When I toured on foot through the villages on San Cristobal I could see that the people possessed relatively few European goods.

Often I came across Solomon Islanders, retired civil servants and the like, who had worked for Europeans all their lives, and in all cases they had re-adopted their traditional pattern of life with no regrets for the comforts of European civilization. Solomon Islanders would tell how they had been fed by the Americans during the war, though they never commented that they had developed a taste for European food.

Undoubtedly the natives appreciated the benefits of the European way of life. Corrugated iron, bush knives, axes, and the like were useful. But the desire to have these things did not seem to have been strong enough to alter the traditional pattern of life. Many of the natives lived in areas where there was an abundance of coconuts, yet they did not make copra. Nor could it be held that the people were lazy; they toiled daily in their gardens during the hottest hours of the day. Young men would leave their home islands to work on plantations for an amount of money which could be earned in a few days in a properly organized copra-producing community. The Solomon Islanders seemed to lack leadership and a desire to have a regular cash income.

These observations led me to wonder about the Melanesian pattern of wants. Were money, tobacco, rice, and calico desired for their own sake, as symbols of European culture, or was something else involved? It appeared that when many of the people on San Cristobal had money they did not spend it on European goods, they kept it in the same way that traditional valuables had been kept—locked in boxes or buried in the ground.

In traditional Solomon Island society, valuables had been a measurement of a man's status, and wealth was often expended to gain status. Did this same value system still apply in the Solomons?

Wahinua, a Melanesian of about fifty years of age, lived in Tawani village near Kira Kira, the administrative headquarters of the eastern district. Nine years previously when the last 'big man' in Tawani village had died Wahinua had announced that he would succeed him.

---

[1] Personal communication from Mr. J. F. Cameron, Manager of the Commonwealth Trading Bank of Australia, Honiara.

Wahinua went to work for the agricultural officer at Kira Kira as a cookboy in 1960, a short while after the death of the 'big man' in Tawani village. At the same time Wahinua's two nephews joined the Public Works Department in Kira Kira as labourers.

They worked for six years until they had saved enough money to buy thirty pigs; then they stopped work and returned to Tawani village. All money-making activities in Tawani village ceased. No copra was made because all the coconuts were required to make puddings, and no vegetables could be taken to Kira Kira market because they were also needed for the feast.

Wahinua had always been an extremely hard-working man and, over the years, through entering into a large number of reciprocal relationships, and as a result of shrewd marriages he had a large number of people obligated to him. By calling on all these people at one time to repay their obligation Wahinua was able to organize the giving of a feast.

A very large feast was made and Wahinua gained the status of 'big man'. The total cost of the feast, which lasted only for one day, was £1,200. Wahinua had had a choice: instead of making his feast, the amount of money he had saved through hard work over the years could have been used to purchase European goods. But Wahinua had chosen the status of 'big man' rather than the kinds of goods that had made up the 'cargo' of 'Marching Rule'. This experience raised a doubt as to whether the Solomon Islanders really had a Europeanized pattern of material wants. In Wahinua's case possession of status had been more important than possession of wealth.

In 1962 the village of Ambu near the administrative centre of Auki on Malaita decided to buy a rice-hulling machine. How or why they decided to buy the machine nobody knew. But they had collected £1,500 towards the total cost of the machine, which was in the region of £3,000. The District Commissioner attempted to dissuade the villagers from buying the machine. He pointed out that there was no road by which the machine could be taken to Ambu village and that the people did not grow any rice. The villagers remained adamant that they were going to buy the machine. Showing considerable enthusiasm they built a road and planted some rice.

Eventually the rice-hulling machine arrived and it was installed in the centre of the village with great celebrations. Four tons of rice were hulled and the machine broke down. Though spare parts were repeatedly brought all the way from Japan, the machine seldom worked again because there was no more rice to hull. In view of the gradual deterioration of the machine the District Commissioner eventually persuaded a Honiara firm to make an offer to purchase which represented two-thirds of the original price. The Ambu villagers refused to sell and their large piece of 'cargo' remained rusting in the village.[1]

My experience also showed me that Solomon Islanders were extremely sensitive to any suggestion that they had no status. There were frequent cases in the Magistrate's court where one native had told another that he was a 'rubbish man', that is a man with no status. Inevitably this insult led to a fight. Knowledge that the law would exact a penalty for assault or breach of the peace seemed of little consequence in relation to the desire to avenge personal honour.

Since the decline of 'Marching Rule' small cults have occurred from time to time which appeared to have strong similarities with that movement although there has been no mention of cargo. Five or six years ago an extraordinary cult grew up under the leadership of a man named Moro on the 'weather' coast of Guadalcanal.[2]

The 'weather' coast of Guadalcanal, containing the Tasimboko sub-District where the cult was centred, is an inhospitable place. The coastline is exposed and it is impossible to get ashore from a ship for a large part of the year. Very small amounts of copra were produced in the area because of shipping difficulties, and there was no other way in which money could be earned locally. The people showed a marked reluctance to work as plantation labourers.

Few Europeans visited the 'weather' coast because of the isolation and because all travelling had to be done on foot. There were no Government schools, and little interest was taken in central or local government politics. The 'weather' coast was socially, economically, and politically backward in relation to other areas on the island of Guadalcanal.

In 1965, when the Acting High Commissioner visited the Roman Catholic Mission station of Avu Avu on the 'weather' coast, the

---

[1] Details of this incident were given by a colleague, Mr. J. L. Pepys-Cockerell, at a South Pacific Commission conference on small-scale business enterprise, Honiara, 1963.

[2] This has now been written up by W. Davenport and G. Coker, 1967.

people presented a list of grievances. They complained about lack of educational facilities and said that the Government had failed to provide a way for the people to earn money. 'Weather' coast people also said that not enough was being done to preserve traditional customs, and that the Local Government Council was inefficient.

These complaints were legitimate to a degree, but it was also true that many of the facilities had been provided by the Government and that the people did not use them. The Council had offered to build a road if the 'weather' coast people would assist by working voluntarily on it; the Agricultural Department had tried to introduce new cash crops in the area but the people refused to grow them; and 'weather' coast people had shown no interest in central or local government politics.

Matters eventually came to a head when a delegation led by a man named Moro went to Honiara and offered to buy their 'freedom' from the Council for £100. The offer was made to the District Commissioner, and it was intended to purchase immunity from all Council taxes and licence fees. But there was no anti-Government or anti-European feeling.

The ideology and organization of the Moro movement were interesting. Myths were in existence which traced Moro's ancestry back to the coming of the first people on Guadalcanal. Moro claimed to be 'King' of the Island. Other myths dealt with the importance of preserving traditions, a feature which had been dominant in the 'Marching Rule' movement. But there was no 'cargo' myth.

The organization of the Moro movement showed a number of similarities with 'Marching Rule'. Taxes were collected, fines were levied, and it was reported that 'courts' had been set up to deal with offences against traditional customs. Moro always had a retinue of 'guards' with him (these 'guards' were reminiscent of the guards of honour that had been provided for 'Marching Rule' leaders) wherever he went. Other 'guards' were stationed at the four corners of Moro's house to protect the movement's money which was inside the house in a very large wooden box.

Under Moro's leadership, 'schools' and new villages were built. Coconuts were planted and plans were made for other money-making activities. Numerous visits were paid to Honiara to explain the meaning of the new movement. But the movement was not repressed by the Government since it contained many admirable features. Even though there were some obvious links with the 'Marching Rule' movement there was no mention of 'cargo'.[1]

One aspect of the Melanesian character which was strikingly demonstrated during the phase of 'Marching Rule' was discipline, rigidly imposed by the autocratic few upon the many receptive adherents of the movement. Of this virtue, for such it must be counted, I was myself a witness when under happier auspices I attended the first meeting of the Malaita Council held at Auki, in January 1953, and I shall not easily forget the spectacle of three thousand persons rising to their feet at a gesture from their leader, and repeating as one man the words of the Lord's Prayer which preceded the ceremony of the appointment of the chosen 'big man' as President. The attentive silence of the crowd during the remainder of the proceedings was no less impressive. This amenability to discipline is of obvious importance in the development of political and social institutions.*

The discipline of the Moro movement was no less impressive than that of the 'Marching Rule' movement.

There were none of the physical symptoms or extreme emotionalism that have been present in other movements. In relation to conventional 'cargo' cult movements the organization was similar though the ideology and declared aims of the movement appeared to be different. But cargo cults had been thought of as millenary movements, as psychological phantasies or simply as irrational phenomena: the Moro movement, which had so many similarities with conventional cargo cults, appeared to be entirely sensible and pragmatic. Moro had not rejected the Government. He had stressed that his people needed Government assistance.

Discipline seemed to be tied up in some way with leadership which in turn was related to concepts of status and wealth. But 'Marching Rule' had been thought of as an anti-white movement containing an implicit demand by Solomon Islanders for a greater say in the determination of their affairs. I found no trace of anti-white feeling during my stay in the Solomons. The Moro movement had no visible anti-white tendencies.

* 'The Political Development of the Solomon Islands.' A note on political progress, written by the High Commissioner at the time of 'Marching Rule', Sir Robert Stanley.

[1] I am indebted to Mr. J. L. O. Tedder, District Commissioner Central District, for information on this movement. Further details were given by a number of Solomon Islanders from the 'weather' coast and by Mr. Robin Plummer, Agricultural Officer.

Late in November 1962, while visiting the Roman Catholic Mission station at Manevovo on the south-east coast of San Cristobal, the European priest-in-charge commented on a request by his parishioners. They asked to put up large wooden signs on their land. The signs bore the inscription: 'This Land Belongs To The Catholic Corporation Of Manevovo.' At the time there seemed to be no reasonable explanation for the signs. The priest said that not only had his people put the signs on their own land, but that they had also placed a considerable number on other people's land. The following day when I visited the Protestant village of St. John Tawarogha, some miles away, I found one of these signs in the middle of the village. As I examined the sign a crowd of very agitated villagers approached carrying clubs and spears. Several spears were thrown into the ground, and I was beginning to wonder what it was all about, when the village chief Henry Fagataro spoke. Fagataro had been a special constable during 'Marching Rule' and was regarded (by my colleagues) as a sound and sensible individual.

On this occasion he was practically incoherent with rage. He said that Government (meaning myself) need not think that they were the ignorant savages that they had been five hundred years ago. They knew that Mr. Sitai (a Solomon Island D.O. who was my predecessor) had given permission for the signs to be put up on their land and that was why they had not taken them down. They also knew that the Pope was going to send an army to the Solomons. All the people who were not Catholics would be killed, and all the land on which signs had been placed would be taken by the Catholics.

The complaint was over Sitai's use of power. He had given permission for the signs to be set up and would punish anyone who took them down. Sitai had failed to curb the power of the Catholics and had failed to look after the village people who were Protestants. The Pope was quite entitled to send an army if Sitai did nothing to stop him.

I gave permission for the signs to be taken down, saying that I was sure that Sitai would want this done. But my bewilderment was considerably increased when the priest from Manevovo walked through the village and was greeted by the Protestants in a friendly manner. It did seem a little unfair, even though we were both Europeans, that Sitai and I should be blamed for everything when the priest was more involved with the Pope than we were.

When I returned to the headquarters of the administration at
Kira Kira I examined all the old records I could find. 'Marching
Rule' in south San Cristobal, where this incident had taken place,
had mainly been concerned with the Pope sending an army to the
Solomons. There had been no mention of 'cargo' or Americans in
the cult ideology of that area. Sitai, the D.O., was a Protestant
from the Tawarogha area. The incident seemed to arise from the
attempt by the Tawarogha people to convince themselves that
Sitai had more power than the priest and that he had their interests
at heart.

If the priest had given permission for the signs to be put up had
Sitai the power to have them taken down? The priest was going to
look after his people by getting them more land after the Pope had
sent an army. Could Sitai prevent this happening? When the signs
were taken down in Sitai's name the people were quite satisfied
that he had more power than the priest and the matter was not
raised again.

I was now convinced that power, status, and 'big men' were connected in some way and that this was relevant to cult movements.
But 'Marching Rule' had been thought of in terms of nascent
nationalism. How did this tie in with the contemporary political
scene?

Before 1962 members of the Legislative Council had been appointed by the High Commissioner on the advice and recommenda-
tion of the local District Commissioner. In 1962, as an experiment,
the 'whispering ballot' was introduced into Eastern District where
I was stationed.

Under this simple system the voters whispered into the ear of
the presiding officer at the election the name of the candidate they
wished to support. Despite lengthy and detailed explanations by
fluent 'pidgin' English speakers, the percentage of votes cast in
relation to the number of registered voters was very low in all
constituencies.

But in the constituency of the 'big man' on the island there was a
100 per cent poll. In all the other constituencies, in which the polls
had been low, the voters had affirmed that they understood the
procedure. But when it came to the actual casting of votes they all
gave the name of the 'big man'. When it was then explained that
one man could only represent one constituency all further interest
in the elections vanished.

The people in each constituency seemed to want a man who was recognized as a 'big man' all over San Cristobal. They wanted him to represent their constituency so that they could think of him as their 'big man'—they did not think it worth while to vote for anyone who was not a 'big man'.

Local government council meetings were quiet, orderly affairs. None of the members appeared to have any strong views. They simply sat quietly while the President of the council and the District Commissioner between them decided all that had to be decided at the meeting. Part of this I put down to shyness. But on occasions when I attended other Solomon Islander meetings they had been lively and vociferous.

At one Seventh-Day Adventist meeting, lively debate, with frequent insults, lasted all the afternoon, until the business of the day was concluded. The meeting decided that the Sabbath was not being observed. No person should be allowed to walk through their village on Saturday (their Sabbath) carrying a heavy load, and everyone must be in bed by nine o'clock on Friday night. Everyone at the meeting had had their say, which was a marked change from the Local Government meetings.

In local government meetings there were 'big men' present (the D.C. and the President) and it was felt that they were the only people who should speak. Ordinary members of the council were thought to have neither power nor status and it would not be proper for them to give any opinion in front of the 'big men'. There was certainly very little political debate and very little discussion of public issues.

How deep a hold had Christianity on the people, to what extent was their acceptance of religion conditioned by traditional notions? An amusing incident in north Malaita confirmed my suspicion that many Solomon Islanders still considered that success was merely the result of applying the right formula, and that they were quite prepared to experiment. One day, as I was passing the fringing reefs of the Lau lagoon in north Malaita, the engine of our small boat broke down. Attempts to restart the engine were unsuccessful and the boat gradually drifted towards the reefs.

I noticed the Solomon Island skipper making use of his rosary beads as we drifted closer, in between his frenzied attempts to restart the engine. Even nearer to the reef he saw one of his old pagan shrines on the headland, he then called on the spirits of his ancestors for assistance. It was all to no avail. We struck the reef and had to swim ashore.

When new religious sects arrive on the scene, Solomon Islanders would often try them out for a while to see what the benefits were like. In this form of experimentation the Jehovah's witness sect were popular. But the millenary nature of the Jehovah's Witness ideology received short shrift from the Solomon Islanders. Promise of future benefits was not enough, and the sect was quickly abandoned. Had this attitude been adopted by Solomon Islanders in evaluating 'Marching Rule'?

As my experience with cult situations and the residual ideology continued, I began to wonder whether there was any explanation which could cover the facts in view of what I had learnt. I remembered Dr. Burridge's comment that the problems which faced Tangu had to be solved in terms of their existing experience.[1]

What was the relationship between the new élite in the Solomons, the absence of 'cargo' cults as such, and the old 'Marching Rule' leaders? In terms of their existing experience had Solomon Islanders regarded the 'Marching Rule' leaders simply as more powerful versions of the traditional 'big man'? I had noticed that the concept of the 'big man' was strong in all those areas that had been affected by 'Marching Rule'. If 'Marching Rule' or other 'cargo' cults were viewed in this light would it be possible to reach a deeper level of understanding?

At every stage during British administration in the Solomons progress has been retarded by a dearth of indigenous leadership. 'Marching Rule' produced leaders of national stature. These 'Marching Rule' leaders have now been replaced by a new élite. But what did the power of the new élite rest on, and why had there been no more cargo cults?

I decided to spend my leave in 1964 at Oxford to see if academic inquiry could give the answers to the problems I had set myself. Dr. Burridge, who became my academic supervisor, suggested that work on the 'Vailala Madness' might be profitable.

The 'Vailala Madness' contained features which later occurred in many other cults, and it has been well documented. With the extensive material which was available it was possible to analyse the cult society before, during, and after, the 'madness'.

F. E. Williams's *Drama of Orokolo*, written after twenty years'

[1] K. O. L. Burridge 1960:209 and C. S. Belshaw 1950b:124.

contact with the Elema people, who were affected by the 'Vailala Madness', is a thorough and painstaking study.[1] The accuracy of Williams's work is supported by books, notes, articles, and manuscripts of missionaries who served in the area. These documents are at the London Missionary Society's headquarters in London. Of particular interest in this collection are the notes which were made by Pryce-Jones, the L.M.S. missionary, who was living among the Elema when the 'madness' broke out.

The 'Vailala Madness' contained many interesting features in addition to the 'cargo' belief; the anticipated return of the spirits of the dead, the physical symptoms of the cult members, and the destruction of the Hevehe ceremony. There is also the problem of explaining why the 'madness' should have broken out at Vailala village while the village of Orokolo only a few miles away was not affected.

In the first few chapters of the book an account is given of Elema life and customs prior to the advent of the 'madness'. Particular reference is paid to the role of the 'big man' and to ideas regarding the nature of power, wealth, and status. The effect that European contact had on the Elema is then examined and this is followed by analysis of the 'Vailala Madness'.

When I returned to the Solomons in 1965, as a result of having analysed the 'Vailala Madness', a number of problems had been posed for further research. I found myself in a unique position to examine 'Marching Rule' in detail. I had access to unpublished official records, and many of my colleagues had been in the Solomons at the time of 'Marching Rule'. Having served in the districts affected by 'Marching Rule', I had taken the opportunity to question former leaders and members of the movement in an attempt to answer questions which had not been answered by standard source material.

Adding this material to data obtained from fifteen months' contact with a cult in North Malaita, together with my growing knowledge of concepts of power and status in contemporary Solomon Island society, I found that problems which had been posed for further analysis by examination of the 'Vailala Madness' could be answered by material collected in the Solomon Islands.

After analysis of the 'Vailala Madness' the book re-examines

[1] A. P. Elkin 1953:45, says that F. E. Williams's work affords a sound background for understanding the Elema.

'Marching Rule' and then deals with the Doliasi 'Custom' movement of North Malaita. This is followed by an examination of the
nature of concepts of power and status in contemporary Solomon
Island society. Comparative analysis of the material collected from
Papua and the Solomons is then undertaken. This information is
then related to existing theories regarding the nature of cargo cults.
Finally, conclusions are given.

I had originally been seeking a theory to cover various facts in
contemporary Solomon Island society which did not seem to be
adequately covered by existing cargo cult theory. In beginning with
the 'Vailala Madness' and following the growth and change in
content of the cult movements through to the contemporary
Solomons I found that the problems I had set myself could be
answered. The solution was intimately connected with indigenous
concepts of leadership, and notions regarding the nature of power
and status.

Traditional notions regarding the nature of power and status had
remained unchanged despite European contact. The traditional
role of the 'big man' and the traditional role of ordinary men had
seen little basic modification. Seen in this light 'cargo' cults were
not a series of dissociated social phenomena, having at best only a
tenuous relationship with 'normal' social life. They were a development episode in the persisting social relationship between
'big men' and ordinary members of society.

The object is to construct a minimal intellectual framework
which will be capable of containing the empirical material relating
to the movements examined. Since this analysis could not be
carried out in isolation from other theories and intellectual frame-
works concerned with 'cargo' cults, it may have some heuristic
value in relation to other movements, and ought to pose problems
for further research.

THE WESTERN ELEMA

T HERE is a substantial measure of agreement among anthropologists that 'cargo' cults are primarily concerned with concepts of power, wealth, and status.[1] And, although this examination takes place within the agreed general area, it is felt that these concepts have not been examined in sufficient detail. These concepts are now examined in relation to the western Elema who were affected by the 'Vailala Madness'.

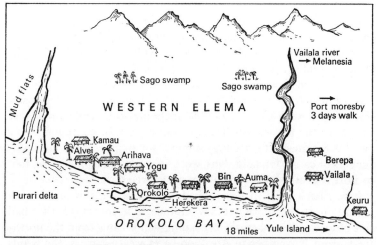

MAP 1. The Gulf Distirct of Papua.

In particular the role of the 'avai' or 'big men' is examined since appreciation of the position that they occupied is of crucial importance in attempting to understand the events of 1919. Attention is also paid to the spirits of the dead and their importance in Elema society. Detailed examination of Elema kinship structure and other institutionalized relationships which were not intimately

---

[1] I. C. Jarvie 1964:74–105, gives a review of existing theories regarding the nature of 'cargo' cults.

concerned with concepts of power, wealth, and status is not germane to this study.

The Elema lived on the south side of the island of New Guinea, and in 1919 they formed part of the administrative area known as the Gulf Division, Papua. The Division was situated 160 miles from the capital, Port Moresby. Commencing at the Purari delta, the Elema lived in a series of straggling villages stretching eastwards for some twenty miles along Orokolo bay towards the administrative centre of the Gulf Division at Kerema.

Orokolo bay contained the five main villages of the western Elema, Vailala, Auma, Orokolo, Yogu, and Arihava. The population was estimated at approximately 20,000.[1]

The western Elema had cultural affinities with their neighbours to the east, the eastern Elema, although their languages were mutually unintelligible and there were considerable differences in ritual and religious practices.[2] Little ethnographic information is available for the eastern Elema. To the west were the Namau people of the Purari delta. The western Elema had little contact with these people or with the nomadic Kukukuku who lived in the swampy hinterland to the north of Elema territory.

From Cape Possession near Kerema to the Purari delta, Orokolo bay, on which the Elema lived, stretched for 100 miles. The coastline was exposed with no suitable anchorage for small ships. Near the shore the sea was shallow causing an almost continual heavy swell which made it extremely difficult for small ships to land passengers or cargo. On land there were no roads and a journey on foot to Port Moresby took the best part of three days.

The Elema lived in a rain-shadow area in relation to the high mountains in the interior of New Guinea. This meant that they had fine clear weather when the prevailing winds came from the northwest, from November to April, and wet weather when the winds came from the south-east, during the remainder of the year.

Fringing Orokolo bay were numerous stands of coconuts. Elema garden land lay behind the coconut groves and this in turn gave way to the swampy land of the interior where sago was grown. The western Elema had an abundance of garden land and the swampy ground was ideal for growing sago.[3] A form of shifting cultivation common to Melanesia and Papua was practised. Communal culti-

vation of garden land was undertaken during the dry hot north-
west season. The first stage was to clear the undergrowth from the
new garden land. Trees were then felled or ring-barked, individual
plots were fenced, and waste timber burned. Finally, crops of
yams, taro, and bananas were planted. Sago palms grew in such
profusion in the swampy ground that it was not necessary for the
Elema to plant young suckers in the normal way to ensure new
crops. Men and women worked together on extracting the sago
pith. A day's work for two people would often yield as much as
45 lb. of sago and a single palm could yield up to 700 lb.

Pigs were occasionally eaten on festive occasions though meat
did not form a staple part of Elema diet. Coconuts were widely
used in the preparation of food. As an indication of their use over
100 words existed in the Elema language for coconut products.[1]

Fish and prawns were obtained from the rivers; sharks and shell-
fish were caught in the sea. The Elema had ample food supplies.
The cultivational pattern was egalitarian, all men had equal access
to the land and the sea and equal opportunities for food-gathering.

The larger villages had a single line of houses stretching out along
the seashore. Some of the Elema villages were over a mile in length.
Houses were small rectangular unfloored leaf structures about
15–20 ft. long. A few were floored with betel nut strips. Each
village had an Eravo or men's house. The men's house was an
imposing building often 110 ft. long and 50 ft. high at the front
descending to about 20 ft. high at the rear.

Adult men lived in the Eravo or men's house where they ate,
slept, and spent the majority of their leisure time. Adult men visited
their wives' houses only for sexual congress. Young men, if they
were not in the process of being initiated to manhood, and young
girls, lived with their mothers. Families tended to reside in one
village and marriage was patrilocal. A young bride occasionally
lived for a period with her husband's mother, but in general each
married woman occupied a separate house together with her young
children. Polygamy was virtually unknown among the Elema and
there was a marked antagonism by the whole society where
instances of adultery occurred.[2]

Western Elema society had eight age grades: Akore Heka, little
boys, Akore Ikua, small boys of about six years of age, Erekaia
Akore, boys of about twelve, Miro Akore, youths of about fourteen

[1] H. A. Brown MSS.   [2] J. Holmes 1924:47.

or fifteen prior to initiation, Haera Eapapo, adults, and Oapau, or old men.

These age grades existed in all Elema villages.[1] Particular kinds of conduct were associated with different age grades: status in the community and the importance attached to a particular individual's views was dependent on age grade seniority. The older a man became, the more weight his opinion carried in discussions. Since the age grades were universal any man visiting a strange village would join other members of his age grade and be treated accordingly by his hosts. Age grades provided clear-cut and universally recognized sets of status.

Each Elema man belonged to a particular totemic group. The groups, known collectively as the Aualari, had ten divisions and were patrilineal. Although the names of the totems were related to geographical places such as the sea, the river Vailala, etc., men belonging to each of the ten divisions could be found in any Eravo. The symbols adopted as totemic symbols were representative of a wide variety of animals and plants in the Elema environment, for example, wild pig, mangrove, lizard, and crocodile.

Totemic activities were essentially concerned with individuals or small groups rather than with society as a whole. A man's totem might indicate to him an auspicious time for pig-hunting or fishing. Men who belonged to the same totemic group helped each other on special occasions such as when a man wanted to build a new house or make a canoe. But totemic spirits who were thought to live in the bush were only helpful to individuals or small groups of people and they were not thought to be as powerful as the spirits of the dead.[2]

The 'avai' or 'big men' were thought to be more powerful than the spirits of the dead or totemic spirits. And the activities of the 'big men' affected all the Elema. A small number of men belonged to what were collectively known as the 'avai'. Membership of the group was not hereditary nor was it confined to the oldest men in the society. The 'avai' was a form of gerontocracy. New members were not elected to it. They were asked to join after they had demonstrated the necessary qualities and attributes for membership.[3]

The 'avai' were 'big men' or the equivalent of chiefs. 'These chiefs without exception were born leaders of men. They were

[1] F. E. Williams 1940:74, 75.   [2] J. Holmes MSS.
[3] H. A. Brown MSS.

endowed with mental powers, a shrewdness of judgement, acuteness of discernment, alertness to seize opportunities, such as the rank and file of the tribes did not possess.'[1] The actual number of the 'avai' was small and the power and influence that they had was very considerable.

These 'big men' were intimately concerned with Elema notions regarding the nature of power, wealth, and status. 'Big men' were the only people who could undertake communal religious technology.[2]

Every Elema man was involved in economic, ritual, and political activities. The standard performance required of a man in all these activities was set by the 'big man'.

The value of wealth is determined socially. Most forms of wealth are either symbolic or intrinsic in value. Elema wealth was symbolic in value; wealth was a measurement of man and an indication of his status. To examine Elema concepts of wealth this involves the two main nexuses in the handling of goods and services. These were, activities concerned with the production of subsistence goods, and complex arrangements made for trade and ceremonial exchange.[3]

This distinction can be further broken down into individual and corporate wealth transactions. Both these kinds of transaction were involved with the question of how wealth forms were created, and the amounts of wealth that were obtained through trade. Analysis of both these categories requires an appreciation of the functions performed by wealth.

Elema forms of wealth were shell ornaments (Huaiea, atiave, and apakoro), dogs' teeth, porpoise teeth, and pigs' tusks.[4] Perishable forms of wealth consisted of pigs, tobacco, yams, taro, sago, and bananas. Balsa logs which were sold to the Motuans were a further form of wealth.

Elema forms of wealth were not factorial like European money. Shell ornaments and pigs were used as bride price, as gifts from a maternal uncle to his nephew, in compensation for injury, or in payment for land purchases. Garden produce was not used as bride price or in payment of compensation. Different forms of wealth were used in distinctly separate social transactions.

---

[1] J. Holmes 1924:38.   [2] Phrase used by P. Lawrence 1964: *passim.*
[3] R. F. Salisbury 1962:39, 40.   [4] F. E. Williams 1940:58, 59.

Expenditure of wealth had no intrinsic merit in itself. The significance of the payment of bride price lay in the fact that the amount of wealth used symbolized the importance of the transaction. A marriage in which a high bride price was paid was more important than a marriage in which a low bride price was paid. Important men gave a large amount of wealth, others gave a small amount. Men gave according to their status.

Pigs were used in a large number of transactions: in feasts, in purchasing a new canoe, payment for a new house, or for performance of important rituals. Since the majority of goods and services were produced by individuals themselves large-scale expenditure was not required for day-to-day living.

The Elema had an exchange economy. Since value is determined by the social use of an object European money had a very limited value. There is no evidence to suggest that European money had replaced traditional wealth forms in important exchanges.[1] Wages earned by labourers were converted into goods before the labourers returned to the Gulf Division. It was the custom for traders to pay the Elema for sago and copra in tobacco rather than money.[2] There can only have been a very small amount of European money in circulation in the Gulf Division. European money could only be used in a very limited number of transactions. These transactions concerned Europeans: Elema had to pay taxes, they bought cooking utensils and gardening implements.

Possession of European goods conferred some status, but beyond their utility these goods were not invested with any particular significance.[3] European goods did not replace indigenous wealth forms in important social transactions. A man's social position was firmly dependent on his possessions of indigenous wealth.

European food was not appreciated by the Elema. An Elema plantation worker, asked why he did not wish to return to his work, said that Europeans did not give him any food—only *Boromakau* (tinned meat), *Kikiki* (tinned biscuit), tea, *suka* (sugar), *raiki* (rice). When asked what was wrong with that he replied that there was no sago.[4]

[1] In the Solomon Islands in 1967 European money had still not replaced traditional wealth forms in many important social transactions.
[2] J. Holmes MSS.
[3] P. Lawrence 1964:63–8 in describing the first cargo belief.
[4] J. Holmes 1924:257, 258.

The characteristic element in individual wealth transactions was the maintenance or preservation of existing status. Corporate wealth transactions had two significant features: the utilization of the economic expertise of the 'big man' on behalf of the community, and the gaining of status through feast-giving and economic leadership activities.

The actions of the 'big man' in the corporate sphere determined the existence, importance, and frequency of individual wealth transactions. Wealth used in the individual transactions came from gardening and trading which were organized communally by the 'big men'.

The Elema coastline had no fringing reefs where shell could be obtained to make traditional wealth forms. All Elema shell wealth forms had to be earned in external trade.[1] During the south-east monsoon season Elema trading canoes called *bevaia* left for Port Moresby where they were able to exchange sago for shell. But the Elema were not good sailors and they were afraid of the sea.

'Big men' decided when a voyage should take place. They organized the collection of sago, and then supervized the exchange of sago for shell.[2] Other exchanges took place when the Motuans visited the Elema. Motuan trading canoes or *lakatois* brought pottery which they exchanged for sago and balsa logs (the balsa logs were used for making canoes). In these exchanges the 'big men' organized the proceedings.[3]

'Big men' were responsible for the provision of public hospitality when representing their village in discussions or meetings with visitors. They also fed a number of young men who came, attracted by the prestige of the 'big men', to stay in the Eravo. Their ability to feed these people was a function of the assistance that they were able to call on from men who were obligated to them.

How did 'big men' gain their wealth, and on what was their personal economic position based? 'Big men' were all personally wealthy. By their personal industry, shrewd marriages, friendships, and other social affiliations they managed to place themselves in a position where a large number of people were obligated to them.

Terms such as 'excess' or 'surplus' were related to social and not economic criteria: any accumulation of garden produce in

[1] H. A. Brown MSS.
[2] See F. E. Williams 1932:139–66 for details of the Elema trading voyages.
[3] C. G. Seligman 1910:108–10.

excess of immediate requirements could be converted into an
obligation to be repaid at a later date by entering into additional
reciprocal relationships until the excess was accounted for. The
amounts of wealth which changed hands in the 'big men's' transactions were not large but the number of transactions entered into
was far larger than that of ordinary men. As a result 'big men' were
able to call on a large amount of support at any particular time.

The corner-stone of the Elema economic system was the production of crops and their transference into shell valuables, or obligations to be repaid at a later date. Corporate wealth activities
involving the initiation, organization, and execution of economic
projects were the function of the 'big man'.[1] They provided a
meaningful framework of organizational activities where personal performances could be evaluated and assumptions about
individual economic expertise verified. By following the 'big man's'
directions garden produce and shell valuables were obtained so that
personal obligations could be honoured. Elema wealth was a function of the existence of 'big men'. Ordinary men knew that if they
worked hard and followed the directions of the 'big man', then
they would gain wealth.

We are now concerned with the 'big men's' ability to perform
actions where the intended consequences were known in advance.
Types of power possessed by the 'big man' can be categorized as
ritual, magical, and political.

In Elema mythology the 'avai' or 'big men' were credited with
the creation of garden fertility. At each stage in the communal
gardening operations, which were undertaken annually, they performed rituals to ensure that the new garden lands would be fertile.
The necessary religious knowledge to perform these rituals was the
exclusive possession of 'big men' and nobody else 'knew' the
formulas that were used. In this way successful gardening was
directly attributable to the existence of 'big men'.[2] But success was
not only a matter of 'knowing'; there was also the implication that
only the 'big men' could prevail.[3] They prevailed because success
was not only attributable to human efficacy but also to possession
of mana.[4]

Effective use of ritual power was necessary for the successful

[1] H.I.Hogbin 1958:157-9.   [2] F. E. Williams 1940:13, 14, 101.
[3] R. G. Lienhardt 1961:138-42 discusses the prophetic powers of the Masters
of the Fishing Spear among the Dinka which raises a similar kind of issue.
[4] R. Firth 1967:174-8.

undertaking of trading voyages. The mariners could meet disaster from sea-monsters which were known as Ma-hevehe. 'Big men' were able to control these monsters and ensure that the voyages were successful. Control of the Ma-hevehe was shown in the Ivaiva ceremony which involved the 'big men' making a ritual sacrifice to the spirits of the dead.[1]

'Big men' provided an organizational framework based on ritual activities which provided a means for individuals to evaluate their own performance. Ordinary men had a passive, ritual role, they awaited the directions of the 'big men'. The essential difference between the ritual power possessed by the 'big man' and that of ordinary members of society lay in the fact that the 'big men's' ritual power had influence over the whole society while the ritual power of ordinary men influenced only a small number of people.[2]

Sorcery was rife in Elema society and it provided a limited form of social control. Feelings of hostility which one man had for another were channelled into sorcery where they might otherwise have resulted in physical violence. Death was, prima facie, evidence that a sorcerer had been at work: a man who enjoyed good health or fortune was thought to be a powerful sorcerer. Sorcerers were thought to be able to 'raise storms, cause drought or famine, give plenty, create lightning, thunder and earthquakes'.[3]

'Big men' were recognized as the most powerful sorcerers. They were reputed to possess incalculable heat or 'ahea' which was needed to perform works of sorcery.[4]

No Elema man was willing to offend a 'big man' lest he use sorcery in reprisal. Very few men knew how rituals were enacted or what the appropriate formulas for success were. 'Knowing' was associated with 'big men' whose actions were thought responsible for the well-being of the community. But 'big men' were reputed to kill by sorcery any men who tried to gain the secrets of their rituals. An important feature of the exercise of power is the ability to use sanctions if commands or instructions were not obeyed: sorcery performed this function for the 'big man'.

Political power among the Elema cannot be examined in isolation; it was inextricably bound up with other notions about economic, social, magical, and ritual power. Although political

[1] F. E. Williams 1940:229–31. [2] F. E. Williams 1940:100, 101.
[3] J. Holmes MSS. [4] J. Holmes 1924:201.

authority was vested in increasing amounts in ascending age grades, ultimate political authority was held by the 'big men'.

In ritual or magical practices the 'big man's' power was largely dependent on his possession of exclusive knowledge. In political activities his position was dependent on his personality and organizational powers. 'Big men' were often involved in arbitration: when quarrels or disputes broke out they were solved by 'big men'.[1] They represented the Elema in negotiations with other tribes.

Traditionally the 'big man' was a leader in war. This was an important activity which provided the most common way in which manhood could be established.[2] War was often the result of insult offered to the 'big man'; he decided when war should be waged and when peace should be made. Elema were disciplined to accept the orders and instructions of the 'big man' without question. Although there were activities in Elema society which could be thought of as political there was a complete absence of any discussion. 'Big men' decided all the issues and ordinary men simply obeyed.

The 'big men's' possession of power was in no way dependent on popular support. But since the 'big man's' power was the only kind of power which affected the whole society, 'big men' were primarily responsible for the maintenance of social cohesion.

STATUS

'Big men', as already indicated, by virtue of their industry entered into a greater number of reciprocal relationships than other members of society; this enabled them to give *sosoka* or a feast.[3] Through feast-giving a considerable amount of prestige was gained.[4] Status was also gained through possession of exclusive religious knowledge and organizational ability.

A 'big man's' claim to possess status could be evaluated empirically. Though feasts and material possessions were visible manifestations of status, possession of exclusive religious knowledge could not be directly tested. But possession of exclusive religious knowledge could be assumed if a man achieved successes in the kinds of ritual activity that were undertaken by 'big men'.

[1] J. Holmes 1924:263.   [2] H. M. Dauncey 1913:8.7,
[3] J. Holmes 1924:158.   [4] H. A. Brown MSS.

The essential difference between the status possessed by a 'big man' and that possessed by other men was that the 'big man' was a microcosm of society. Thus the status of a 'big man' was a matter for the concern of the whole society while individual status was of import for only one man. The status of the 'big man' was the status of the group. Acquiring status was a matter of competition. If an individual wished to increase his status he had to demonstrate superior performance. When this was done status was granted. The Elema status system was completely egalitarian. It was also mobile: men could gain and lose status.

The position of 'rubbish men', 'nothing men', or men who were 'something nothing' is now examined. How did 'rubbish men' achieve their comparatively low status and what was their function in society? 'Rubbish men' were not pariahs, they provided a back-drop for social endeavour. These men were lazy and indolent. They entered into a very small number of reciprocal transactions, and only produced small amounts of food from their gardens. 'Rubbish men' could not call on extensive support if they wished to build a new house. They were unable to pay a respectable bride price. At feasts, as a mark of their low status, they were given the smallest portion.

'Rubbish men' had no magical, ritual, economic, or political power. Their opinion was of no account in meetings. Elema called 'rubbish men' *haera merava*, meaning bush pig[1]—that is, one who scratches for a living. These people were unable to participate in communal activities; they did not have the necessary equipment to become useful members of society. 'Rubbish men' did not have the same rights as other men: they could not demand compensation if men committed adultery with their wives; if someone assaulted a 'rubbish man' this was not a serious matter. They were not really men.

The bulk of society's members were 'solid' citizens, neither so industrious and powerful as the 'big man', nor so indolent and impotent as the 'rubbish man'. To progress to 'big man' status, ability and driving ambition beyond the capacity of most men was required. For the man who became lazy or who was unable to meet his obligations the downward path to the status of 'rubbish man' was accompanied by strong feelings of *maioka* or shame and a sense of no longer belonging to the community. To accuse a man

[1] F. E. Williams 1940:98.

of being a bush pig was an insult. Manhood was precious to the Elema.

By reference to the social position of 'big men' and 'rubbish men' ordinary members of society were able to evaluate their own position. 'Big men' provided the organizational framework and the means for ordinary men to establish their manhood. 'Rubbish men' provided an example of how manhood could be lost.

LIFE CRISES

Among the Elema, youths of fourteen or fifteen underwent initiation rites marking the change from boyhood to manhood. The importance of the rituals lay in the education of youths about the meaning of manhood, the responsibilities of a man and the conduct expected of him.

When a large number of youths were ready to be initiated, a high walled enclosure was built near the Eravo. There the youths, who were known as 'parrot boys', lived during the period of their seclusion, which normally lasted six months. Elema initiation rites showed a common pattern of exclusion and separation followed by ritual rebirth, purification, and re-incorporation into society.[1]

Seclusion of the initiates was emphasized. If they left the enclosure they did so while covered by a wrap made from coconut leaves. No person was allowed to see the youths during their seclusion. The only exceptions were old women, who were beyond all suspicion of sexual activity (sexual intercourse was thought to weaken a man and the emphasis during seclusion was on growth of physical power), and the 'big men'.

Those who were physically large among the Elema appealed as 'big men'.[2] Attempts were made to stimulate the growth of the initiates as much as possible. The young men were given very large quantities of food to eat. They sprayed each other with coconut oil which was thought to assist growth. If this treatment did not have the desired results then red ochre or charcoal was used. Considerable stress was laid on the physiological changes that were thought to take place during the youths' seclusion. Physical power was an important attribute of manhood, being indicative of a man's ability to work, to fight, and his sexual prowess. In this as in so many other things the 'big men' represented the ultimate standard.

[1] R. Hertz 1960:76–86.   [2] J. Holmes 1924:39.

Two ideas are implicit in this emphasis on physical growth, the change from boyhood to manhood, and Elema ideas on the physical attributes of men. Seclusion normally took place during puberty coinciding with normal physical changes. The use of red ochre carried with it connotations of menstrual blood emphasizing symbolically[1] the change from boyhood to manhood. Charcoal was the colour associated with the 'big man', the colour associated with his power, and was only used if other attempts to stimulate growth failed.

At puberty a clear distinction was drawn between male and female powers and attributes; the physiological change at puberty for young girls was striking, but to the Elema the physical change in young men who underwent seclusion was more impressive. Tattooing or circumcision were not used, the sole distinction marking the physical change from boy to man being physical growth.

Initiation ceremonies and rituals were the responsibility of the 'big men'. During their period of seclusion the youths were instructed in Elema customs and traditions—knowledge which was possessed by adult men.

Youths were cautioned against stealing and adultery, warned to respect other people's property, and exhorted to be industrious. They were warned of the supernatural penalties that they would incur if they disobeyed their elders. This instruction buttressed the position of the 'big man' in two ways: young men learnt that the ideal standard of manhood was that of the 'big man', they also learnt that they must obey the 'big men' or run the risk of supernatural sanctions.

Only the 'big men' could successfully perform the initiation rituals. They prevailed because they alone possessed the necessary mana. The physical changes that took place in the initiates during the period of seclusion were directly attributable to the power of the 'big men'. Women were amazed at the changes that took place and this emphasized the effectiveness of the 'big men's' exclusive religious knowledge. They were in a sense makers of men.

After their six months' seclusion the young men left their enclosure. Re-entry into the world was marked by a purifying bathe to remove harmful influences that they had been exposed to. After an elaborate gift exchange with their maternal uncles, the initiation

[1] B. Bettelheim 1955:178–9.

rituals were finally concluded. But 'big men' did not have to take the purifying bathe, they were immune to harmful influences. This showed the 'big man's' ability to identify himself with the sacred and the profane.

Mortuary practices in Melanesia and Papua reveal large opportunities for individual variation within any particular social grouping. South of a theoretical line drawn between the Admiralty group and Santa Cruz the dead were thought to live under the ground. North of this line the dead were thought to live on the earth, on reefs or on neighbouring islands.[1]

'Horovu Harihu', the Elema land of the dead, was thought to be a place in the west where coconuts grew. Death among the Elema was a 'rite de passage' in which two objectives were accomplished. The deceased was prepared for his new life among the spirits of the dead and sent on his way; those who had been connected with the rituals surrounding death had to be purified before they re-entered society.

When an Elema man died his house was soon filled with women. Women prepared the dead man for his journey; they performed what was essentially a male role. To emphasize this they exchanged their skirts for male perineal bands. Death rituals were too dangerous for ordinary men, although 'big men' had nothing to fear from a corpse.

The dead man was dressed in a new perineal band. He was then placed on part of a canoe, symbolizing the journey he would take to the land of the dead.[2] In many instances death by sorcery would have been suspected. The corpse was closely watched. If it grinned or urinated while rigor mortis was setting in, then this confirmed that death had been due to sorcery and that the man responsible was in the room with the dead man. Sorcerers who knew that they had been responsible for death would stay away from the dead man. The dead were very powerful and every attempt was made to ensure that they were not angered.

The spirits of the dead were thought to be white in form. This idea had resulted in the Elema thinking that the first Europeans who visited them were spirits of the dead.[3] These spirits were thought to be present during the interment rituals.

[1] R. H. Codrington 1891:*passim*, and C. H. Weadgwood 1927:*passim*.
[2] G. Landtman 1927:214–17; 257 mentions a similar practice among the Kiwai Papuans.
[3] J. Chalmers 1902:42, 43.

The grave was dug by old women, who also carried the body to the graveside. During the time when the body was decomposing the grave was guarded night and day to prevent sorcerers taking pieces of the corpse which they needed for their magic. After the burial no drum could be sounded in the village for a period of six months—the sound of a drum was associated with the spirits of the dead.[1]

When the body had decomposed it was time for the spirit to go to the land of the dead. In preparation for this journey coconuts, roast fish, and bananas were left by the grave. A firestick was placed nearby to light the way. But sometimes the spirit of the man lingered in the vicinity of his house. It might make small noises or cause small objects to fall down. This indicated that the spirit had insufficient food. A special plea might be made to the spirit to depart to his new home: 'Your bow, your bag, your belt; your pearl shell, arm shell, feathers; your perineal band, axe, knife, dog's teeth—these your things, take them and go, your ornaments and your property'.[2] When spirits of the dead were thought to be near food was placed on funerary platforms. After the deceased had gone to his new home a feast was made for all the people who had come into contact with the corpse. These people then had a purifying bathe to get rid of the harmful influences that they had been exposed to. 'Big men' did not take any purifying bathe.

The spirits of the dead were thought to be very powerful, capable of doing great harm or of giving help and assistance.[3] Their attitude was thought to be ambivalent and to depend on the use of the right formula. They were difficult to control, they answered no laws and there was no guarantee that they would behave themselves. The dead were known to be conservative. They were angered by breaches of traditional customs and failure to execute funerary rites in a proper manner. Spirits of the dead also upheld the traditional moral code and were thought to be angered by stealing, adultery or disobedience. The code of the dead strengthened the power of the 'big men'—if benefits were to be obtained from the dead then the 'big men' had to be obeyed.

'Big men' were credited with the ability to control the dead. This ability came from the 'big man's' possession of *ahea* or heat.

[1] F. E. Williams 1940:114.   [2] F. E. Williams 1940:118.
[3] B. Blackwood 1935:477 mentions propitiation of the dead when their help was required.

The process of inducing heat was known as *siahu*. To induce *siahu* a man fasted for several days. Then large amounts of ginger were chewed, and since this acted as a physical stimulant the 'big man' felt that he was hot.[1]

The dead did not give assistance to individuals. Assistance was obtained from the dead as a result of the 'big man's' exclusive knowledge. This assistance was given by the spirits of the dead to the 'big men' and they in turn used it for the good of the community. In this way the 'big men' were able to ensure garden fertility and successful trading voyages.

[1] H. A. Brown MSS.

II

MYTHOLOGY, SYMBOLISM, AND THE HEVEHE CEREMONY

ANALYSIS of Elema mythology is necessary since it can provide a key to understanding the main ritual of the Elema, the apa-Hevehe ceremony. This ceremony was discarded during the 'Vailala Madness'.

The Elema had a rich body of myths, primarily concerned with providing accounts for the origin of physical and spiritual order. Explanations were given for the origin of social institutions and for the 'big man's' role. As part of the non-empirical background to social action mythology was thought out in religious context—it was composed of a body of knowledge directly related to ritual.

In Elema society, which had a comparatively simple technology, epistemological assumptions about events and about the nature of the universe were unsophisticated. Myth provided the sole means for innovation: new events could be explained or new courses of action justified.[1] However, these explanations or justifications had to be contained within the existing cosmological framework. New concepts were not created in a vacuum. New ideas and theories had to be linked to old ideas and theories. Innovation was limited by myths which were in existence at the time. In the event of doubt or confusion over any new event, an explanation could be sought in mythology. Elema myths were a sole repository of truth.[2] 'Big men' were the only people who possessed, and who were able to interpret, details of all the Elema myths. They instructed young men about the meaning of myths, and they were expected to interpret new events in the light of their knowledge of mythology.[3] The heuristic power of myth was unlimited.

Elema symbolism was a form of communication. In an attempt to understand the method of communication it is possible to break the material down into binary oppositions. 'To the extent that the

---

[1] R. Firth 1967:159. [2] K. O. L. Burridge 1960:150
[3] H. A. Brown MSS.

ethnography is comprehensive and reliable, the form of classification by which a people order their world imposes itself on the analytical construction.'[1] Dualism is to some extent the essence of primitive thought dominating primitive social organization. Powers which maintained or increased life, health, and courage were all thought sacred while all diminishing influences were held to be impure.[2]

The analysis which will now be undertaken is only concerned with 'big man' aspects of the Elema myths.

ELEMA MYTHS

(i) Evarapo, an ugly person, figure of fun (a ' rubbish man '), lived in the west. Avaiara, a beautiful girl, lived at the mouth of a river some distance away and her brothers, two long-legged fishing birds, gave Evarapo news of her. Evarapo sent the girl a message in the form of a betel nut with markings on it, then he sent his younger brother as envoy. After several mishaps his younger brother, by donning a mask ('rura'), was able to meet the girl. Eventually he returned to tell his brother that she would marry him. A canoe (the basis for the Bevaia or trading canoe) was then launched by Evarapo who, transformed into a handsome young man, carried off the girl Avaiara. Her father, a monster named Oa-Birukapu, was angry at the elopement and gave chase. After several narrow escapes Evarapo reached his new home where the Elema later lived. Oa-Birukapu, arriving shortly afterwards, hid on the beach, and later, by mistake, he ate Avaiara and Evarapo's son. In return for sexual intercourse with Avaiara, Aikere and Maikere, 'big men' from a nearby village, killed Oa-Birukapu by shooting their arrows into his anus. Oa-Birukapu's bones were buried in the east and they caused yams, taro, and bananas to grow.[3]

Oa-Birukapu was a ma-Hevehe or sea monster. These monsters came from the land of the dead in the west. A later myth will make the connection between the sea monsters and the dead more clear. Of importance at this stage is the fact that 'big men' can kill or control harmful sea monsters, and by doing this they are indirectly responsible for the creation of garden fertility.

(ii) A woman named Ape lived near the mouth of the Purari river in the west. Ape was jealous of the son of a woman named Mare. She managed to kill and eat him. Ape then chased Mare into a tall tree. Mare poured

---

[1] R. Needham 1960:31. [2] R. Hertz 1960:95, 96.
[3] F. E. Williams 1940:173–9.

boiling water on Ape who fell to the ground and was buried in the sand. Aikere and Maikere who were walking along the beach where the incident took place then rescued Ape. Ape chased Aikere and Maikere, but they eventually succeeded in killing her in the same way that Oa-Birukapu had been killed on a spot where their Eravo later stood.[1]

This myth associates women with sea monsters. Ape sometimes took the form of a pig and she came from the Purari river in the west. The Purari delta was also associated with the ma-Hevehe sea monsters: the one who lived in the mouth of the river could assume the form of a pig. 'Big men' again overcome a harmful creature.

(iii) Ope and his mother were the only two survivors from a village which had been attacked by a snake. After more adventures they were attacked by a hawk, Hekeke, who had enlisted the support of the sea people. In the struggle that followed Ope was swept away and became a ma-Hevehe sea monster. An old man named Ira was journeying east with some young men in a canoe. The old man was swept overboard. Rising to the surface he told the young men not to worry about him because he would be happy in his new life. Ira became a ma-Hevehe sea monster and he and Ope were often seen together.[2]

This myth connects the spirits of the dead and the ma-Hevehe sea monsters. Ira and Ope died and they became sea monsters. They were attacked by a snake. Snake was the generic word for Hevehe or 'big men'. This myth illustrates the power of the 'big men' to control the spirits of the dead.

(iv) After a long series of struggles Iko, a legendary figure, beat his rival Ipavu in a hand-to-hand struggle, but did not kill him. But Ipavu's people, believing him to be dead, killed Iko, cut him up and ate him. Iko, who was still not dead, appeared to his uncle who was mourning his death in the Eravo. Iko was killed again and he went to live in Horovu Harihu which was later known as the land of the dead. But before he remained in the land of the dead for all time Iko returned to the Eravo once more and told Kapai how he could kill his enemies by sorcery.[3]

'Big men' were credited with the creation of the whole of the Elema environment. Iko and Ipavu were 'big men' and their fight resulted in the creation of the land of the dead. Aikere and Maikere the other 'big men' had killed Oa-Birukapu and had created garden fertility. Another 'big man' had made Ira flee and had thus been responsible for the creation of the first sea monster.

---

[1] F. E. Williams 1940:334, 336.   [2] F. E. Williams 1940:332–4.
[3] F. E. Williams 1940:118.

This myth is also concerned with the maintenance of life. 'Big men' make sure that the dead go and live in their proper home.

(v) On her way back from working in the garden a young woman named Lauara used to sit down and rest on the butt of a tree. A man named Haraua, hiding secretly within the tree, inserted his penis through a hole in the tree and had sexual intercourse with Lauara—this happened a number of times until Lauara was pregnant. Mystified as to the cause of her pregnancy Lauara enlisted the aid of two axes named clitoris and vagina to cut down the tree. Haraua and his brother who lived in the tree realized that they would be discovered, and so they dressed themselves in all their finery. The tree was cut down and the two men married Lauara and her sister. Lauara and Haraua had a son named Hoaro. One day while his wife was away Haraua baked some sago and gave it to his son and this made Lauara very angry. By this time Haraua and his brother had built an Eravo or men's house and they went into the house taking the boy Hoaro with them. Their wives stood in front of the Eravo demanding the boy, the men then came out of the Eravo and after walking among the women they disappeared into the ground becoming lizards, trees, and snakes etc., which were later adopted as the totemic symbols.[1]

This myth shows the 'big man's' role in the ordering of Elema culture. Men live apart from women in the Eravo. Women are responsible for cooking and they live in their own houses. Men belong to the totemic groups which are associated with the land and the bush. The importance of this myth lies in the fact that it indicates that the roles of men and women were created by 'big men'. It also illustrates the 'big man's' ability to cross cultural divisions—in this myth he does the work of a woman.

(vi) The bull roarer was a small elliptical piece of wood with a hole in it. When whirled around the head it made a loud noise. This was used in several initiation ceremonies where the noise made by the bull roarer convinced the young initiates that the spirits were near. When the bull roarer was a young man named Apu he travelled from Kauri in the east to the Purari delta. There he lay roaring all day long by the hearth of the men's house. An old woman named Oro-ipi-avu, known as the Eravo grandmother, succeeded in quietening him by pouring sago and meat balls down his throat. He then lived on quietly in the Eravo as a bull roarer. Elema mythology recounts that the original bull roarer was found in the intestines of Oa-Birukapu by women.[2]

[1] F. E. Williams 1940:339, 340.   [2] F. E. Williams: 1940:204, 205.

This myth illustrates ideas on the maintenance of Elema culture. Apu came from the east which was associated with fertility. The original bull roarer was found in the intestines of Oa-Birukapu. Sea monsters were associated with the spirits of the dead and with women. Women feed men who live in the Eravo, who then become strong and are able to insert a child/bull roarer into the womb of a woman.

In the myths that have been examined the 'big man's' position has come through as one of strength. 'Big men' control the dead, initiate communal activity, organize society, and kill harmful mythical monsters. But has the Elema system of communication anything else of importance to say about 'big men'?

A deeper level of analysis is required. Using material from the myths and other ethnographic data it is now possible to construct a series of binary oppositions. This method is a useful heuristic device and it is required to perform two functions: (a) it should assist in reaching a satisfactory level of understanding about the main rituals of the Elema, (b) more knowledge may be gained about semantic aspects of Elema symbolism.

	Categories	
Left	Transcendent	Right
Profane	'Big Man'	Sacred
Woman		Man
Useless old man		Virile young man
Dead		Aualari
ma-Hevehe		Bush spirits
Sea	Snake	Bush
Sky		Ground
Anger, inhospitality		Kindness, hospitality
Dirt, ugliness		Beauty, cleanliness
Burial		Birth
Coconuts		Yams, taro, bananas
South/west		North/east

Opposition is the basis for thought: differences, oppositions, and contradictions are encountered in the phenomena of experience and in the process of thought. In examining Elema symbolism the system must be dealt with holistically by concentration on synoptic or transcendental principles.[1] The structural morphology exhibited by Elema symbolism shows signs of the operation of these transcendental principles. There are two basic categories of left and right, but there also exists a third category. This third category shares attributes of the left and right categories.[2] The binary oppositions were co-ordinates for the map of social life. 'Big men' accounted for both sets of co-ordinates while ordinary people were in between these co-ordinates. 'Big men' could be associated with sacred and profane attributes. They could do the work of a man or woman, they had all the attributes of the dead and yet were thought of as living men. 'Big men' are shown as having transcendental qualities. Elema mythology shows that the 'big men' were thought responsible for the creation, maintenance, and ordering of Elema social life.

'Big men' presented a synthesized cultural image of Elema society. They could be connected with attributes associated with the left and with the right. These two sets of attributes were not contraries precisely articulating difference, they were also contraries dividing the cosmos between them. Both sets of attributes were each apparently in opposition, though each were capable of characterizing the qualities held by the 'big man'.[3]

These men transcended the limitations of opposition. They were a particular in which the universal was reflected.[4] Society contained 'big men' and 'big men' contained society. They encapsulated all that was valuable, and without them nothing had value. 'Big men' expressed the Elema, or in Mauss's terms, they were a 'total social fact'[5] because, in terms of symbolism, 'big men' were sacred and profane, and they were man and woman. This apparent symbolic incoherence can be clarified when it is appreciated that 'big men' *were* society.

THE APA-HEVEHE CEREMONY

The apa-Hevehe ceremony is of importance because of the iconoclasm of the 'Vailala Madness'. During the 'madness' the ceremony was discarded. Apa-Hevehe, or drum carrying Hevehe, constituted the centrepiece of Elema ritual life. The term 'Hevehe'

[1] R. McKeown 1954:17.   [2] E. Leach 1964.
[3] G. R. G. Mure 1940:140 for a discussion of the operation of the dialectic.
[4] This approach has been stimulated by L. Dumont's discussion 1960 on the position of the Sanyasi in Indian religion.
[5] M. Mauss 1954:45.

was a generic word for snake. Other kinds of Hevehe were ma-Hevehe, a sea monster, and be'ure Hevehe, a monster that lived in the ground.

The number, size, and frequency of the colourful ceremonies which made up the Hevehe cycle exhibited considerable complexities. Each of the component parts of the apa-Hevehe's dress was collected in a separate ceremony. And each of these ceremonies had its own initiation and mask. The materials which were used in the apa-Hevehe mask appeared to be connected with the bush and the sea. Williams was unable to find that there was any system of logic in the Hevehe cycle of rituals.

There is on one hand Hevehe Karawa (sea ritual) with its own initiation, and on the other, there are the Hevehe (i.e. land ritual) with their initiation. It is the writer's opinion that the former represents an accretion upon the latter, the incorporation of a sea cult on an earlier land cult. What I presume to be the newer cult has imposed its interpretation upon the Hevehe masks en masse: they are the daughters of sea monsters. But the results of our examination of the individual masks, their names and associations point in the opposite direction—to the bush.[1]

The apa-Hevehe ceremony had a common meaning for all Elema. People from Auma, Vailala, Arihava, Yogu, and Orokolo attended each other's Hevehe rituals. A cycle of rituals lasted a very long time, often as long as twenty years. It can be assumed that at any time a part of the cycle was in progress in one of the Elema villages. Duration of the ceremony was coterminous with the life of the Eravo: an Eravo was built to house the masks and when the ceremony was over the Eravo was abandoned and allowed to fall to pieces. Later stages of the ceremony were almost millenary. The staging of a cycle required large amounts of food. In the later stages, while the people were waiting for the apa-Hevehe to appear, no work was undertaken in the gardens. This state of affairs lasted for almost a month.

Williams's ambiguity can be resolved using information which has been gained by analysis of Elema myths and construction of the table of binary oppositions. The method of analysis involves examination of the ways in which the materials which were used in the apa-Hevehe's dress were collected (Fig. 1).

Stages in the ritual are described in physiological terms to give more impact and meaning, although these are not the actual terms

[1] F. E. Williams 1940:291.

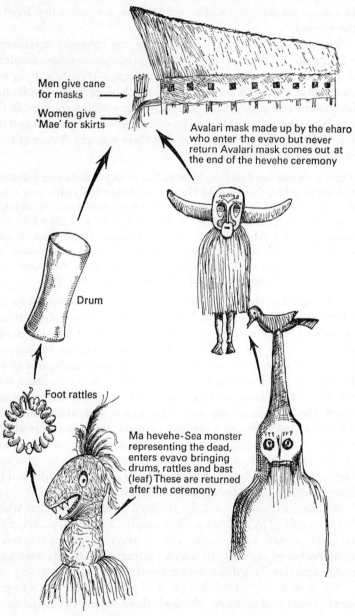

Men give cane for masks

Women give 'Mae' for skirts

Avalari mask made up by the eharo who enter the evavo but never return Avalari mask comes out at the end of the hevehe ceremony

Drum

Foot rattles

Ma hevehe-Sea monster representing the dead, enters evavo bringing drums, rattles and bast (leaf) These are returned after the ceremony

FIG. 1. Contributions to the 'Hevehe'.

used by the Elema themselves. Apa-Hevehe were conceived in the Eravo—they also died in the Eravo. In order to appreciate the significance of the apa-Hevehe's existence, examination can be broken down into the following sections: the Eravo as a womb, the collection of semen, impregnation of the Eravo, the gestation period, the birth, life, and death of apa-Hevehe. Use of these terms is not intended to emphasize 'subconscious' elements of Elema symbolism but to stress that apa-Hevehe had an almost human existence. As far as the Elema were concerned they were conceived like children, they lived as adult men, they were destroyed, and then bade farewell like spirits of the dead.

As a new Eravo was being constructed the builder would refer to a pillar being the grandmother's backbone, another pillar being her shinbone and so on.[1] The Eravo grandmother was a mythical woman who was thought to live under the Eravo. Further sexual symbolism was added by referring to the front and rear entrances as 'vagina' and 'anus'. It was in this womb that apa-Hevehe were born.

Collection of semen, as this section is called for heuristic purposes, is concerned with the collection of the materials used in the dress of the apa-Hevehe (Fig. 1). These materials were cane for the masks, totemic symbols which were used to decorate the masks, and drums and rattles which were carried by apa-Hevehe.

'Big men' initiated the Kovave ritual which was connected with the bush spirits by going to the bush and cutting cane. As the 'big men' cut the cane which was to be used to make masks they called on the bush spirits to come. The bush spirits came and eventually some of the cane that was associated with the bush spirits was placed in the Eravo.

The 'big men' summoned the bush spirits and they also told them to go home. 'Go back to your homes in the bush. We have fed you: do not be angry with us. When other strong men (big men) of our village have pigs for you they will sound the shell trumpet. Hearken and come again.'[2]

Totemic symbols were then collected. Mythology recounted that the 'big men' had been responsible for the creation of the totemic groups. In the apa-Hevehe ceremony 'big men' supervised the making of Eharo—figures which represented the totemic symbols.

[1] F. E. Williams 1940:159, 160.   [2] F. E. Williams 1940:149.

Drums and rattles were collected from the spirits of the dead who came to the Eravo in the form of ma-Hevehe sea monsters. By splitting a coconut 'big men' established communication with the spirits of the dead. Coconuts were associated with the land of the dead. Spells which were used by the 'big men' when they called on the spirits give some indication of the meaning of the apa-Hevehe ritual:

(a) Master Havae, rise up and sit here, I pray you with my lips. Your own Eravo men, your mat, your headrest, your sleeping place are here. Depart not to any other Eravo. Remain here and here alone. As we are about to do these things do you guard us. Go not to any other place;
(b) If my village people are about to die, then split the coconut badly. If they are to keep well then split the coconut well;
(c) I am about to open Apu's jaws. I Oro-ipi-avu am about to pour into them meat and sago;
(d) I am splitting open Oa-Birukapu's belly.[1]

Spells (a) and (b) were straightforward prayers for assistance directed towards the dead—Havae was the ancestor of the Eravo—who were traditionally thought to respond to calls for assistance. The idea is given that the well-being of the people is involved.

Spells (c) and (d) connect the ritual with mythology. The first deals with Oro-ipi-avu who fed the bull roarer (this was connected with fertility). In the other spell a reference is made to garden fertility. The death of Oa-Birukapu was responsible for the creation of garden fertility.

This appeal was addressed to the dead and in reply to the summons a sea monster visited the Eravo. The 'Hevehe Karawa' visit dealt with the contribution made to the apa-Hevehe's dress by the spirits of the dead. This contribution consisted of drums, bast (used for the apa-Hevehe's skirt), rattles, mats, and headrests which the apa-Hevehe used when they slept in the Eravo.[2]

The spirits of the bush and the spirits of the dead paid several visits to the Eravo. On each occasion they brought their distinctive contributions. The spirits had been warned to hold themselves ready for a summons from the 'big men'. 'Big men' organized the final visits of the 'Hevehe Karawa' and the entry of the Eharo totemic symbols into the Eravo. During the process of impregnation the Eravo was like one of the temples of the 'Vailala madness':

[1] F. E. Williams 1940:200–5.   [2] F. E. Williams 1940:210–20.

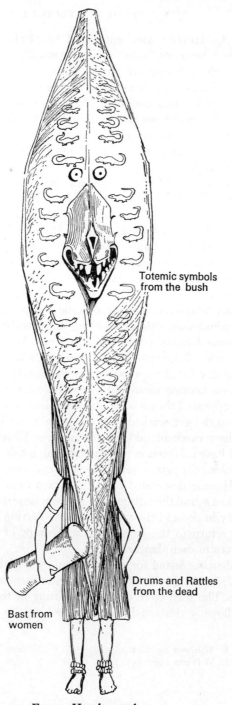

Totemic symbols
from the bush

Drums and Rattles
from the dead

Bast from
women

FIG. 2. Hevehe mask.

'When the Hevehe have entered it the Eravo acquires a new sanctity—it becomes "aiha" or supernaturally dangerous; and it is now, like those temples of the "Vailala madness", though not in the same disreputable sense, an "ahea-uvi" or hot house.'[1]

Impregnation was complete when the door of the Eravo was bound up in a ceremony known as 'dehe'. The door was not opened until the apa-Hevehe emerged. When the door had been bound up the Eravo was under a very strong taboo and only the 'big men' could go inside.[2]

During the period of gestation the apa-Hevehe developed their final form. From the cane that had been placed in the Eravo the masks were made. These masks were often over 20 ft. high and were decorated with totemic symbols (Fig. 2). Women made *mae* or grass skirts for the apa-Hevehe.

Fiction growth of the apa-Hevehe, as if they were like a 'foetus', was maintained by three excursions of the partially completed masks from the Eravo. These excursions served two purposes: young men who were to dance with the masks gained experience in their manipulation, delicate painting which was not possible in the dark crowded Eravo could be carried out. When the masks had been completed the apa-Hevehe were ready to be born.

As the day for the appearance of the apa-Hevehe came closer, the women became more and more excited. On the day the apa-Hevehe appeared they stood outside the Eravo. 'Come out, I want to see you, I have worked for you. In rain and heat I have made sago; I have carried food from the gardens; I have paddled up the rivers; I have shivered in the water catching fish; I have burnt my hand cooking for you; I want to see you and touch you, come out.'[3]

Apa-Hevehe descended from the Eravo each day for a month and walked round the village dancing from time to time. The masks were very heavy and the men who were wearing them had to frequently return to the Eravo to rest. Groups of women attached themselves to each dancer.

The dancing lasted for a month and during this time no work was done in the gardens because everyone was involved with the dancing. The men were dancing or sitting in the Eravo, women were following the apa-Hevehe or cooking. As the apa-Hevehe

[1] F. E. Williams 1940:226.   [2] F. E. Williams 1940:271, 272.
[3] F. E. Williams 1940:353, 354.

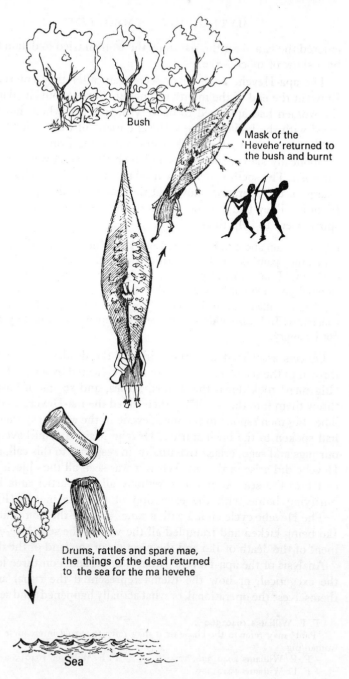

Bush

Mask of the
'Hevehe' returned to
the bush and burnt

Drums, rattles and spare mae,
the things of the dead returned
to the sea for the ma hevehe

Sea

FIG. 3. The close of the 'Hevehe' ceremony.

entered the Eravo for the last time, the women tried to detain them by a show of mock force.

The apa-Hevehe were never seen again after they entered the Eravo at the end of the month's dancing. Throughout the dancing the women had appeared to be very happy, but when they were faced with the loss of the apa-Hevehe many of them cried.[1]

Men wearing Aualari masks came out of the Eravo. They were symbolically slain with arrows and then the masks were burnt in the bush. The spells which were used by the 'big men' who were in charge of the operation show that they expected the spirits to feel friendly. They had fed the spirits of the bush, and in return the spirits were to help them:

(a) Now I am about to burn you. Look kindly on the men of the Eravo. When they pant[2] do not let the arrow stick in the ground but in the eye of the pig. I do not harm you. Constantly from long ago I have fed and fostered you. Do not be angry with us;

(b) I have called you up because of my pigs and sago I have fed you constantly. In future other strong men ('big men') will call on you. Do not be angry.[3]

Objects associated with the spirits of the dead were taken and thrown in the sea where they were to be collected by a ma-Hevehe. 'Big men' took down the drums, rattles, and scraps of bast and threw them into the sea. They then called the ma-Hevehe to come. The 'big men' spoke to the ma-Hevehe in the same way that they had spoken to the bush spirits. 'Hevehe Maiavu. You have eaten our pigs and sago, arise.' Eventually, in response to this call, a ma-Hevehe did arise in the sea. When it was seen all the objects were cast into the sea. After this ceremony all the participants had a purifying bathe with the exception of the 'big men'.[4] (Fig. 3)

The Hevehe cycle ended with a cane figure of the mythical hero Iko being kicked and trampled all the way to the sea. A re-enactment of the death of Iko and the creation of the land of the dead.[5]

Analysis of the apa-Hevehe ritual is undertaken on three levels: the exegetical, or how the Elema represented the ritual among themselves; the operational, or what actually happened; and seman-

---

[1] F. E. Williams 1940:360–7.

[2] 'Pant' may refer to the chase or it may refer to sexual intercourse with a woman/pig.

[3] F. E. Williams 1940:376, 377.   [4] F. E. Williams 1940:382–4.

[5] F. E. Williams 1940:390.

tic analysis, or the significance of the ritual in relation to the role of the 'big man'.[1]

Exegetical analysis is confined to spells and formulas used by the 'big men' during the collection of semen and the bidding farewell to contributions associated with the spirits of the dead and bush spirits. Attention is also paid to myth-charades which were enacted at various points during the ceremony. How did the Elema represent these things to themselves? Many actions were referred to as re-enactments of the mythical role of 'big men'. During the myth-charades that accompanied the collection of semen Aikere and Maikere re-enacted their mythical roles. They killed Oa-Birukapu and Ape. Iko was symbolically slain at the close of the cycle. Summoning the bush spirits and the spirits of the dead was referred to as the work of 'big men'. But there is no information on how the Elema represented the apa-Hevehe among themselves.

Things which actually happened are now dealt with. Materials which were widely representative of Elema cosmology were collected and placed in the Eravo which was likened to a womb. After a period of gestation the apa-Hevehe which emerged had a dress which represented the spirits of the bush and the spirits of the dead —the left and the right. These contributions were eventually returned in the same order that they had originally been collected.

The entire ceremony was organized by the 'big men'. They initiated action in each successive stage of the ceremonial cycle, they used their personal wealth in the feasts and their exclusive ritual knowledge in summoning the spirits. Spirits of the dead and spirits of the bush had been given food by the 'big men' and in return they were expected to help the Elema people. The dead were to help by making sea voyages safe and ensuring garden fertility; the spirits of the bush were supposed to help in hunting. The bush spirits were told to go home. Spirits of the dead had to behave themselves and go home at the close of the rituals because the 'big men' had the Iko myth re-enacted.

Semantic analysis begins by assuming that apa-Hevehe were a symbol; and examination is directed towards finding out what was symbolized, i.e. the referent. The 'big man's' role was shown in the examination of Elema myths to be one of instituting, organizing, and maintaining Elema culture. Creation of apa-Hevehe meant a

[1] A modified form of the analysis discussed by J. Beattie 1960.

reassertion of that role. It involved a reaffirmation of the 'big man's' superiority. His ability to control the Elema environment and his ability to look after his people. Apa-Hevehe like the 'big men' were an integrative social force. Among the Elema, as with any society, there was conflict between man and his environment to obtain a living from the soil and the sea, between man and woman, and between man and the supernatural. Apa-Hevehe transcended these conflicts.[1]

Apa-Hevehe like the 'big men' presented a synthesized cultural image, a microcosmic view of the cosmos. They too were a total social fact. They were concerned with the restatement of basic truths about Elema cultural life and social organization. They were a symbol of the 'big man's' power, their creation was a reaffirmation of Elema social values. Maintenance of Elema life and culture was the work of the 'big man'. Apa-Hevehe symbolized the 'big man's' ability to carry out this task.

[1] See the Introduction to *African Political Systems* 1940:16–18 for a discussion on this point.

III

EUROPEAN CONTACT

EXAMINATION of experiences the Elema had with Europeans before the 'Vailala Madness' deals first with the role of the administration, then with missionary and commercial activity. However, among these types of European there were considerable differences of opinion on what the European role in the territory should be. In this chapter examination of administrative, missionary, and commercial activity as it affected the Elema is prefaced by a brief outline of the general situation. The nature of European contact is then related to indigenous concepts of power, wealth, and status.

ADMINISTRATIVE ACTIVITY

Australian connection with Papua began in 1884, when the State of Queensland declared the territory a Protectorate.[1] This move was in part the result of a desire to safeguard the commercial interests and welfare of Queenslanders working in Papua. It also aimed at counter-balancing possible German expansion from New Guinea by establishing a first line of defence against possible incursions on the vulnerable northern Australian coastline.

During the period of Queensland's control, the top administrative staff of the territory were drawn from the British Crown Colony of Fiji, necessary because the Australians had no Colonial Service of their own. Recruitment at lower levels in the territory's civil service was undertaken locally.[2]

Conflict between administration and commercial interests over policy on land and labour was evident from the declarations of the Protectorate. This conflict was to reach considerable proportions during the period of Hubert Murray's Governorship. It arose because the administration conceived its role in terms of protecting native interests while the commercial expatriates thought that the Government had a duty to create favourable conditions for trade. In 1892 legislation was enacted forbidding natives to work more

[1] L. P. Mair 1948:11. [2] J. D. Legge 1956:2, 3.

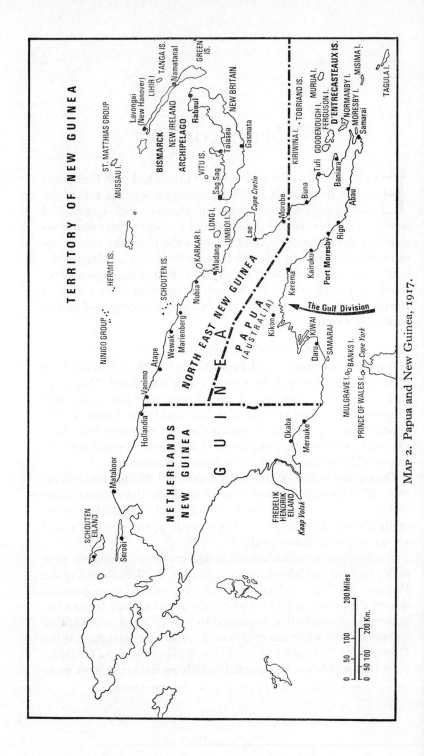

MAP 2. Papua and New Guinea, 1917.

than twenty-five miles from their homes. This law had obvious repercussions on recruitment. Further legislation was enacted forbidding the alienation of native land without Government permission.[1] A number of early laws laid down conditions for the employment of native labour. Land legislation militated against the building up of large native estates.

Commercial expatriates favoured easy purchase of native customary land, favourable rates of taxation, financial backing from the Government, and a plentiful supply of cheap labour. The administration's refusal to comply with these requests was not made any the more palatable by the knowledge that these conditions existed in German New Guinea.

The administration took a strong line in enforcing the rule of law. Papuans were left in no doubt that the murder of Europeans would attract savage reprisals. The Goarabari, who murdered the L.M.S. missionary, Chalmers, at the turn of the century, were punished severely by two punitive expeditions.[2] Houses were burnt down and all the women and children in sight were shot.

After the formation of the Royal Papuan Constabulary the administration was able to punish inter-tribal murders. It was firmly believed that the humiliation of rebellious tribes was essential to the inculcation of respect for the governing power. Dignity must be upheld by force. One severe lesson at an early age was thought to do away with the necessity for repetition.[3]

During the Protectorate era there were very considerable difficulties facing the administration in the government of Papua. Although the officer in charge was drawn from Fiji, his staff had no specialized training or colonial experience. It was not until 1924 that the need for pre-service training for Papuan administrative staff was recognized.

The number of Government officers in the territory was pegged at a very low level due to lack of finance. In 1904 there was only an allocation of £22,000 from Queensland to cover all expenses.[4] Added to these staffing problems, the territory was rugged and inhospitable, divided by fast-flowing rivers and clothed in dense tropical rain forest.

Despite these drawbacks, and the unhealthy nature of the climate, the administration was able to adopt a progressive agricultural

[1] J. D. Legge 1956:75, 77.   [2] J. D. Legge 1956:71, 108, 109.
[3] L. Lett 1942:59, 74.   [4] L. P. Mair 1948:25.

policy aimed at realizing the potential of Papua's natural resources. This agricultural planning was due to the efforts of Stanniforth-Smith who hoped to succeed Dr. Macdonald (who was then Governor). Stanniforth-Smith established experimental plots to assess the commercial possibilities of growing rubber, tea, and coffee. However, some three years after the Commonwealth of Australia had assumed responsibility for the administration of Papua, Hubert Murray was appointed Governor.

Murray's Governship of Papua was extremely long, lasting from 1908 till 1939. During this period Murray achieved international recognition for his ideas on the theory and practice of Colonial administration.

Hubert Murray was an unusual man. Born in Australia, he read classics at Oxford, was called to the English bar, became an amateur boxing champion and then went to Papua as a judge.[1] His brother, Gilbert Murray, later became Professor of Greek at Oxford.

Hubert Murray believed that the situation in Papua called for a type of administration which differed from the African model.[2] He accepted the idealism which was inherent in the League of Nations concept of Colonialism and he agreed with the great African administrator, Lord Lugard, that priority of native interests must be regarded as of prime importance.

Gilbert Murray was a humanist and it is evident that his views struck a chord of sympathy with his brother Hubert. They corresponded regularly until Hubert's untimely death in 1939. The influence of Gilbert's humanism was platonic in form. Both Murrays were concerned with the development of man as a unique moral being. Their views were unallied to any comparative judgements based on the superiority of European society by virtue of its technological and material achievements.

Humanism means the building of a better society. Some people measure progress by man's material inventions, but material possessions do not themselves constitute progress. We can certainly think of great individuals and simple societies that were quite as good and happy as we are without any of these inventions. Even the supposed supernatural revelations, different in different parts of the world, which the local population accept as superhuman truth, are all in the language of man, shaped by man.[3]

[1] J. A. La Nauze 1963:1-4.   [2] J. H. P. Murray 1925:viii.
[3] G. G. A. Murray 1944.

In his reviews, books, and papers Gilbert Murray made a plea for two special features to be incorporated in Colonial administration: there should be special legislation to reinforce the protecting codes administered by Imperial officers (who would be free from local bias); administrators must start, as his brother Hubert had, by liking the natives in order to understand them.[1]

Hubert Murray knew that change was inevitable. He was deeply sensitive to the effects of European material culture on the Papuans. Writing about the disappearance of native customs he said:

We may think it a good thing that they disappear, but they have during many generations been the protection of men and women in times of stress and trial, and, when these customs and traditions are weakened, the morals of those who have to battle through life without them must surely be weakened also.[2]

Murray's cautiousness in the face of change is exemplified by another statement:

In suppressing a practice which seems to you silly and useless, you are at the same time perhaps affecting a dozen other practices which may in other ways be desirable.[3]

In dealing with those who wished to maintain Papuan culture as a 'closed' society Hubert Murray said:

Papua is full of people who 'understand' the native thoroughly; these are a very dangerous class, for they really believe what they say and are quite unconscious of their limitations. The capacity of thinking 'black' or 'brown' is in fact possessed by few, for this is an art which, it is said, requires more sympathy and insight than is given to all men. It is an art which is as valuable as it is rare, but the man who possesses it labours under a corresponding defect, for he is apt to attach an exaggerated importance to native culture and tradition, and, in fact, to anything native. I can sympathize with those who regret the disappearance of old customs and religions, but really the people who affect a regard for all these matters of the old régime in Papua often idealize them out of all relation to reality.[4]

Hubert Murray's views on change were not shared by Williams, the Government anthropologist. He was shocked by the iconoclasm of the 'Vailala Madness', and he made a passionate plea for the retention of the colourful Hevehe ceremony. Williams maintained

[1] G. G. A. Murray 1900:154.   [2] J. H. P. Murray 1925:222.
[3] J. H. P. Murray 1925:234.   [4] J. H. P. Murray 1925:224.

that Papuan culture was like a watch. You only had to remove one wheel to stop a watch, or one stone from the social structure to have it tumbling about your ears.[1]

Viewing the effects of the impact of European civilization on the Papuans, Murray was able to adopt a realistic standpoint. He believed that efforts must be made to check revolutionary social change, by observation, analogy, and imagination. Anthropologists, he thought, worked by analogy; they did not give advice in specific instances, but attempted to formulate general principles. Administrators based their actions on deductions which stemmed from direct observation. The defect was that the anthropologist had the learning without the experience, while the administrator had the experience without the learning.

Despite his humanist leanings, Hubert Murray carried the moral convictions of his class: work hard, play hard, cleanliness is next to godliness, etc. The effects of social change, the introduction of steel tools, and the Pax Britannica had meant that the Papuan had more leisure time on his hands. Murray, in appreciating this, felt that if the Papuans could be given plenty to do then the effects of social change could be minimized. Murray believed that the Papuan had not yet acquired habits of sustained industry.[2] But he achieved only limited success with his plans to fill the vacuum which he believed had been created in the lives of the Papuans through contact with Europeans.

The early Papuan administration had neither the finance nor the staff which would have been necessary to implement large-scale development schemes. As Lord Hailey said: 'Nor is it any disparagement of Murray's reputation to say that his system of administration amounted to no more than a well regulated and benevolent type of police rule. Appointment of village constables and subsequently of village councillors appears only to have amounted to the creation of local auxiliaries to the police organization.'[3]

The appointment of local councillors and constables was resented by the Papuans. Those who were chosen often had no standing in the community—they were not 'big men'. These officials were usually chosen because they were the only people who could understand simple English.

[1] F. E. Williams 1939b.   [2] J. H. P. Murray 1925:219.
[3] L. P. Mair 1948:xvi.

Hubert Murray's ideas are of importance not only because they set the tone for the administration but also because his brother G. H. Murray had to deal with the 'Vailala Madness'. The attitude he took showed the influence of Hubert's thinking. Papua was divided into administrative Divisions each under the control of a resident Magistrate. The headquarters of the Gulf Division was established at Kerema in 1906.[1] The technique of administration was by direct personal contact. Magistrates undertook long foot tours of inspection in their Divisions. They were accompanied by detachments of the Royal Papuan Constabulary, an armed disciplined service. Magistrates had vast areas to cover, they often spent weeks on tour in pursuit of murderers or simply trying to cover their Divisions. Murder of Europeans by Papuans was punished very severely. But Hubert Murray had made it plain on his assumption of office that he would not tolerate officers taking the law into their own hands. Officers who were attacked by natives could only use firearms as a last resort.

The native constabulary regarded their commanding officer as a 'big man'.[2] They were trained on infantry lines,[3] and complaints had arisen about their 'arrogant, high handed treatment' of village officials.[4] Papuan constables were recruited from tribes who were renowned for their warlike qualities. It seems clear that they found their duties congenial at times, particularly when they were taking reprisals against their traditional enemies. During a punitive expedition to the Gulf Division in 1881, an Elema 'big man' was killed and his house destroyed. Chalmers of the L.M.S. was informed that only a very 'big man' could act in this manner.[5]

Magistrates imposed rigid discipline. The kinds of instructions that they gave to the Papuans showed they had the same moral convictions as Hubert Murray. Dirtiness and inactivity were characterized as laziness; idolatry and poor hygiene were deplored. But in getting their ideas over to the Papuans the Magistrates had little time for pleasantries. The territory they had to cover was so large that they had only a short time to spend in each village. Orders had to be given quickly and Papuans had to be made to appreciate that failure to carry out the Magistrate's instructions would be punished.

[1] L. P. Mair 1948:27.   [2] J. G. Hides 1938:38.
[3] H. M. Dauncey 1913:31.   [4] L. P. Mair 1948:40.
[5] W. Seton 1909:80, 81.

Resistance was patently futile. The Magistrate was backed by his armed Constabulary who in many cases came from tribes that were traditional enemies. Magistrates were physically and mentally strong and self-reliant; in many cases they had been recruited locally from the ranks of those who knew how to 'manage' the natives—the expatriate planter class. The Magistrate appeared as an isolated individual. He gave orders, imposed discipline, and organized the village communities.

Magistrates had considerable powers in addition to their role in enforcing the rule of law. They gave orders to clean villages, they made the villagers line up for inspection, and they laid down standards for housing. Papuans were required to keep open such roads as the Magistrate might direct and to act as carriers if required.[1]

Murray's main attempt to inculcate habits of industry among the Papuans was in the sphere of agriculture. In 1894 a Regulation had been passed requiring the natives to plant coconuts; this had had little effect—planting was not supervised, nor was any stipulation made about spacing between the seedlings. However, in 1918 additional Regulations were passed which provided for the supervision of planting by Magistrates. These measures were enforced. The Gulf Division was chosen for a number of the agricultural experiments—possibly on account of the topography and the plentiful supply of land, though more probably in view of the proximity of the Division to Port Moresby.

Before 1918 the Elema were forced to grow rice. By 1923 476 acres were under cultivation on thirty-one plantations in the Gulf Division. These ranged in size from half an acre to fifty-two acres. As with the compulsory coconut planting, rice cultivation had little impact on the economy of the Gulf Division because there were no compulsory marketing arrangements. The Elema, who were basically sago eaters, protested that they did not want to grow rice, and as a measure of their refusal to co-operate in the scheme, convictions, for failure to cultivate rice, were running at the rate of 200 per annum.[2]

The impact of these agricultural schemes must have resulted in a considerable amount of intervention in the lives of the Elema. In these activities the Elema made no decisions. There was no person

---

[1] J. Holmes MSS. and J. D. Legge 1956:78.
[2] L. P. Mair 1948:86, 87, and J. D. Legge 1956:171, 172.

or social mechanism capable of taking note of the changing circumstances or of making explicit decisions regarding reorganization. Consequently the individuals concerned could only collide with their own outmoded community values.[1]

In 1918 compulsory native taxation was introduced for the first time to raise badly needed revenue for the administration. The Regulations provided a contingency clause in the event of the natives being unable to pay. If a village was unable to pay then an adjacent area was declared a plantation by the Government. Government supplied tools and seed, the natives supplied the labour. Profits, if any, were to be equally shared between the natives and Government.[2]

Magistrates, like 'big men', were known as 'men of many things'.[3] They did not enter into reciprocal relationships with the Elema but they did feed their followers. Among the Elema the ability to call on large-scale food supplies had been the hall-mark of a 'big man'—Magistrates possessed large quantities of food.

The economic expertise of the Magistrate affected the Elema to the same extent, and had the same impact, as the traditional economic role of the 'big man'. Coconut planting and rice cultivation affected all the Elema. The Elema were unfamiliar with these activities although they could appreciate the organizational implications of the Magistrate's role. He initiated action, organized the community for work, imposed discipline, and achieved visible results. In doing these things he had a role which was similar to the role of the 'big man'.

Obviously the Magistrates were in possession of a great deal of ritual power. The results that they obtained in their agricultural ventures had to be due to the intervention of the spirits of the dead. Alternatively, the Magistrates received their supplies, like the traditional Elema trading, by sea, which involved the ability to control the ma-Hevehe sea monsters. But there were other rituals which the Elema had not performed. The Magistrate worked in an office which was like an Eravo. He sent letters and there were impressive flag-raising ceremonies. Orders were given to line up and to keep the village clean.

Good health, good fortune, and success in ritual activities showed possession of the powers of a sorcerer. Magistrates fell into

---

[1] K. O. L. Burridge 1960:260–3.   [2] L. Lett 1942:124.
[3] H. A. Brown MSS.: all Europeans were known as 'men of many things'.

this category and no one had been able to harm the Magistrate by using sorcery.

The Magistrate's political power could be thought of in the same terms as the 'big man's' political power. It was dependent on his personality and organizational ability together with his ability to impose sanctions if his wishes were not carried out. A further similarity with the 'big man' was provided by the fact that the Elema had no opportunity to discuss the Magistrate's executive decisions. They were forced to accept the instructions of the Magistrate without question. Magistrates upheld the traditional moral code. They solved disputes and punished stealing and adultery. Operating with the native Constabulary, who were often employed on punitive expeditions, the Magistrate could be thought of as a war-leader.

'Big men' gained status from their organizational ability and because they possessed exclusive religious knowledge—Magistrates had the same status among the Elema. They could call on large-scale food supplies and had the ability to feed their followers. But the Magistrate's status was not the same kind of status that was possessed by the 'big man'. Traditional 'big men' had presented a synthesized cultural image of their society. The Magistrate ignored Elema culture and his status was of a personal nature—the Elema could not think of him as their 'big man'.

MISSIONARY CONTACT

A gentlemen's agreement was made in Port Moresby in 1890 between the Roman Catholic mission and the London Missionary Society, the only two missions at that time in the territory, defining their respective spheres of influence. The southern half of the island of New Guinea fell to the L.M.S.[1]

The early evangelists had few doubts about the value of the message that they were bringing to the Papuans. As Holmes of the L.M.S. said: 'I have lived, dined and slept with the cannibal . . . but I have never met a single man or woman, or a single person, that your civilization without Christianity has civilized. . . . Gospel and commerce but remember that it must be the Gospel first.'[2] There were frequent differences of opinion between the missionaries, the Government, and the commercial expatriates.

---

[1] J. D. Legge 1956:82.   [2] R. Lovett 1903:180

Missionaries believed in the inevitability of change. But their views differed from Hubert Murray's in two respects: the vacuum which had been created in Papuan social life through contact with Europeans was to be filled with religious works, and the missionaries believed in the superiority of European civilization. One missionary went so far as to say that he was sorry that the Papuan was no cleaner in his mind than he was in his body.[1]

But the more liberal view of Holmes prevailed: 'Retain native customs as far as possible—only those which are very objectionable should be forbidden—and leave it to the influence of education to raise them to more civilized customs.'[2]

Mission policy frowned on general engagement in commerce which might prove detrimental to evangelical work. However, as far as possible mission stations were encouraged to be self-sufficient, by doing their own repairs, executing their building programmes in local materials, and by growing their own food.

The L.M.S. divided their territory into Districts, and each District had its own head station where the European missionary lived. The head station for the Gulf Division was established by Holmes at Orokolo.[3]

Holmes paid his first visit to the Elema in 1881. He was struck by what he termed the Orokolo people's 'responsive attention' to the Christian message.[4] Having established a base at Orokolo a missionary compound was then built, containing a church, a school, workshops, and expatriate housing. Holmes lived in Orokolo village for seven years and was then succeeded by Bartlett, Schlenker, and Pryce-Jones who remained among the Elema up till the outbreak of the Second World War.

The station at Orokolo was supplied by the missionary ship the *John Williams*. The *John Williams* brought L.M.S. native missionaries from Tonga and Samoa to Orokolo where they helped to teach and train Papuan missionaries. At the same time new varieties of vegetable were introduced from Polynesia.[5]

Bartlett, who arrived in Orokolo in 1905, found a ready-made mission compound, and even a wind-driven water-pump. The new missionary was an energetic man. He constructed a steam press to shape planks and made a small boat. Rickshaws were imported

[1] C. W. Abel 1907:23. [2] L. M. Link 1915:18.
[3] J. Holmes 1924:67, 134, 204. [4] W. Seton 1909:86.
[5] H. A. Brown MSS.

from Singapore to help in travelling quickly on the land. Alderney cows were brought to Orokolo to provide milk and a buoy was constructed off-shore so that ships could leave mail when the weather was too rough to permit a landing.[1] Early L.M.S. missionaries paid a considerable amount of attention to the temporal needs of their parishioners. They not only wanted to 'missionize' the Elema, but also wanted to make them into useful citizens who could take their place in the new society that had been created as a result of European contact. While appreciating the value of the training he could give the younger Elema in his station workshops Bartlett wanted to do more: 'Once again we feel the necessity of placing our boys on an independent footing, by giving them, in addition to the usual mission training, the knowledge of an industry. Without detracting in any way from the spiritual side of the work we must do more for the temporal needs.'[2]

The L.M.S. missionaries lived in Orokolo, they learnt the Elema language, and shared their food with the people. Holmes and Pryce-Jones gave their children native names. Pryce-Jones entered into reciprocal relationships with the Elema and wrote bitterly that he was judged to the extent that he gave.[3] The Orokolo missionaries adopted Elema culture and became a part of it. Orokolo was later to become the one western Elema village which was not affected by the 'Vailala Madness'.

When Christian concepts were translated into the Elema language misunderstandings arose which had the effect of convincing the Elema that the missionaries had the power of 'big men'. A sermon began: 'Erita maso toae soi,' meaning, 'let us make a spell'. The name chosen for Heaven was 'Horovu Harihu', the traditional name for the land of the dead. The church was called an Eravo or men's house.[4]

There were strong similarities with the traditional pattern of religious technology. If benefits were to be obtained from Heaven (the land of the dead) then the people must be worthy. This meant that God (the spirits of the dead) had to be propitiated. Adultery, stealing, or disobedience were likely to destroy any hope of benefits.

The missionaries gradually gained the confidence of the people.

[1] T. W. Reid 1960:38, 40, 57.   [2] L.M.S. Annual Report 1910.
[3] Pryce-Jones MSS.   [4] H. A. Brown MSS.

Never, perhaps, do the old customs and indulgence in sorcery show more than in preparation for the trading expedition to the west. Delema (a village not far from Elema territory) fitted out two *lakatois*, and when they were ready for sea a deputation of those to sail in them came to ask if I would hold a farewell service, and commend the *lakatois* and those travelling in them to God's keeping while they were away. With joy I consented, and rarely have I seen a larger congregation in our little church. The captains, each at the head of his crew, marched up and took the front pews. Their relatives and friends filled the church, and some of us are not likely to forget the service, which for the first time took the place of heathen rites. The prayers were answered. Both *lakatois* returned in safety with all on board.[1]

Although progress in the work of converting the Elema was made, it was slow, and by the time of the outbreak of the First World War the L.M.S. had only established a foothold in a few villages. Despite the fact that a native Regulation had been passed in 1907 making it compulsory for children to attend a school where English was taught, the 664 pupils in the L.M.S. schools in 1909 all came from Christian villages.[2]

Individually the missionaries were 'men of many things' like 'big men'. They entered into reciprocal relationships and it can be assumed that they carried out their obligations in a satisfactory manner. But like the traditional 'big man' the missionary made his main impact in the sphere of corporate wealth transactions. Missionaries could call on large-scale food supplies, and they fed their followers. Communal economic expertise was evident from the way in which they grew food for the whole station[3] and organized trading with the *John Williams*.

Missionaries performed rituals which affected all the people in the village. In traditional religious technology there had been no appreciation of the means/end relationship—the same reasoning applied in relation to Christian rituals. Missionaries, like 'big men', had exclusive religious knowledge; and though this was not empirically testable, it was a logical deduction in view of the results that the missionaries obtained. Their success in gardening and trading showed that they had the power to control the spirits of the dead.

But there were other rituals which the pagan Elema did not take part in and which appeared to have certain similarities with rituals

[1] *L.M.S. Annual Report 1910–11.*   [2] H. A. Brown MSS.
[3] T. W. Reid 1960:72.

which were used by the Magistrate. The Magistrate made his men
do drill: Bartlett had established a contingent of the Boys' Brigade
at Orokolo. They had uniforms, they drilled, they had twenty pipes,
one drum, three kettle-drums, and a pair of cymbals.[1] Missionaries
and Magistrates used flags; the missionaries at Orokolo used flags
to signal to ships, and they were also raised on Sundays in Christian
villages.[2] On the Government station the flag was raised and
lowered with great ceremony each day. Both kinds of European
also received and sent letters and received supplies by ship.
Although these rituals were new they had semantic associations
with the rituals that were performed by the 'big men'. Missionaries
appeared to get benefits from the spirits of the dead.

Due to their successes and good health, the missionaries possessed, prima facie, the powers of sorcerers. Their medical and religious roles gave the missionaries two further attributes of a sorcerer.
In healing the sick and curing hitherto incurable diseases they
overcame traditional prejudices. And the Christian message
emphasized the power of God, his ability to strike his enemies.
The way to avoid this was to follow God's commandments which,
by implication, involved obeying the missionary. So that like the
'big man' the missionary was buttressed by sorcery.

Missionaries had the same kind of political power that was
associated with the 'big men'. They had very considerable
organizational ability and, in relation to the Elema, strong personalities. They initiated, organized, and executed communal projects.
Missionaries took executive decisions involving the Elema without
reference to the views of the community. They solved disputes
between Elema, and within their church organization they imposed
fines and sanctions for breaches of church discipline.

The missionary had the same kind of status that had been possessed by the 'big man'. This came from his organizational ability,
command of food supplies, communal economic expertise, and
possession of exclusive religious knowledge. And the missionaries
to a certain extent identified themselves with Elema culture.[3]

COMMERCIAL ACTIVITY

Hubert Murray's humanistic approach, with its protective
attitude towards Papuan interests, was bitterly resented by the

---

[1] *L.M.S. Annual Report 1910.*   [2] T. W. Reid 1960:43.
[3] W. Seton 1909:82.

commercial expatriates in the territory. By 1914 Sir Hubert had clashed with the powerful Burns Philp company on a question of labour policy. The company had illegally recruited 500 natives, due to a misunderstanding, and they maintained that the contract should stand, but Murray, who declared the contract void, had his way. Other incidents of this nature did little to help relations between the two camps.[1] Antagonism against Murray had reached its climax when one individual, without consulting any of the other expatriates, sent a telegram to the King demanding Murray's withdrawal. The telegram was sent to the Prime Minister of Australia who returned it to Murray without comment. The commercial section felt that sending a telegram had been too extreme, and sympathy swung in Murray's direction.

Plantation owners wanted labour. For this reason Burns Philp company had advocated the introduction of taxation for some years prior to 1918. It was thought that compulsory taxation would force the natives to work on plantations to earn money to pay tax.

Papuans resisted indenture very strongly since work on the plantations was very unpopular. This resistance lasted till about 1922. 'Native labourers, their time completed, went to their homes firmly determined that they would not again be tempted to undergo the tyranny of indenture.'[2]

Commercial expatriates felt that Papuans should be kept in their place. Their object was to make money and they did not feel that they had any responsibility for native welfare. The following newspaper extracts show the prevailing climate of opinion:

How to Succeed as a Coconut Planter in New Guinea.—Never talk to the boys themselves under any circumstances, always do it through bossboys. Apart from your own houseboys, never allow any native to approach you in the field or on the bungalow verandah.

As soon as the natives are made to work the healthier they will be, and the less call there will be for the expenditure of the Government on large quantities of medicine for the curing of native ailments which are nothing more than laziness on the part of the Kanaka. In addition to making him healthier it will make him more honest, though there is no getting away from the fact that corporal punishment until the Kanaka is taught honesty is the best and most painless policy.[3]

The commercial attitude was much more harsh than that of the

---

[1] L. Lett 1949:182.   [2] L. Lett 1942:115.
[3] *Rabaul Times*, 27 Aug. 1926 and 22 Mar. 1929.

Magistrate. Plantations were boycotted. The commercial expatriate was recognized as an enemy. But even though the plantation
owners could be ignored, it was not possible to ignore the traders
who lived among the Elema.

Burkman, a European trader, lived at Vailala. He traded in copra
and sago, buying it for tobacco, dogs' teeth, calico, knives, and
axes. Bartlett, the L.M.S. missionary, commented:

He's a brute. . . . He is one of those men whom one finds about the
Pacific—good family, well educated, can talk and act like a gentleman;
traded, mined, and ran cargoes all about Australia, New Zealand and the
islands, will end his days in New Guinea unless he is chucked out. He is
a white haired old man, aristocratic looking Johnny, tall, thin, got a nose
that shows signs of having been in contact with an irresistible force in
the past. He wanted to be carried down to Orokolo a week or so back,
got so weak he cannot tramp as he did. Natives refused to carry him, he
got his gun and blazed about to frighten them, and managed to shoot
some small shot into a woman's shoulder, also shot a child, not fatally,
but that does not excuse the man.[1]

The Vailala people could not take reprisals. They were by that
time well aware of what had happened to other Papuans who had
killed Europeans.

In addition to their unsatisfactory plantation experiences, a
number of Elema must have been involved in mining operations
when gold was discovered up the Lakekama river at the turn of the
century. Conditions in the mining camps were rough and primitive. By 1910 there were 120 Europeans in the area. The death rate
among the Papuan workers reached 35 per cent of those employed.
Fortunately for the Papuans the war intervened, and by 1918 there
were only five Europeans left. Also, at the turn of the century, oil
surveying was carried out near the Vailala river by the Anglo-
Persian oil company. The survey did not last long and no base was
established on land.

There is evidence that the Elema were residing in an area which
had received a considerable amount of expatriate commercial
attention. Kerema, the Government station, was only forty miles
away and the station's first annual report mentions that twelve
trading posts had been established in the Gulf Division. Copra,
sago, sandalwood, and bêche-de-mer were exchanged for trade
goods.[2] But there can be little doubt that, despite the administra-

¹ T. W. Reid 1960:53.   ² H. A. Brown MSS.

tion's protective attitude, considerable pressure was put on the Elema to trade with the Europeans.

European traders were 'Men of many things'. They had power, wealth, organizational ability and warlike attributes. Commercial expatriates entered into a large number of reciprocal relationships. But the commercial expatriates did not identify themselves with the Elema. They ignored them, they beat them, and the Elema were unable to retaliate. These commercial 'big men' were like those of an enemy tribe. The traditional response would have been war. The only alternative open to the Elema was to ignore them as far as possible.

THE EFFECTS OF EUROPEAN CONTACT ON THE ELEMA

The concomitant effect of European contact on the Elema was to convince them that in every field of activity their performance was markedly inferior. No matter how hard they tried, the Europeans treated them as 'rubbish men'. At the same time the status of the 'big men' was completely eroded away. Traditionally a tribe with an unpopular leader could move their village; this was not possible —the Europeans were everywhere.

The 'Pax Britannica' removed the main activity for which leadership was required. It also did away with one of the main activities in which the Elema could prove their manhood. Large men had appealed as 'big men'—physically the Europeans were larger than the Papuans and they were demonstrably better soldiers.

Europeans took over the economic role of the 'big man'. His initiation, organization, and execution of the annual economic projects, the gardening and the trading, were replaced by European agricultural activities. The Elema no longer had time to follow their traditional way of life.

Missionaries and Magistrates assumed responsibility for control of the spirits of the dead. Trading voyages had in any case become virtually obsolete through the activities of the resident commercials and the missionaries. Europeans sent ships to collect the goods. But there was no longer any ritual framework in which the Elema could establish their identity. The Europeans, like the traditional 'big men', kept their exclusive religious knowledge to themselves.

Curative medicine and missionary influence had destroyed the 'big man's' claims to superior powers of sorcery. Europeans were able to cure sickness, and Christian concepts were phrased in such a way as to be in direct competition with traditional ideas on the role of the sorcerer.

Due to the shortage of wealth the transactions of Elema became like those of 'rubbish men'. It was increasingly difficult to carry out traditional obligations. The cessation of overseas trade meant that it was no longer possible for the Elema to obtain the same quantity of shell money as they had been able to obtain under the 'big man's' directions in traditional times. Failure to execute obligations meant a loss of status. The 'big men' were champions or symbols of Elema culture—they guarded and sustained it. They stood for Elema cultural integrity and in terms of its symbolism they *were* Elema culture. What was left when Elema culture was treated as being of no account?

The 'big man's' loss of status had important organizational implications. He had established a framework of organizational activities within which men had been able to establish their manhood. Standards had been set by the 'big men' which, when reached, had automatically resulted in ascription of manhood status. This organizational framework had been modified by European contact. The Elema were unfamiliar with the new activities and no matter what they did the Europeans would not recognize that they were men. In this situation anomic tendencies were bound to gather momentum.

IV

THE 'VAILALA MADNESS'

CONFUSION existed among the Elema as to what kind of men the Europeans were. Could they be spirits of the dead, as was first supposed, or were they simply more powerful versions of the traditional 'big man'? This ambivalence was evident before the outbreak of the 'madness' in 1919, for a number of individuals attempted to identify the Europeans as dead kinsmen, at the same time giving them presents. But this was an attempt to rationalize the existence of the Europeans—an attempt to account for their existence.[1]

Although Pryce-Jones had established friendly relations with the people in Orokolo village, he had had little success in the pagan villages and, appreciating the strength of custom, he was prepared for a long wait.

Between 1910 and 1918 the missionary had a number of unusual experiences. Pryce-Jones had given his children native names and he found that the pagan Elema were beginning to take a great interest in his children. Men came from distant villages to ask the missionary the names of his children and 'on hearing the names of the children they went away apparently satisfied with their strange behaviour'. The pagan Elema were confirming that Pryce-Jones was identifying himself with Elema culture.

In 1910 a small group of Elema men visited Pryce-Jones although they were not members of his church. But they were dressed like mission natives in clean white 'ramis' or loin cloths. They shook hands with the missionary and told him that they had come to give him money because they were happy. After this they went away leaving a very perplexed missionary.[2] This incident was another attempt by the pagan Elema to identify themselves with the Missionary—by accepting money he entered into a reciprocal relationship with the natives.

[1] P. Lawrence 1964:63–8 describes how the southern Madang natives accounted for Miklouho-Maclay (the first European they had seen) as a deity.
[2] Pryce-Jones MSS.

In 1912 Pryce-Jones received an invitation to visit the pagan village of Iokea, which was later a village of the 'Vailala Madness'. When the missionary arrived he found the people engaged in killing all their pigs. He was told: 'Perform here the works which we hear you are performing elsewhere.' Traditionally pigs had been killed before the 'big men' had produced apa-Hevehe, the symbol of their power[1]—the Iokea people had killed their pigs and asked Pryce-Jones to produce evidence of his power as a 'big man'.

Later that night Pryce-Jones preached to the Iokea people taking as his text, 'I am but human with a nature like your own, the Gospel I am preaching is to turn from such futile ways to the living God.' And as the sermon progressed: 'The power of the spirit seemed to shimmer in our midst.' The tension became so great that Pryce-Jones stopped his sermon prematurely and retired to his tent. The Iokea people wanted a solution to the problem of explaining the Europeans. They wanted Pryce-Jones to show them a solution.

After the sermon a number of men came to the missionary's tent. He told one visitor that he would only learn by way of Christ: 'He looked at me with such pathetic perplexity and said he did not know the way.'[2] Pryce-Jones became like other Europeans in the eyes of the Elema. He guarded his power jealously, he would not let anyone else 'know'. At this stage there was no coherence in the Elema attempts to explain the Europeans. There was no leadership in the search for a solution, and these isolated experiences of the missionary serve to illustrate the gradual growth of *anomie*.

The Europeans were given gifts and the Europeans were asked for gifts. It was a time of experimentation, of testing, searching, and attempting to reach conclusions about Europeans. But the European attitude towards the Elema was unrelenting. The erosion of the 'big man's' status had been gradual, but in 1918 European pressure on the Elema intensified considerably. This pressure emphasized the Elema's painful inability to deal with the problem of reaching a satisfactory *modus vivendi* with the Europeans. No matter what they did the Elema were treated as 'rubbish men'.

In 1918 'Luluais' were appointed in all the Elema villages to act as the local arm of the administration. These appointments were designed to secure more effective implementation of administrative policy. But they introduced an element of uncertainty into the

[1] F. E. Williams 1940:346.   [2] Pryce-Jones MSS.

European/Elema relationships at a time when the Elema were trying to consolidate their ideas about Europeans. This meant further
administrative interference in Elema lives at the village level.

1918 was also the year when the Elema were forced to cultivate
rice and plant coconuts. In the same year compulsory taxation was
introduced. When war broke out, manpower was drained from the
territory leaving the Elema to face a smaller number of Europeans.
But these Europeans had more to do and so the nature of their
relationships with the Elema became less friendly. The pace of life
quickened.

Pressure was exerted on the Elema to supply more labour. As a
result of the war there was a world shortage of vegetable oils and
fats—copra prices soared and the plantations enjoyed a boom
period which would only be sustained through a continuing supply
of labour.

The Elema endured this increasing European intervention in
their lives for a year. Then in the latter months of 1919 'extraordinary' events, which were later to be known as the 'Vailala
Madness', took place in the Gulf Division, Papua.

G. H. MURRAY'S ACCOUNT OF THE 'MADNESS'

10th September 1919—Mr. —— visited the Government station on
the evening of the 9th September to report extraordinary conduct on the
part of the natives from Keuru to Vailala. According to him, the natives
were saying that the spirits of their ancestors had appeared to several in
the villages and told them that all flour, rice, tobacco, and other trade
belonged to the New Guinea people, and that the white man had no
right whatever to these goods; in a short time all the white men were to
be driven away, and then everything would be in the hands of the
natives; a large vessel was also shortly to appear bringing back the spirits
of their departed relatives with quantities of cargo, and all the villages
were to make ready to receive them. Platforms were being erected in the
villages and these were being loaded up with presents. Bosses or 'big
men' were appointed, presumably self-appointed, who seemed to be
acting as masters of ceremony in these preparations, and making the
other natives 'fall in' with a pretence of drilling them and making them
salute. These bosses also instructed the natives that they were not to sign
on to the white man any more. . . .

A number of natives who were interrogated, in describing the way in
which they were affected, stated that their 'heads went round'. I suggested that possibly too much betel nut or other stimulant was the cause of
their feeling of excitement, or whatever else it may be called, but they

are fully persuaded that it is entirely due to supernatural causes, and not to any drug. . . .

20th November—Mr. —— brought a Me-i native, named Kari, affected with the Orokolo madness[1] to endeavour to learn the cause of the complaint. The boy is well known as being of a very quiet disposition, and not the least inclined to be impudent, but about midday he was sent to Mr. ——'s house and walked straight into Mr. ——'s room smoking a cigarette. Although unable to read or write, he had a book, the Gospel of Luke, in Toaripi, in his hand, also pencil and paper on which he had scribbled a number of marks, and which he said was a letter he had just written. Mr. —— ordered him out of the room, and he then went to the store to be attended by Mrs. ——. Shortly afterwards Mrs. —— was seen running out of the store, and she explained that she was afraid to stay there, as the native seemed to be mad. Mr. —— investigated the matter, and finding that the boy was certainly acting like a lunatic, brought him straight to the R.M.'s office. As they entered the office the boy was making an attempt to sing, slapping his chest with his hands, and gave quite an exhibition of dancing, as if he were attempting to perform the highland fling. When ordered to be quiet he came to his senses somewhat, but could give no explanation for his conduct. All that could be got out of him was, 'I no savvy; God he savvy'. He was told that he was not considered a fit and proper person to be at large, and would be detained for a time at the station to be under observation.

21st November.—A native simply says, 'I no savvy', then looking up at the sky adds, 'God he savvy'. Quite a number have lost flesh to such a degree that, although well known to me, I did not at first recognize them. They appear to have worked themselves into a frenzy in a semi-religious mania, and have not been attending to their physical wants. The 'Witnesses' and P.O. houses were turned into a temporary lunatic asylum, and they were all quartered there, while the other villagers were instructed to supply them with abundant sago and other foods.

29th November.—The Me-i and Uaripi natives who have been detained on the station now state that they are quite well, and were all sent back to their village.

5th January, 1920.—In open spaces throughout the village were to be seen ornamented flag poles, long tables or forms or benches; the tables being usually decorated with flowers in bottles of water in imitation of a white man's dining table. On one of the forms a large number of men were seated with their backs to the table, all being dressed in new clothing, some in clean ramis and singlets and others in new suits of European garments. They sat quite motionless and never a word was spoken for the few minutes I stood looking at them.

[1] In fact Orokolo was one of the very few villages which were not affected by the 'madness'.

4th February.—Arrived at Vailala in the late afternoon and inspected the village, which was fairly clean, with houses and fences in good order. A tall flag pole painted red with native paint, and several tables and seats were erected in the village, and I was told that there were still several natives who kept watch for a large ship which is to bring back their ancestors in the form of white men. A number of men were sitting or strolling about in clean new ramis, as, according to the new belief, it is beneath their dignity to work unless it be at the erection of tables in the village, at which they sit once a day. I was informed that the lunacy is gradually wearing itself out and there is not the excitement amongst them now that was so noticeable on previous visits.

22nd May, 1920.—This Madness, which started last September at Arihava, and passed like a wave through all the coastal and a few bush villages, has now quite subsided, except for a few mild cases in which natives still ape being white men.

F. E. WILLIAMS'S ACCOUNT OF THE 'MADNESS'

It must be understood, however, that different villages are affected in different degrees. Orokolo and the neighbouring village Iogu appear to have resisted the new influences successfully: and here all the paraphernalia of the ceremonies are to be seen as in the old days. Yet the next village of Arihava—only a mile or so removed—has been a veritable hot bed of the cult, and is still one of its most active centres.

In practically every village will be found a certain number of men who from time to time are overtaken by the Madness; and, for lack of a better term, these may be called by their Pidgin English name of 'Head-he-go-round Men', an expression which has the advantage of being entirely non-committal. . . .

. . . But there are undoubtedly individuals who assume symptoms of a similar nature for reasons of their own: indeed, impostors of this kind must constitute a fair proportion of the 'Head-he-go-round Men'. It is noticeable that probably the majority of these recognized 'Head-he-go-round Men' have been signed on and that they are proficient in Motuan and even in English.

Perhaps one of the most fundamental ideas was that the ancestors, or more usually the deceased relatives, of the people were shortly to return to visit them. They were expected in a large steamer, which was to be loaded with cases of gifts—tobacco, calico, knives, axes, foodstuffs, and the like.

A feature of interest and importance is that in some places the returning ancestors or relatives were expected to be white; and indeed some white men were actually claimed by the natives to be their deceased relatives returned.

The really fundamental fact in the whole cult is the tremendous interest in the dead: and perhaps the most important regular duty connected with it is the making of mortuary feasts. In all the affected villages are to be seen roughly made tables, usually with benches surrounding them. These tables and benches are always fixtures and usually placed in some central position in the village. The relatives of a deceased person make a series of mortuary feasts which are set out upon the tables and consumed al fresco by men and women alike.

There is nothing new in the fact of these mortuary feasts in the Gulf Division; they are apparently part of the old culture; they illustrate this keenly felt interest in, and, to some extent, fear of the dead or rather of the spiritual entity that is believed to survive death. It would be a surprising thing if a new cult could abolish an interest so deeply grounded. Thus it would appear to be only in the highly pretentious style of arraying the feast that there has been here any great deviation from former custom.

The special house is called 'ahea uvi' in Arihava and the Vailala villages. The expression means literally 'hot house'. Informants found a difficulty in explaining the rationale of the name, but it appears, on the information of one or two, to rest upon the supposition that, when a man enters the house he becomes 'hot', i.e., inspired, afflicted with the Madness, or simply excited. In the more easterly villages of Motu Motu and Lese, the corresponding building was called 'the office'.

The house is usually closed, and frequented only by the automaniacs. A general quietness, and indeed an air of sanctity, pervades the place. Before a feast the dishes may be set on the tables, but the actual meal is, I am told, not taken inside. As was previously mentioned, the victuals, after being allowed to remain some time in the 'ahea uvi' are distributed by the automaniacs towards sundown: and it was explained at Vailala that during the day the Hae (spirits of the dead) actually enter the place and partake of the feast.

But the most important function of the 'ahea uvi' is that of a rendezvous between the souls of the dead and the automaniacs; or a holy place to which the latter repair for inspiration. It is with the dead that the automaniacs hold communication according to popular theory.

Besides these special houses—one might at a stretch call them temples —there is a further very typical medium of communication between the automaniacs and the souls of the dead. This is the flag-pole.

In many cases the pole bears a personal name, and in some is possibly given a real personality. The automaniac Ua Halai, prominent in Arihava, had raised the flag-pole ive kera, and had said to it: 'I have made you stand: stand firm, then, and do not let sickness come to this village.' When the flag-pole was first set up, said Ua Halai, there had been sickness; but now some people were dying. Formerly he had cared well for it, but now 'too many people looked at him, and talked to him'. Besides that, 'some had grown tired of the flag-pole, and did not make feasts around it when they should'.

The main function of the flag-pole has been mentioned: there are certain individuals who can receive messages from the dead through its agency.

Thou shalt not steal, commit adultery, nor break the Sabbath are the three commandments most frequently heard; though it is a question whether they are observed more obediently now than in former times. The cardinal sin, however, is to neglect feasting the dead: and this, no doubt, largely because it is an omission by which the community suffers.

It cannot be denied that there is much good in the general code advocated by the 'Head-he-go-round Men'. Many of the messages they profess to receive and utter are well meant and often laudable enough. An informant at Motu Motu occasionally fell into the 'Head-he-go-round' condition, when he saw his deceased parents and daughter; they told him it was wrong to steal, and that those who did would 'find big trouble on top', i.e., at the hands of God. Old Evara, of Iori, preached the same rule with a different sanction: those who did wrong would die. Biere, of Vailala West, claimed to receive and pass on such messages as these: To make a feast; to tidy the village thoroughly; to be cleanly in eating; to wash the hands.

There is one respect in which a very praiseworthy but sometimes amusing effort has been made; that is in the imitation of plantation, or possibly police, discipline. The 'fall in', for example, appears to have been regularly enforced upon the communality by the leaders.

In Arihava, when a great mass of people was dancing somewhat aimlessly together, one man was regulating start and finish with whistle blasts.

In Motu Motu the old nine o'clock curfew was in full vogue, and said to be a very fine institution; though no doubt its stringency is modified by the fact that no one is in a position to tell the time.

In reality the Vailala Madness appears to have been spread in two ways: first, by the common method of acquiring the ceremonies, i.e., by going to see them and then reproducing an imitation at home; and second, by the new method of active proselytism. From accounts received in various villages along the coast, it seems that, from Vailala westwards, the most zealous spirit has been Kori, the present V.C. of Numu; toward the East, one Harea, of Haruape, Vailala West.

Now in certain villages, at any rate, these men enjoy very considerable power; and it sometimes appears that they have superseded the former chiefs. In one of the villages of Vailala West, there were three leading automaniacs named, of whom the principal was Biere. The former Chief, or Abua, of the village was Kauka, now an old man; his proper successor it was said, would be a younger brother named Kaivu Ko. But neither of these men was regarded as first in the village—that position belonged to Biere. Whereas Kauka had been formerly, Biere was now Karikara Kiva —responsible for the village. It was said that Biere's claim to this position rested upon the fact that he had been the first to introduce the Madness into Vailala West, but it must be admitted that he appeared a very strong character, and deserves to be a man of influence.

In most instances there seems to be a small clique of such men in the village whose power will naturally vary according to their personalities, but who are to no small extent respected and obeyed. It is not too much to say that in many villages there is a 'Head-he-go-round' régime.

It is possible to view these men from another aspect, viz., as constituting an incipient priesthood. Their more or less exclusive right of entry to the 'ahea uvi's'; their duties of distributing the feasts; their supposed intercourse with the dead, or in some cases with Heaven, and their function as mediums of the oracle would all in some degree justify the use of such a term.

It is with the utmost disappointment that one finds in village after village the devastation which this movement has caused; with disgust also, and something like incredulity, that one hears on all hands the condemnation of the old customs. It seems nothing less than preposterous that old men, who have been brought up among the ceremonies, and who have taught their sons that their prime moral duty is to carry on the ceremonies, should of their own accord come to despise and abandon them. Yet no old man has the initiative to speak a word in defence of his dishonoured tribal customs. Too often in a group of witnesses, it is the Automaniac, who, being the leading personality, acts as spokesman, while the others sit in silence, not venturing to contradict him, even if it occurred to them to do so.

No more thoroughly deplorable instance could be found of the power of suggestion than this, when at a time of uncontrolled excitement, agelong traditions were thrown aside in favour of the absurdities of the Vailala Madness.

Williams saw the 'Vailala Madness' as a pathetic desire on the part of the Elema to be like the white man. He felt that the strain of contact with the Europeans and the loss of 'customary means of social excitement'[1] had caused the Elema to become mentally deranged. To Williams it seemed as if the Elema were suffering from a sort of mental indigestion. The anthropologist found the 'madness' inexplicable. For him the most terrible thing was the destruction of the colourful Hevehe ceremony. With the destruction of this ceremony Williams believed that the whole Elema

---

[1] F. E. Williams 1934:377.

culture was bound to collapse. Elema society had to be preserved
as a 'closed' society with a minimum of European intervention or
it could not be preserved at all.

Murray, the Magistrate, felt that the 'madness' had been caused
by insufficient contact with the Europeans. He felt that the cult
leaders were unscrupulous persons, and if the Elema had learnt
habits of sustained industry then they would have had little time
for such foolishness. The Magistrate did not find the 'madness'
inexplicable. To Murray there was nothing abnormal about the
physical state of the cult members. This was simply the result of
too little food and too much betel nut or other stimulant.[1]

THE NEW MYTH

Traditional Elema mythology formed part of the non-empirical
background to social action, and it had stressed the 'big man's'
role in the creation, ordering, and maintenance of Elema culture.
'Big men' had been in exclusive possession of the entire body of
Elema myth which was regarded as a sole repository of truth. New
events and situations had been explained by the 'big men' in the
light of their mythical knowledge. Myth had expressed the relation
between past and present and between experience and belief.[2]

The myths of the 'Vailala Madness' followed the traditional
pattern. They were formulated by 'big men'. They accounted for
the creation, ordering, and maintenance of the new society in which
the Elema found themselves living. These myths may have been on
an individual level, psychological projections, products of the
unconscious archetype.[3] But they performed the same social function as traditional myth in providing a charter for ritual action.

Myths of the 'Vailala Madness' may be termed moral and enabling. Moral in that they provided mythical justification for the idea
that it was inconceivable that the spirits of the dead would not help
the Elema. Enabling, in the same sense as enabling legislation, in
that once the non-empirical background to social action was interpreted it was possible to proceed with new rituals.

The 'big man' in Heaven was Ihova; under him were Noa, Atamu;
Kari a very 'big man'; and Areva and Maupu, both children of Ihova.
The land of Ihova was like earth only much better; there was no forest
like New Guinea; the houses were built of the ground itself and not of

---

[1] See pp. 53–55.   [2] K. O. L. Burridge 1960:150 and 1954a:*passim.*
[3] See Jung's thesis on Flying Saucers 1960:*passim.*

stone. There was food in abundance, white man's food, such as limes and oranges, water melons and also sugar cane and bananas. There were sheep, and a certain kind of animal of another kind called 'arivava'. Everyone wore long garments reaching from the top of the head down to the feet and resembling those worn by the white men on Yule island.[1]

This myth deals with two separate issues: social organization and modes of living, and habits of cultivation. In traditional mythology the land of the dead (which in missionary terminology was the same as Heaven), had been organized by 'big men'—the situation in the new land of the dead was similar.

The way of life for the living had been set by the spirits of the dead. In the new mythology the land of the dead was like a European station, cleared of undergrowth and with European houses. If this was really the way the spirits of the dead lived then this mode of life could be adopted by the Elema. The myth also said that the land of the dead had European kinds of food. This was important because the kinds of food that were grown by the Elema were thought to have come from the land of the dead originally. Such myths created the moral and ideological climate for dealing with the problems which had been raised by the Europeans.

The Vailala cargo myth in its structural and semantic implications had a genetic relationship with the original Oa-Birukapu fertility myth. 'All the rice, flour, tobacco, and calico belonged to the New Guinea people; white men were to be driven away. A ship would come bearing their ancestors and goods; the villagers were to make ready to receive them.'[2]

Oa-Birukapu had brought garden fertility which had been obtained when he had been killed. Spirits of the dead were to bring goods which would be obtained when the white men were driven away. These structural and semantic similarities indicate that, as in the traditional myths, the 'big man's' role is of prime importance.

Although the mythology of the 'Vailala Madness' consisted of images and situations which were in themselves open to rational criticism they were based on a foundation which was unassailable by reason. The myths were put forward by the new 'big men'. Within terms of their existing experience the Elema knew that the kinds of truth put forward by 'big men' in myth form had to prevail, because they 'knew'. Myth, as in traditional society, provided directives to action under the 'big men'.

[1] *P.A.R. No. 4*, 1923:17.   [2] *P.A.R. No. 4*, 1923:14.

Control of the dead was a vital factor in the success of the 'Vailala Madness'. The Elema religious technology employed was a synthesis of traditional epistemological assumptions and deductions which had been made about the success of Europeans. Europeans had given an impressive demonstration of their ability to control the dead through their sea voyages which had suffered no harm from the Ma-Hevehe sea monsters and through their ability to achieve success in agricultural activities. The Elema must have realized in the light of the Orokolo Christians' experience, that European beliefs about the dead were much the same as their own. Benefits came from the land of the dead which the missionaries called Heaven and men had to be worthy to receive them. To prove themselves as men the Elema had to regain the control of the dead that they had lost to the white man.

Traditionally three things were necessary to control the dead: funerary practices had to be executed correctly; prohibitions against stealing, adultery, and disobedience had to be observed; and 'big men' had to perform the necessary rituals. Heat or 'ahea' was needed to perform rituals and control the dead.

Great attention was paid to funerary rites. The dead were propitiated in every possible way. Lavish feasts were set up on funerary platforms because the dead were expected to visit the Elema. Every inducement was offered to persuade the dead to visit the Elema and to let them know that they would be welcome.

Prohibitions against stealing and adultery were zealously enforced.[1] But it was the third condition for securing the assistance of the dead which gave rise to the greatest amount of misunderstanding among European observers. This was the generation of 'ahea' or heat.

The attempts which were made to generate heat gave rise to the physical aberrations of the cult members. These physical aberrations were not general among the cult members. They were confined to the 'big men'. These new 'big men' knew that heat was required to perform the necessary rituals for controlling the dead. As a result of very energetic measures taken to induce heat the 'big

[1] See F. E. Williams's experience with the pole, *P.A.R. No. 4*, 1923:33, 34. The pole had interesting symbolic connotations. It was decorated with a snake's head. A snake sheds its skin to reveal a new skin—the symbolic implication behind the use of this pole in the 'Vailala Madness' is that the process was involved with the birth of a new society. And the symbolic analogy with the circular motion of a snake carries with it the connotation of a circle which can be taken as symbolizing the order of the psychic totality: C. G. Jung 1959:19.

men' suffered physical disturbances. Heat had been induced by the process of 'siahu'. This called for the taking of large amounts of ginger which acted as a stimulant while at the same time giving an impression of heat being generated in the stomach.[1] 'One reason for chewing ginger and those hot barks was to harden the stomach . . . (there were frequent references to the stomach by the affected cult members); but more usually it is explained that they make him hot and thus ready for magic making. . . . He makes a pretence of being ill to give colour to his action, but his real purpose is to make himself hot for magic.[2]

But European rituals, as well as traditional Elema rituals for controlling the dead, were used to ensure success. European rituals which were thought to be part of their success in controlling the spirits of the dead were added by the new 'big men' who had claimed to have familiarity with the European way of life.

These rituals were a mixture of deductions which had been made about the Magistrate and the missionary. There was flag raising and drilling which were common to both kinds of European. Christian influence can be seen in the ritual of sitting at tables with clean clothes.[3] But the Elema had no way of empirically evaluating these formulae. Ritual was the product of exclusive religious knowledge. The new 'big men' who introduced these rituals claimed to have this knowledge—their claim could only be tested by testing the effectiveness of the new rituals. Concentration on the return of the spirits of the dead in the 'Vailala Madness' was not so much concerned with revolutionary eschatology as with restatement and reaffirmation of traditional truths.

THE NEW HEVEHE CEREMONY

The new Hevehe ceremony of the 'Vailala Madness' was an eclectic mixture of European and Elema culture involving a blend-

---

[1] Personal communication from Dr. I. Porteus of the B.S.I.P. Medical Department. In his opinion the taking of excessive amounts of ginger would have been consistent with the symptoms of the cult members. In these circumstances it would seem that Murray's analysis was correct.

[2] F. E. Williams 1932:149, 150. This, of course, was written long after Williams's first account of the 'madness'.

[3] The 'Vailala Madness' ritual of sitting quietly at tables seems to have had a resemblance to the conduct of the Orokolo Christians in Church: 'And the congregation sits, amazingly quietly, and listens. There is a look of indifference on their faces, as though this story has nothing to do with them.' T. W. Reid 1960:44.

ing of new ideas with old in the light of epistemological assumptions about the nature of European power. But the new ceremony was still on the traditionalist pattern with the old features: the arrival of the dead, the Eravo as a ritual centrepiece, and production of a symbol of the 'big man's' power, that is 'cargo' instead of apa-Hevehe.

The centrepiece of the new Hevehe ceremony was the 'office' or 'ahea uvi', meaning literally 'hot house'. Europeans possessed tremendous power to control the dead, and the spirits of the dead were naturally thought to visit the office of the Magistrate. 'Ahea uvi' with its connotation of heat showed that there was intercourse with the spirits of the dead in the 'office'. It was a synthesis of traditional ideas about the Eravo and deductions which had been made about Europeans. Traditionally the Eravo had been taboo to all but the 'big men' when the spirits of the dead were present. The 'office' was taboo to all but the new 'big men'.[1] A further link with the traditional Hevehe ceremony can be seen in the presence of Aualari totemic symbols in the 'office'.[2]

The bush spirits were no longer thought to be important. They had never had the power of the spirits of the dead, and Europeans had convinced the Elema that they must concentrate on controlling the dead (but they did place Aualari totemic symbols in the Eravo).

Spirits of the dead were to be summoned by the new 'big men' in the traditional manner and by using the new European rituals. Traditional norms were followed, together with the new rituals—the flag raising, and sitting round tables. Formulae used by the new 'big men' in addressing the spirits of the dead in these new rituals show a relationship with the formulae used by the traditional 'big men' in the Hevehe ceremony: 'I have made you stand, stand firm then, and do not let sickness come into the village.' This was very similar, semantically, to the formula used by the 'big men' when splitting the coconut and slaying the apa-Hevehe.

Apa-Hevehe had symbolized the 'big man's' power. But the traditional 'big men' had been discredited in their relationships

---

[1] Paradoxically, F. E. Williams, who had seen nothing reprehensible in the way the 'big men' had deceived the women by maintaining that the Ma-Hevehe sea monsters actually visited the Eravo, felt that the new 'big men's' claim that the spirits of the dead visited the 'office' was a disreputable deception. F. E. Williams 1934:376.

[2] F. E. Williams 1920:f.n.22.

with the Europeans and this symbol was no longer valid. This symbol had had credibility for the old way of life. It had symbolized the traditional 'big man's' ability to control the old environment. But if new 'big men' were to have any validity as a cultural symbol they had to produce a symbol of their ability to control the new environment. The symbol of the new 'big man's' power was to be a ship carrying the spirits of the ancestors and 'cargo'. 'Cargo' was to be the motif for the new way of life.[1]

THE IDEOLOGICAL FRAMEWORK

The new 'big men' were concerned with corporate wealth transactions. Traditional 'big men' had been responsible for the organization of trade and feast-giving in the corporate wealth sphere. But the Elema did not expect money in the 'cargo'.[2] They wanted the kinds of goods which in terms of their own experience they associated with the corporate wealth transactions of 'big men'/Europeans —trading by ship and (European) kinds of food. 'Cargo' was to belong to the new 'big men'. No arrangements were made for the division of the 'cargo'. It was not supposed to be a vast miscellany of goods but a meaningful unity.[3]

In examining notions regarding the nature of power in the 'Vailala Madness', change in relation to the traditional pattern is evident. Traditionally, claims to power were evaluated on the basis of results that were achieved. This could not be done during the 'Vailala Madness' and the new 'big men's' claim to power was accepted provisionally on the implicit understanding that results would be forthcoming.

The new 'big men' in using European rituals were not emulating or trying to be like Europeans. They *were* European/'big men'. The young man who had written a 'letter' even though he was illiterate illustrates this idea: to the Elema this young man *had* written a letter, he *had* performed a European ritual with success. Since the means/end relationship was not appreciated the Elema could not interpret the young man's action in any other way.

Traditionally only the 'big men' knew how to perform ritual, and because of their possession of exclusive religious knowledge

---

[1] W. E. H. Stanner 1958:*passim* on 'cargo' as the motif for a new way of life.

[2] Due to high copra prices and rice cultivation, the Elema must have been better off financially than they ever had been before. See the Appendix on Papuan Exports, Mair 1948 and P. Worsley 1957b:34.

[3] W. E. H. Stanner 1958:2, 3.

this claim could not be tested. The situation was similar in the 'Vailala Madness'. The new 'big men' spoke in an unintelligible tongue (thought to be German): this showed that they had entered into a special relationship with the spirits. This claim could not have been tested. For the gift of speaking in an alien tongue when understood loses its evidential value.[1] Axiomatically the new 'big men' had the same ritual power as the traditional 'big man'.

Sorcery was not in evidence during the 'Vailala Madness'. Traditionally sorcery had been employed by the 'big men' to make the spirits of the dead stay in their homes: during the 'madness' the emphasis was on attempting to convince the spirits of the dead that they would be welcomed by the Elema. But sorcery had also buttressed the position of the 'big men': during the 'madness' the Elema were aware that their moral salvation lay in the hands of the 'big man'.

A military function, as a war-leader, was implicit in the drilling and in the expectation that rifles would be contained in the 'cargo'. Political power was not exercised on any democratic basis. 'Big men' initiated, organized, and executed communal programmes while at the same time imposing discipline in the traditional manner. These political functions were the same as the political functions of the Magistrate and the missionary. But when they exercised these new functions the new 'big men' *became* the Magistrate and they also *became* the missionary. In ensuring that the traditional code was observed the new 'big men' acted in a judicial role, and in their dealings with the administration they represented the cult.

There were two clear-cut kinds of status in the 'Vailala Madness': that of the new 'big man', and the status of the ordinary member of society. Traditionally status had been earned on the results of past performance;[2] in the 'Vailala Madness' status was described provisionally. This status would be confirmed when the Europeans no longer treated the Elema as if they were 'rubbish men'.

The new 'big men' attempted to organize, and set standards of excellence in, both the old and the new activities. New myths and rituals accounted for his role in the creation, ordering, and maintenance of this new society. It was a society which was neither

[1] R. A. Knox 1950:554.
[2] Unfortunately there is little information on this point. It is, however, possible that in traditional society, as in the 'Vailala madness' the 'big men' went through a kind of probationary period.

wholly Papuan nor wholly European in form or content. The new 'big man' presented a synthesized cultural image of this new society. A new organizational framework was provided by the new 'big men'. Traditionally ordinary men had been able to establish their status as men within the organizational framework; this process was the same in the 'Vailala Madness'. There was no new role and no new kind of status for ordinary men, only new activities and rituals within the old organizational framework. There was no ascribed role of 'rubbish man' during the 'Vailala Madness'. This position would inevitably have been filled by those who could not live like men.

The administration took repressive measures against the cult and a number of the new 'big men' were imprisoned. When this was done the organizational framework was destroyed and the new symbol of the Elema's cultural integrity was removed. Ordinary men were not able to establish their manhood because there was no longer any series of activities. This meant a return to *anomie*.

Arrival of 'cargo' and the spirits of the dead was an empirical test of the validity of the new 'big man's' ritual power and status. When the 'cargo' and the spirits of the dead failed to arrive the new 'big men' were discredited and the things that they did and said no longer had any validity, and so they lost their following.

But the ship and the 'cargo' had only been a means to an end. 'Cargo' was a way of forcing the Europeans to recognize that the Elema were men and not 'rubbish men'. This failure to produce 'cargo' and the spirits of the dead could be explained in terms of the Elema's experience by assuming that the wrong rituals had been used.[1] The 'Vailala Madness' was really a failure because the Europeans continued to treat the Elema as 'rubbish men'.

[1] See R. Firth 1951:233-6.

V

THE SOLOMON ISLANDS
AND 'MARCHING RULE'

THE islands which now make up the British Solomon Islands Protectorate lie in a scattered archipelago stretching approximately 900 miles in a south-easterly direction from Bougainville in the Australian territory of Papua-New Guinea to the tiny Polynesian islands of Tikopia and Anuta in the eastern Solomons.

Six major islands, Choiseul, New Georgia, Santa Ysabel, Guadalcanal, Malaita, and San Cristobal, form a double chain from Bougainville converging again at San Cristobal. The topography of these major islands is extremely rugged. They vary from 90 to 120 miles in length and from 20 to 30 miles in width. Typically the large islands have a mountainous spine which on one side drops down steeply to the coast and on the other drops through a series of foothills to the sea. The islands are clothed in dense tropical rain forest and cut by fast-flowing rivers.

The climate is equatorial but is modified by the surrounding ocean. Normal midday temperature is between 86° F. and 90° F. with a very high degree of humidity, though at night-time the temperature sometimes drops into the upper sixties. There are two seasons. From April to November the south-east trades blow from 10 to 15 knots, and from November to April the winds are gusty, coming from the north-west and frequently of cyclone proportions.

TRADITIONAL SOCIETY

Although there were differences from island to island in ritual and ceremonial activities, this chapter concentrates on their commonly held notions regarding the nature of power and status. The traditional pattern of life is broadly outlined in the following extracts dealing with warfare and the residence pattern, the economic environment, and the indigenous system of leadership.

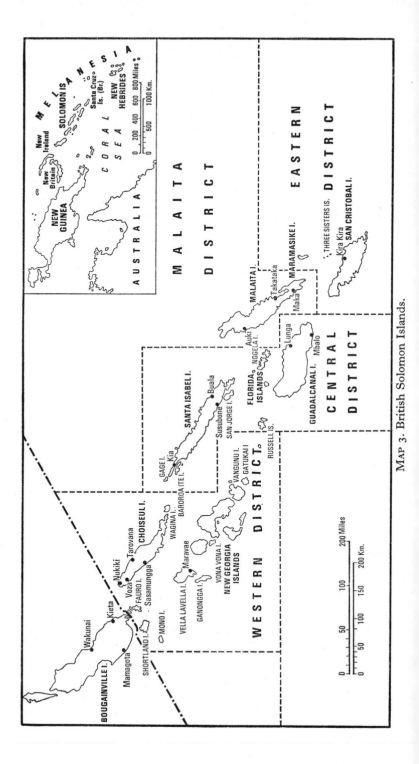

Map 3. British Solomon Islands.

In the smallest island a constant state of suspended warfare may exist, the two opposing districts being separated by a sort of 'no man's land' which in days gone by was a traditional battle ground. . . . Hostilities took on an elaborate ceremonial nature and the observance of the etiquette of war was a religious obligation. The rules for making peace were as ceremonial and elaborate as those controlling hostilities.[1]

Certain fertile areas support larger population. . . . But less than 200 people go to make up a village in most parts. The people live by cultivating basic staples: root vegetables such as taro or yams, sago in the lowlands, or sweet potatoes in the highlands. Formerly, they used stone, wooden or shell tools. . . . Although there was some individual specialization and although some whole communities traded objects—pots, baskets, feathers, even songs and dances—in whose production they specialized, for the most part every man cultivated his own garden, and the limited technological equipment inhibited the development of specialization and trade. Under these circumstances surpluses could not be stored, they could not be used to extend trade, or to acquire capital equipment; instead they were used as a means of acquiring prestige. A man's personal material wants in perishable commodities like yams and taro were soon satisfied; he therefore gave his surplus away in feasts. But he gave it away in a manner which created an obligation on the part of those who participated in the feast to render him respect, service or some return in the future.[2]

Physical forms of wealth were pigs, garden produce, either dog or porpoise teeth, pig's tusks, shell ornaments, and long strings of shell wealth made up of thousands of small ground shell discs threaded on a length of coconut fibre string. The economic system was static. There was no conception of profit in social relations, the norm was exchange or equivalence in goods and service. And the system was egalitarian since everyone had equal access to garden land.[3]

There was no hereditary authority, not even hereditary ranks or statuses.

A man could by virtue of his diligence in the gardens, his skill in warfare or trade, or his personality, quickly acquire high social status. He would use his wealth to mobilize people for activities such as building a clubhouse, which would reinforce his importance, or he would organize trade expeditions or war parties. If his son was a man of few parts, he would be unlikely to benefit much from his father's material and social power, as there was often no real material wealth to be handed down. It

[1] H. W. Krieger 1943:55-7.   [2] P. Worsley 1957b:14, 15.
[3] P. Lawrence 1964:11.

was largely open to any man to advance himself socially by his own endeavours . . . society was so unspecialized that there were no formal courts, police officials etc.,—political and legal security depended on support by relatives and kin, and the impermanent authority of the 'big men'.[1]

Religion was primarily concerned with ancestor worship. These putative relationships with the dead were merely an extension of the field of social relationships beyond the confines of human society. Relationships with the spirits of the dead presented an additional complex of reciprocal relationships whose satisfactory conduct was thought to help men in fishing or hunting. Failure to discharge the obligation might mean death or ill health.

There was no communal organization of the spirits of the dead. The complex of relationships with the dead was static. A man could not gain increased benefits from the dead by entering into a greater number of relationships than other men. He had to confine his relationships to male ancestral kin in direct line of descent from the mythical progenitor of the clan or lineage.[2]

Individuals sought help from the spirits when they wanted to know whether the time was auspicious for the initiation of a new project: 'Without religious sacrifice there is no fishing, no hunting; no field labour; without invoking the help of the spirits no canoe is built; without submitting it to the will of the Gods no sea voyage is undertaken.'[3]

Myths were concerned with the exploits of 'big men'. The ancient myths of Malaita, Ulawa, and San Cristobal are voluminous and fragmented but in the structure of the myths there are semantic similarities. 'Big men' who could overcome any obstacle were credited with the creation, ordering and maintenance of Melanesian culture.

The 'big men's' power to overcome difficulties came from their possession of mana. Basically mana refers to a kind of power beyond the ordinary—not just physical strength but power of a less tangible kind though it must be demonstrated by physical results. Mana is often translated as success or reputation. Human success and the use of a superior weapon in war with devastating effect were attributable to possession of mana. In fact human success was not

[1] P. Worsley 1957b:14, 15.
[2] Results from investigations carried out at pagan settlements at Manus on Malaita; Su'umoli on Ulawa; and Oke Oke on San Cristobal.
[3] L. A. Mander 1954:306.

attributable to physical prowess alone.[1] Great achievements could be empirically ascribed to possession of mana. For this reason the Melanesians did not have to understand or be confused by the means/end relationship of unusual happenings and events. The only relationship affecting the whole society, and consequently the only channel for adapting to change, was the multipurpose organizational framework.[2] The Melanesians could explain failure by supposing that the wrong rituals had been employed. Success could be evaluated empirically: it did not stem from possession of exclusive religious knowledge but from mana. 'Big men' possessed more mana than anyone else and they controlled the multi-purpose organizational framework.

The system of feasting was egalitarian and competitive—any man who was already a 'big man' could summon help in making a feast or a village canoe or in planting his garden.[3] And a 'big man' had the assistance of a retinue of young men who, attracted by his growing prestige, attached themselves to his household.[4] These young followers had to be fed and in addition a 'big man' normally gave between two and four feasts in his lifetime.[5]

In addition to the kinds of wealth that were used in reciprocal transactions 'big men' also had custody of 'public wealth'. They were given gifts or tribute which did not have to be returned. But this kind of wealth could not be spent by the 'big man' on himself, it had to be spent on the welfare of the community.[6] Wealth was a measurement of his status.[7] This wealth which was given by the tribe to the 'big man' was kept in his house which was thought of as a bank.[8]

A 'big man' was thought to have a special responsibility for maintenance of the traditional way of life. If he did not use his authority to enforce traditional mores then he ran the risk of losing status. 'Big men' imposed fines or sanctions for swearing, unlawful sexual intercourse, or any action, such as a man entering an area reserved for women who were menstruating, where the sacred and the profane were brought into contact.[9]

[1] R. Firth 1967:174–94.
[2] See P. Lawrence 1964:11 on the multi-purpose organizational framework.
[3] W. G. Ivens 1927:7.
[4] R. H. Codrington 1891:52, 53 and H. W. Scheffler 1965:186.
[5] Results of personal survey.   [6] C. S. Belshaw 1950a:33.
[7] A. I. Hopkin 1928:113.
[8] W. G. Ivens 1927:32 and R. H. Codrington 1891:63.
[9] L. A. Mander 1954:307.

'Big men' possessed exceptional organizational powers which were demonstrated in their initiation, organization, and execution of all communal projects. Since there was no specialization, the same organizational structure performed multiple functions. In supplying this organizational framework the 'big men' set standards. Standards that resulted in recognition of manhood when they were achieved by individuals working under the direction of the 'big man'. In this way certainty was introduced into the system. Feelings of confidence were important because the sum of knowledge was so small and the means of modifying the environment so slight.[1] 'The chief was the root of the land . . . the living stock whence came life and fruition. . . . Chiefs were said to succour the land, to draw up people who came to them for protection.[2]

But the status of the 'big man' was not the status of a chief; it was the status of a leader. And maintenance of leadership status was dependent on personal performance.[3] In peace and war the 'big man' represented the whole society.[4] An insult to a 'big man' was the most frequent cause of war. It was not merely an insult to the 'big man' but an insult to society.

The 'big man' was a symbol of the society's cultural integrity, presenting in himself a synthesized cultural image of his society. He occupied a nodal point in the network of social relationships: groups combined in a small way, so that small groups like lineages opposed other lineages, and clans opposed clans. 'Big men' transcended these oppositions—they were society and society was 'big men'.

'Rubbish men', 'nothing men', or those who were 'something nothing' occupied the lowest status category. They supplied the backdrop for social endeavour. These 'rubbish men' were lazy and indolent' they entered into a very small number of reciprocal relationships' produced very small amounts of food from their gardens; and never gave any food to the men's house. 'Rubbish men' were poor warriors, and if an enemy killed one of these men, it was not considered a sufficient cause for war.

A 'rubbish man's' opinion was of no account. An ordinary member of society could commit adultery with a 'rubbish man's' wife, swear at him, have intercourse with his unmarried daughter or steal his best fish-hook and the 'rubbish man' could only ask for

[1] H. I. Hogbin 1939b:109, 110.   [2] W. G. Ivens 1927:128, 129.
[3] H. I. Hogbin 1939b:81.   [4] R. F. Salisbury 1962:38.

compensation—he could not demand compensation as of right, like other men.[1] All that was necessary to rise from the position of 'rubbish man' was hard work: 'The worker has the meat, the lazy one the bone'.[2] Ordinary men were neither so industrious and ambitious as 'big men' nor as lazy and indolent as 'rubbish men'. They discharged their obligations in a satisfactory manner and worked hard enough to maintain their families. By working hard and following the directions of the 'big man' they established their identity as men.

The 'big man's' power was the only form of power which affected the whole society. Basically it stemmed from his status[3] and control of the multi-purpose organizational framework. Although the function of this organizational machine at any particular point in time might be political or economic its efficient operation inevitably had ritual overtones. This was because the power that was exhibited through its operation was thought to come as a result of the 'big man's' human attributes and, in addition, his possession of mana.

The 'big men' were normally warriors of renown. They decided when war should be declared and when peace should be made. Native names for 'big men' on Ulawa, Malaita and San Cristobal, 'Ma'eraha and Ma'alaha', meaning literally great death or war,[4] show that they were regarded primarily as warriors.

'Big men' gave executive directions. They punished disobedience, and solved disputes within the society. In the exercise of power intensity of effort and harshness in application were the criteria used in deciding how much power a man had. Those who gave a great number of executive orders and prohibitions and who punished failure severely, while maintaining rigid discipline, were thought to be more powerful than those whose efforts succeeded in merely maintaining cultural integrity. The greater a 'big man's' status the more rigid the discipline: 'If his reputation for mana spreads abroad, he will have a wide influence in his island and even beyond it; young men from other parts as well as youths from his own village . . . will carry out his orders even to the punishment of death in peace, and fight for him in war.[5]

'Big men' had economic, political, judicial, and representative

---

[1] Results from personal enquiry. [2] H. I. Hogbin 1939b:46.
[3] C. S. Belshaw 1950a:33. [4] R. H. Codrington 1891:f.n.51.
[5] R. H. Codrington 1891:58.

functions. Performance was dependent on organizational ability and possession of wealth. A 'big man's' recognition came through demonstration of superior performance. Power had to be exercised frequently and discipline was harsh. Success was attributable, not only to human effectiveness, but to possession of mana. Ordinary members of society accepted the discipline imposed by the 'big man' and followed his directions. In doing this they were able to establish their status as men within the organizational framework of activities that the 'big man' provided. Achieving manhood status was a matter of working hard, following the traditional norms, and obeying the 'big man'.

'Rubbish men' were socially unimportant and unable to conform to the existing pattern. Consequently they had no status and were not thought of as men.

ADMINISTRATIVE ACTIVITY

Alvaro de Mendaña discovered the Solomons in 1568. Despite his subsequent unsuccessful attempts at colonization and the later efforts of his compatriot Quiros to rediscover the islands, the existence of the Solomons remained almost a myth until the voyages of Bougainville, de Surville, and d'Entrecasteaux in the eighteenth century.

The establishment of British influence in the Solomons was due to the importance of the labour traffic and a desire to protect European missionaries.[1] Towards the end of the last century plantation owners in Fiji and Queensland required cheap labour. This demand resulted in the notorious 'blackbirding' or recruitment voyages to the Pacific Islands.

Many Solomon Islanders were taken against their will to the plantations; the death rate among the natives was high, and few returned to their homes. Solomon Islanders retaliated by killing the crews of the recruiting vessels on every available opportunity.[2] Unfortunately, the Solomon Islanders did not only kill 'blackbirders', they also killed a large number of missionaries.

Relationships between Solomon Islanders and the Europeans worsened. The natives obtained an increasing number of firearms. Recruiters were forbidden to take the law into their own hands when attacked by natives. They had to report the incident to the nearest Naval officer. The Navy frequently shelled villages in the

---

[1] W. P. Morrell 1954:331.　　[2] C. M. Woodford 1890:16.

Solomons in reprisal for the murder of Europeans. But it became obvious that a policy of minimum intervention on the part of the Metropolitan power was no longer practicable.[1] A Protectorate was declared in 1893, and in 1896 Mr. C. M. Woodford the first Resident Commissioner arrived and assumed duty in the Protectorate.[2]

The guiding theme in Papua was humanism and the development of indigenous resources. Solomon Islanders were thought of in terms of Rousseau's 'noble savage'; emphasis was on evolution, once objectionable customs had been eradicated, with conformism to European standards for those who chose 'civilization'. Britain's role in the Solomons was simply to keep the peace and help to create the right conditions for commercial expansion. Educational and medical work were, from the declaration of the Protectorate until after the Second World War, considered mission responsibilities.[3]

The Civil Service grew slowly. In 1900 four Europeans were in Government employment. By 1924 eight Districts each with a District Officer had been established. In 1937 there were 42 Europeans and 417 native officers and five Chinese. Districts were divided up on a geographical basis, one District Officer looked after Malaita, one looked after Aola or Guadalcanal and one officer was in charge of San Cristobal and Ulawa.[4] By 1938 Government expenditure had risen to $138,000 per annum which was slightly more than 30 per cent of the equivalent Papuan figure. Little of this money was spent on development. Most of the budget went on personal emoluments, shipping, and upkeep of prisons.[5] As in Papua, this resulted in direct personal administration.

The administration was not welcomed: uprisings were followed by punitive expeditions led by the District Officer. Measures for the enforcement of law and order were pursued vigorously but the Melanesians continued to resist strongly and Europeans were frequently murdered.[6]

District Officer Bell and his Cadet, Lillies, were murdered while collecting tax in the Koio sub-District on Malaita in 1927. The

---

[1] J. M. Ward 1948:328.   [2] L. A. Mander 1954:323.
[3] L. A. Mander 1954:316.
[4] B.S.I.P. Annual Reports 1924-25, 1937-38.
[5] B.S.I.P. Annual Reports.
[6] W. T. Wawn 1893 gives details of many of these incidents and of the reprisals taken by the Royal Navy.

official inquiry commented: 'All administrative measures for the establishment of law and order must, on their inception, appear repressive to primitive natives who have previously lived under the *Lex Talionis*, and much depends on the tact and discretion with which they are introduced, particularly among tribes of a warlike nature and a reputation for bravery such as the hillmen of Malaita.'[1] But the early administration did not feel disposed to use tact. On San Cristobal and Ulawa the murder of Europeans had been answered by Naval shelling, but after the murder of Bell and Lillies Europeans in the Protectorate felt that the Melanesians should be taught a final lesson. A European punitive expedition was mounted against the Koio people. This took place after the Government's retributive measures which had resulted in the hanging of eight men and a further thirty dying in Tulagi gaol.[2] This punitive expedition was known as the 'red band army' because of the distinctive armbands that they wore. It was officered by Europeans. Many willing followers were enlisted from the Koio people's traditional enemies in north Malaita. Men, women and children were shot, villages were burnt, ancestral shrines were destroyed, and coconut groves were cut down.[3] News of this incident spread all over the Solomons. There was no longer any doubt that District Officers and Europeans in general were very powerful war-leaders and that resistance against them was patently futile.

Although the principle of pre-service training for Colonial Service Officers had been accepted by the mid 1920s, no trained Cadets reached the Solomons until the outbreak of the Second World War. The pre-war District Officers were men with either a military or a plantation background.

While on patrol the D.O. was accompanied by an armed detachment of Native Constabulary. 'Government' for the Melanesian was a single D.O. in the same way that in traditional times it had been a 'big man'. The Melanesian's only contact with Government was when the D.O. made his rounds: 'The difficulty is that such visits must nearly always be disciplinary; the District Officer does not have time to give complimentary and friendly visits.'[4] The D.O. was a harsh disciplinarian. He gave executive orders like a traditional 'big man', and he sent the Melanesians out to work as if they

[1] Command 3248.   [2] Command 3248.
[3] Personal communication from ex-Headman Maekali of Malu'u, North Malaita, who was one of Hogbin's informants.
[4] A. I. Hopkins 1928:236.

were his dependants. By the mid-1920s village headmen and constables had been appointed to ensure that the D.O.'s orders were carried out.

In Melanesia, probably to a greater extent than in Africa, the character of the D.O. was of more importance than the law itself.[1] The D.O.'s powers were laid down in the Native Administration Ordinance of 1922. Natives were responsible for keeping open roads, constructing village meeting-houses, and keeping their villages clean. Village people had to work one day every week for the Government on these communal projects for which they received no pay. When the D.O. visited the village the people had to line the section of the road that they were responsible for and if the D.O. did not find it satisfactory they were fined.

Twice a year, at the celebration of the King's Birthday and at New Year, the D.O. gave a large feast at his headquarters. This feast was much larger and more impressive than the feasts given by the 'big men'. The D.O. rationed his followers in the same way that the 'big men' had rationed youths who came to live with them.

In 1920 Native Tax Regulations were passed. Under these Regulations every able-bodied male native had to pay 5s. a year to the District Officer. This tax payment was like the traditional payment that had been made to the 'big man'. Tax money was like the 'public money' in traditional society. It was used on native welfare and was kept in the D.O.'s quarters.

The District Officer's judicial functions were like those of a traditional 'big man'. Failure to obey his commands resulted in a fine or imprisonment under the Native Administration Ordinance of 1922. The D.O. was ex officio a Magistrate. He punished theft, and resolved disputes over land. A King's Regulation passed in 1924 made adultery a criminal offence. The District Officer maintained the traditional way of life. But his power to uphold the code was far greater than the traditional 'big man's'.

Government was a single D.O. in the same way that the traditional 'big man' had been society. The Government machine was also a multi-purpose organizational machine and it was capable of coping with every demand. The D.O., in organizing communal projects, had shown his organizational ability. And his success in all these activities showed that he possessed a great deal of mana.

Within terms of their existing experience the Melanesians could

[1] M. Fortes 1936:53-5.

see that the D.O. gained his status in the same way as the traditional 'big man'. But the D.O. was a paradox, for although he gave justice and was thought to have the welfare of the people at heart, he never gave friendship.[1] District Officers did not identify themselves with Melanesian culture. Instead they treated the Melanesians as if they were inferior. They did not learn the local language, did not marry the local women or enter into reciprocal relationships. Thus the D.O. could not be thought of as a Melanesian 'big man'; he did not in himself present a synthesized cultural image of their society.

The District Officer had very extensive powers which were used in the same manner as the powers of a traditional 'big man'. But in all his actions his performance was superior to that of the traditional 'big man'. He was a more powerful war-leader, he was more effective in enforcing the traditional code, and his executive decisions carried far more weight than those of the traditional 'big man'. These successes indicated the possession of mana. This power stemmed basically from the District Officer's status and from his control of the multi-purpose organizational framework.

MISSIONARY CONTACT

Before the establishment of the Protectorate in 1893, there had been a long record of missionary martyrdom in the Solomons. Roman Catholic Priests of the Marist order were murdered at Makira Bay on San Cristobal in 1845 and Bishop Selwyn of the Melanesian Mission was killed at Nukapu in the Reef Islands in 1874. The Melanesian Mission (Anglican), founded in 1850, the Marist Mission, established in the Solomons in 1898, and the South Seas Evangelical Mission, founded in 1904, are the only missions represented on Malaita, Ulawa, and San Cristobal.

In the years following the establishment of the Protectorate, and as the Government gradually introduced law and order, the missions consolidated their positions by establishing stations on all the major islands in the Solomons.

The Melanesian mission founded a station with a hospital at Fuambu in the Kwara's sub-District in north Malaita. By 1930 the S.S.E.M. had stations at Rama in the Bauro sub-District on San Cristobal, and at Su'u, Onepusus, Takwa, and Araki in north and south Malaita. The Marists had stations at Manevovo and Wainoni

[1] C. E. Fox 1964:134.

bay on San Cristobal, and at Takwa, Buma, and Tarapaina in north and south Malaita.

The Melanesian and Marist missions followed the ecclesiastical order characteristic of them in other parts of the world, with native priests having the same standing as their European counterparts.[1] In practice the Catholics have preferred to work intensively through strategically placed stations. The Catholics have had a smaller number of converts. But their priests have always learnt the local language and they have tried as far as possible to make their mission stations economically self-sufficient.

The Melanesian mission was fortunate in its early years to have men of the calibre of Ivens, Codrington, and Fox. These men quickly passed on responsibility for mission affairs to local priests. And the mission was also fortunate in being financially independent because of the subvention it received from affiliated bodies in the metropolitan countries.

Since the majority of the adherents of the 'Marching Rule' movement were members of the S.S.E.M., the activities of that mission are now examined in detail.

The S.S.E.M. was originally founded to cater for the spiritual needs of Solomon Islanders working in Queensland during the 'blackbirding' days. In the Solomons the mission worked through strategically placed stations, each of which was in the charge of an expatriate missionary.

In addition to the expatriate stations the mission had village stations on all the major islands. Each of these was under a native pastor and contained a school and church. Figures available for San Cristobal and Malaita show that the S.S.E.M. had 295 stations in comparison with 39 for the Marist mission and 123 for the Melanesian mission in the early post-war days.[2]

The S.S.E.M. had vague Baptist leanings, and was organized on the congregationalist pattern. Mission teaching was 'light' on theology and 'heavy' on Christian ethics. Most mission weaknesses were attributable to a lack of financial resources and to difficulties experienced in obtaining the right kind of European workers in sufficient numbers. In both these respects the mission was singularly unfortunate. They had few funds and the majority of their staff were not of the same intellectual calibre as the Anglican or Roman Catholic missionaries.

[1] J. W. Burton 1949:108.   [2] J. W. Dovey 1950:*passim.*

Mission teaching and the mission way of life emphasized that there was a difference between natives and Europeans. The mission continued to encourage its members to work on plantations, and Solomon Islanders were taught to know their place. Native officials in the mission were discriminated against: they had to speak respectfully to Europeans, they were not invited to eat or stay at the houses of their European superiors, and they were taught that service of any kind to Europeans was the highest form of native attainment.

God was referred to as a 'big man' in pidgin English, which was the missionaries' method of communication. The Bible contained myths showing the power of God to overcome any difficulty—this was like the power of the traditional 'big man'. Missionaries concentrated on the all-pervasive power of God, who was thought to have a great deal of mana. God had to be obeyed; he punished adultery, swearing, and sex offences. God was like the D.O. and was thought of as a more powerful version of the traditional 'big man'.[1]

Those who worked for the D.O. spent at most one or two days a week on Government work, those who worked for the missionary spent nearly all their time on mission work. Solomon Islanders who lived near the European-run stations spent a great deal of their time planting coconuts and tending mission gardens; and those who lived near a village station had to support the pastor. 'When a village professed Christianity a pastor teacher was appointed, and it became the communal duty of the people to build him a house, provide him with gardening land and with the use of schoolboys to cultivate it.'[2]

Financial demands made by the mission were heavy. Followers had to make copra to pay for their churches, their pastor's wages, and for educational materials. Government asked only for annual tax.

The missionary had the power and status of a 'big man' but he did not appear to have the welfare of his people at heart. He taxed them and sent them out to work like his dependants, but his demands were excessive and instead of preserving the traditional culture he seemed to be intent on destroying it.

COMMERCIAL ACTIVITY

Europeans had been actively engaged in negotiations for land in the Solomons for some years before the declaration of a Protector-

---

[1] Personal communication from Mr. Baetalua of Bita'ama, North Malaita.
[2] J. W. Burton 1949:109.

ate. By 1900 a shipping link with Sydney had been established and Mr. C. M. Woodford the Resident Commissioner was able to write: 'With an export trade to Sydney larger than that of the New Hebrides, and, excluding gold, far larger than that of British New Guinea, the Solomons should be worth encouragement from the point of view of New South Wales.'[1]

There was none of the difficulty about alienation of native land that had been present in the early days of Papuan development. The Government felt that the development and expansion of European commercial interests was of paramount importance.

William Lever started to acquire land in 1905. By 1939 Lever had 20,000 acres of planted coconuts and the total planted acreage in the Protectorate was 60,000 acres. The number of expatriates in the Solomons rose from 44 in 1896 to over 500 before the outbreak of the Second World War.[2]

Solomon Islanders who did not work on plantations earned very little money. The amount of copra produced annually by Solomon Islanders varied from 1,000 to 1,500 tons. The majority of this copra came from the western District. Very little copra was produced by Malaita, Ulawa, or San Cristobal. Solomon Islanders also made money through sale of crocodile skins, bêche-de-mer, turtle shell, trochus shell, and green snail (used in making buttons). But these products all came from lagoon areas. Neither Malaita, Ulawa or San Cristobal have any sizeable lagoons and they earned little money in this way.[3]

Solomon Islanders disliked working on plantations and they earned very little money in this way. Labour Regulations were passed in 1922 and full-scale recruitment started soon afterwards. In 1927 there were 6,000 labourers, in 1932 this had dropped to 3,927, and there was a further drop in 1938, when only 1,129 labourers were engaged. The pre-war reluctance to recruit was so marked that Levers approached the Government in 1939 to see if they would import Asian labour.[4]

Solomon Islanders living on the islands of Malaita, Ulawa, and San Cristobal were not dependent on the European economy to maintain their pattern of life. But what did they need European money for?

[1] B.S.I.P. Annual Report 1900.   [2] J. M. Ward 1948:423.
[3] Personal communications from Mr. T. Elkington of Tulagi and Mr. E. Palmer of Gizo who were trading in the islands in pre-war days.
[4] B.S.I.P. Annual Reports 1922–37 and L. A. Mander 1954:313.

Money had only a very limited utility. It was used in the payment of taxes and in purchasing clothing, cooking utensils, and gardening implements. But a man who could not pay his tax could work it off—fewer than 25 per cent of those who were supposed to pay ever did pay.[1] Clothing in pre-war days was still traditional: men wore a breech clout and women a grass skirt. Cooking utensils and gardening implements were made to last for a very long time, and in many cases for as long as fifteen or twenty years.[2] The Melanesians produced all their own food, grew their own tobacco, and manufactured their own salt—in terms of food they were self-sufficient.

Money did not give status or power to the same degree that traditional kinds of wealth did. It could not make a feast nor be used as bride price. As Hogbin wrote: 'It is a striking fact that money is in no way regarded as a substitute for the old type of valuable and that all ceremonial transactions are carried out today as in the past with Tafuliae (shell wealth).'[3]

Melanesians who worked for friendly Europeans came and worked until they had enough money to buy their axes and knives, and then they returned to their homes—their pattern of wants was satiated.[4]

Expatriate commercials felt that Solomon Islanders were lazy and that they would not work unless they were forced to. The Europeans who worked on plantations were tough, physically and mentally. The plantation ratio was four Europeans to 1,000 labourers which meant that strict discipline had to be imposed if plantation production quotas were to be achieved.[5]

Corporal punishment was thought to be a good thing. Europeans rode round their plantations on horseback, and stockwhips and savage dogs were used to keep the natives in order.[6] Solomon Islanders frequently retaliated by assaulting their European overseers.[7] The commercial expatriates acted like an enemy, and by 1939 the Solomon Islanders were adopting the traditional reply to

---

[1] Native Tax Registers, Malaita, 1935–39.

[2] On Tikopia with Professor R. Firth in 1966, for example, he showed me axes which he had given to the Tikopians in 1929 which were still in use.

[3] H. I. Hogbin 1939b:223 and B. Blackwood 1935:85, 116, 445, 458, who mentions a similar feature on Bougainville.

[4] Personal communication from the Hon. J. Campbell, Kira Kira, B.S.I.P.

[5] C. H. Grattan 1963:393.   [6] S. G. C. Knibbs 1929:70, 73.

[7] Personal communications from Mr. K. H. Dalrymple-Hay of Honiara, former planter, and Mr. Ben Ngarii of Kira Kira, former plantation 'bossboy'.

an unpopular 'big man': they boycotted the plantations.[1] Stronger reprisals could not be taken against these Europeans: they were too powerful and they were backed up by the administration.

THE EFFECTS OF EUROPEAN CONTACT

The S.S.E.M. forbade their followers to give any feasts. Hogbin described the effect of this measure in 1939: 'Since authority and leadership are traditionally dependent on the giving of feasts, it follows that in the Evangelical mission today no one can rise to the position of nwane inoto ("big man").' Feasts could not be given in honour of the dead. And the children of evangelical converts learnt to challenge the authority of their elders at school.[2]

Mission prohibitions prevented Melanesians from gaining status but other prohibitions made the natives like 'rubbish men'. Mission followers were not allowed to accept or pay bride price. They were not allowed to sue for or receive compensation in cases where adultery or unlawful sexual intercourse had been committed. The mission view was that such money was 'tainted'. The social importance of a marriage had been characterized by the amount of bride price that was paid or received—the S.S.E.M. converts became like 'rubbish men' unable to pay and unable to expect a bride price. They were also like 'rubbish men' because other men could commit adultery with their wives or have sexual intercourse with their daughters without being forced to pay compensation.[3]

The power and status of the traditional 'big man' was destroyed. The traditional multi-purpose organizational framework was replaced by Government and missionary activities. The demands made by the Europeans were excessive and the only communal activities which were undertaken were European-inspired. The Melanesians were unable to exercise any power over their own affairs. Many of these new European-directed activities were unfamiliar. The natives were unable to establish their status as men in their relationships with the Europeans.

[1] C. S. Belshaw 1950b:122 mentions that the traditional reaction to an unpopular leader was to abandon the village where the man lived. From my own experience I know that as recently as 1961 the entire village of Fa'adila in central north Malaita moved to Guadalcanal because they did not like the administrative officer in charge of the District at the time.

[2] H. I. Hogbin 1939b:214, 224.

[3] Results of personal investigation on Malaita.

8—B.M.C.C.

Europeans refused to identify themselves with the Melanesian way of life. They did not share their food with the natives, or live with them.[1] No matter how hard they tried or what they did, the Melanesians found that the Europeans treated them as 'rubbish men'. But a solution of some kind to the problems that were posed by the Europeans had to be found. The plantations could be boycotted but the other kinds of European were everywhere; it was impossible to escape them, impossible to escape from the problems that they posed.

THE 'MARCHING RULE' MOVEMENT

In 1942 the Japanese invaded the Solomons and in August of the same year the United States Marines landed on Guadalcanal. A local Defence Force was organized and a Labour Corps was formed to assist the Americans in handling their supplies.

When the Japanese invasion of the Solomons became imminent the Resident Commissioner had moved his headquarters from the island of Tulagi to the administrative centre of Auki on Malaita. A large number of European officers left the Solomons to join the Australian forces and those who remained had to keep a very firm hand on things.[2] The administration was faced with the possibility of severe food shortages and measures were taken to ensure that the local people grew extra food in case the allied troops should run short of supplies.[3]

Solomon Islanders in the Labour Corps had found the Americans friendly and for the first time they were able to establish satisfactory relationships with Europeans. But they found that this made no difference to the British who continued to treat the Melanesians as 'rubbish men'.

European contact with the Malaita people increased. Administrative patrols increased in frequency, to gather information about aircraft and shipping movements. Coast-watching was organized, and in some places towers were built on the tops of hills to give maximum visibility.[4] But relationships with the British did not improve and in 1944 the 'Marching Rule' movement broke out. A

---

[1] C. E. Fox 1964:134.   [2] 'Among those Present' 1966:*passim*.
[3] Large communal gardens were established at all sub-District H.Q.s and the natives were ordered to grow food.
[4] Personal communication from Rev. Fr. Camphuis of the Roman Catholic Mission Takwa, North Malaita.

comprehensive account of the movement has been given by Allen:[1]

During the year 1944, at a time when the British Administration was actively concerned with the increasing American drive towards Japan, there began in the Districts of Koio and Ariari on the island of Malaita an apparent quasi-nationalist movement known as the Marching Rule.* It is believed that it originated in the Solomon Island Labour Corps on Guadalcanal in 1943 and was spread through the hill villages of South Malaita by repatriated members of the S.I.L.C. By 1945 it had penetrated throughout North Malaita and by the same year had made its appearance in Guadalcanal, Ulawa and San Cristobal. In 1947 it spread to Florida and Ysabel and since then its strength has been diminishing. During the past six years Marching Rule has presented the Government with its most serious problem, for, at a time when the Protectorate has been striving desperately to rehabilitate its economy, stricken by the war, the movement has consistently preached non-co-operation with practically all political, social welfare and development programmes.

This movement, which has combined admirable and progressive objects with preposterous and mystical promises and terrorist tactics, has developed a studied system of civil disobedience which unfortunately compares more than favourably with similar campaigns in far less primitive countries. Had it not been for the intelligence, industry and imagination of the Western Solomons people and those in other isolated districts who withstood its insidious propaganda, this small Protectorate of only about 100,000 natives would indeed have been in a serious position.

The essential characteristic which differentiated Marching Rule as a political movement from that of a mere cult was its organization. The two main founders of the movement, Timothy George and Nori, divided Malaita into nine districts which roughly corresponded to the administrative divisions of the island. They despatched circular letters and emissaries to each district with instructions for the people to choose a 'head chief'. Six of the nine men chosen were mission teachers and all held considerable power in their areas. Occasionally they met together to decide matters of broad policy, but for the most part they ran the movement in the districts according to their own ideas. Each 'head chief' was assisted by several 'full chiefs' in charge of small sub-districts. Every Marching Rule town had its own 'leader chief' and, assuming the town

---

*'Marching' is an anglicized pronunciation of the word 'Masina' which in the Ariari language of South Malaita means 'brotherhood' or 'the young shoot of the taro'. One British newspaper referred to it as the 'Marching Rule (Marxian Rule) Movement'. This is nonsense.

[1] C. H. Allen 1951:93-100.

a large one, each clan had a 'line chief'. The chiefs on the different levels were all assisted by clerks responsible for the despatch of instructions, the listing of members and the preparation of the local custom that was to be adopted by the movement. Each 'leader chief' was supported by a bodyguard of young men, armed with truncheons, called 'duties'. These men picketed the towns day and night and provided a guard of honour for visiting 'head chiefs'. When not engaged in some official Marching Rule duty they were drilled by 'strife chiefs' who functioned as non-commissioned officers. The 'duties' were used to threaten recalcitrant members of the movement, who objected to being subjected to its pressure, and were responsible for marshalling the people for work in the communal gardens. Discipline in the gardens was handled by the 'duties', but the actual work was directed by 'farmer chiefs'.

In the middle of 1947, the movement began the establishment of its own courts to deal with breaches of Marching Rule custom. The courts were in the charge of 'customs chiefs' or *alaha'ohus*. It had been found that the 'head chiefs' were unable to find the necessary time to dispense justice and the *alaha'ohus* were appointed as a kind of gestapo to maintain unity in the ranks and ensure that the directions of the Nine Chiefs were fully understood and obeyed. They summoned offenders to their courts, tried them, and either issued fines or committed the convicted to the local Marching Rule gaol. The *alaha'ohus* were just beginning to develop their functions when Government started to take action against the Marching Rule as a subversive movement. Offences which came under the notice of the tribunals of the movement included refusal to accept the principles of the movement, disobedience of communal orders, non-payment of Marching Rule taxes, and breaches of native custom which had been recognized by the movement.

Articulate natives on Malaita had for many years before 1939 complained of the lack of attention which the Administration paid to native custom. For instance it was claimed that the six months penalty for adultery was absurd when in pre-annexation times adultery was punishable by death. While Government had begun the establishment of Native Councils and Courts in 1943, the Marching Rule insisted on boycotting these and 'head chiefs' instructed the lower level authorities in the different areas, to discuss and write down 'the custom'. It was envisaged that such codification would provide the law of the Marching Rule government. The meetings discussed and the clerks wrote out laboriously the different codes of behaviour to be followed in regard to such institutions as single women, suitors, wives, sexual intercourse, childbirth, swearing, land ownership and usage, pigs, and so on. It was made quite clear, however, that the more serious crimes such as murder, manslaughter, rape, and assault were too difficult and dangerous to be handled by these courts and therefore such offences would be reported by the 'head chiefs' to the District Officer, who would deal with them in the usual manner.

An important symbol of the Marching Rule was the large village or 'town'. Tribes which had lived in scattered villages and districts in the bush for countless generations suddenly uprooted themselves and came down to the coast to establish the Marching Rule 'towns'. These were built for the most part on eminently suitable sites and were rather a cross between the model villages advocated for years by both Government and Mission and the American camps which had been seen during the war years on Guadalcanal. While it appears that the reasons for this tremendous energy were largely tied up with the ridiculous rumours which the movement was propagating, the Marching Rule in the beginning did have an avowed belief in better housing.

In the 'towns' were built the meeting houses. Here were welcomed the high officials of the movement; here were argued 'the customs' and the policy; the latest news and instructions were disseminated, the census taken and the tax collected; here, day after day in 1946 and 1947, the latest orders and moves of the Government were argued and confused. To the ordinary native to whom government had never meant very much, life suddenly became full of purpose. Never was betel nut chewed with such vigour as new and more fantastic rumours spread through the meeting houses of what the movement was going to do for Malaita and of measures to be taken against anybody who tried to stop it.

The leaders discussed, planned and promised their followers elaborate social services, Marching Rule schools and communal farms directed by a European 'farmer'. Finance was to be forthcoming by overall taxation, fines and the controlled leasing of Malaita's physical resources to Europeans. The traditional social system on Malaita had always provided for the aged and infirm. For many years before the war young men had gone off in their thousands to the European-owned plantations and had left the old people to shift for themselves. Marching Rule preached of the evils of this exodus and, while not expressly forbidding young men from going to the plantations, said they must not leave their communities unless they were paid wages at $24 a month and found. (The pre-war rate had been ten shillings a month and found.) The Leaders knew that no plantation manager could possibly afford such a wage and that they were safe in making such demands. The effect was that Malaita as a source of labour dried up completely and the economic stability of the Protectorate was endangered. And so the young men stayed at home to dig the gardens of their aged families and, when they tired of that, would gather in the meeting houses in their hundreds, listening to the oratory and promises of their leaders, scratching the dust, chewing Marching Rule betel nut, talking of the new excitements that were promised them in the days to come, being drilled by their 'strife chiefs' and enjoying a form of indolent life which their fathers and their fathers before them had seldom known. Occasionally they made trouble in the 'towns' and, as they got more and more bored and brawling became frequent, their elders began to shake their heads and wonder whether or not the old balances of power and divisions of work could ever be really established again and whether or not it might be better for all concerned for the young men to go away for a few years before they married instead of idling about the villages.

The 'Cargo Myth' of the Marching Rule movement has taken rather a different form. It is believed by adherents that there are two varieties of white men, British and Americans. While both possess great property, it is the British who refuse to disgorge. It is the Americans who are going to be the saviours of Malaita. On a given day, to be revealed by the leaders, the Americans will return in their L.S.T.s and Liberty ships to Malaita and there on the beaches will be unloaded tons and tons of cargo, amongst which will be cigarettes, tobacco, candy, tinned food, knives, fish lines, hooks, axes, calico and all the hundred and one items of the PX and trade stores. All these goods will be stored in huts already prepared and be distributed as free gifts to good adherents of the movement. Non-adherents will be punished by being deprived of their lands and gardens and driven far back into the bush. So runs the myth of the Marching Rule. The version differs from village to village and island to island but basically the principle is the same.

POWER, STATUS AND 'CARGO'

As a general rule the belief in 'cargo' was strongest in all those areas where the traditional 'big man' or 'alaha' had exercised authority over a wide area. Exercising authority over a wide area had meant that the 'big man' had to give very large feasts to gain his status and that he had had to use large amounts of food in rationing his followers.

'Cargo' was not money, nor was it radios or bicycles. It was thought of primarily as food. But it was not thought of as American food: there was no mention of ice cream or chicken. 'Cargo' was Australian and British food, rice, tinned meat, and stick tobacco.[1] It was the kind of food which in indigenous terms gave the British their status—would it do the same for the new 'big men'? 'Cargo' belonged to the new 'big man'. Although arrangements were made for the reception of this cargo there was no arrangement made for division.[2]

[1] Results of inquiry among former members of the 'Marching Rule' movement.

[2] W. E. H. Stanner 1958:24, and personal investigation.

The ideas about wealth in the 'Marching Rule' movement were a synthesis of traditional notions and experience which had been gained about European forms of wealth. Considerable secrecy surrounded the aims and actions of the 'Marching Rule' leaders, and the Government did not discover until the movement had been in existence for some time that tribute was being collected from the members.

This tribute was the same as the tribute that had been traditionally paid to a 'big man' and was also like the tax paid to Government. In some areas this tribute was in American or Australian currency, while in others it took the form of traditional valuables. The tribute was levied regularly and physical sanctions were taken against those who refused to pay. Traditionally tribute had been kept in the 'big man's' house in the same way that the D.O. kept the tax in his H.Q. The 'Marching Rule' tribute was kept in the new 'big man's' house which was called a 'bank'.[1]

Traditionally status could be lost if the traditional code was not enforced. 'Marching Rule' leaders took strenuous measures to ensure that this did not happen. The laws to be enforced were traditional but the methods of enforcement were modern. Customs were codified and written down. Penalties were fixed for swearing, adultery, and unlawful sexual intercourse. This pointed to a desire to preserve rather than to create a new social order.

The new 'big men' possessed exceptional organizational powers which were demonstrated in their initiation, organization, and execution of all communal projects. Since there was no specialization the same organizational structure performed multiple functions. In supplying this organizational framework the 'big man' set standards. Standards that were meant to result in recognition of manhood when they were achieved by individuals working under the direction of the 'big man'.

Traditional Melanesian society in 1944 had undergone change as a result of European contact; European ideas and attitudes had been added to it. 'Marching Rule' was an attempt to give validity and impact to indigenous notions regarding the nature of status and power in this new society where the Melanesians found themselves without power or status. These new 'big men' provided a

---

[1] Personal communication from Mr. Salana Gaa's former 'Marching Rule' leader and conversations with Government officers serving in the Protectorate at the time of the movement.

synthesized cultural image of the new society. They had achieved successes in the European world as well as in the traditional world.[1] These new 'big men' were, like the traditional 'big men', a symbol of the society's cultural integrity.

The new 'big men's' power was the only form of power which affected the whole cult society. Basically it stemmed from his status and control of the multi-purpose organizational framework. Although the function of this machine at any particular point in time might have been judicial or military, its efficient operation inevitably had ritual overtones. This was because the power that was exhibited through its operation was thought to come as a result of the 'big man's' human attributes and, in addition, his possession of mana.

Did the 'Marching Rule' movement intend to take military action against the British? The object of 'Marching Rule' was to force the British to co-operate, not to kill them. All through the war it would have been easy to have had the D.O. or D.C. killed. During the 'Marching Rule' period it would also have been easy to have had the D.O. or D.C. killed. But in six years of full-scale cult activity only one Government supporter was killed.[2] And during the war the Solomon Islanders had demonstrated with the unfortunate Japanese that they had not forgotten how to kill.

On south San Cristobal it was thought that the Pope would send an army,[3] on Ulawa it was thought that the U.S. Marines might come, and on Malaita massive preparations for self-help were made. The common idea was that a large military presence would force the British to co-operate.

The Solomon Island leaders of 'Marching Rule' respected and liked the D.O.s—they had been through the war together. Vouza, who was bayoneted six times by the Japanese for refusing to divulge military information, said that he held out because when he had been a policeman he had been naughty and he wanted to make amends to his King.[4]

The whole military organization was more impressive than that of the British. The ceremony was more elaborate, the drilling more rigorous, and the discipline more harsh. Military nomenclature was

---

[1] All the successful leaders had very good war records and many had achieved success in the pre-war Civil Service.

[2] Personal communication from ex-Sgt.-Major Vouza, G.M., former 'Marching Rule' leader.

[3] Above.   [4] 'Among Those Present' 1956.

not that of the American army, nor of the S.I.D.F., but that of the administration. The structuring was the same as the British administrative hierarchy. The 'custom chief' *was* the D.O.; the 'head chief' a Government headman; 'leader chiefs' and 'line chiefs' were the same as the Government's village officials.

Military activities were a mixture of old and new. The new activities were concerned with drilling,[1] carrying messages, forming guards of honour, etc. And old ideas on warfare can be seen in the movement. The building of fortified hill towns in 1947, and the elaborate peace-making ceremony in 1953. War drums were used to communicate between villages on San Cristobal. Eagles, the traditional symbol of a chief, were put up on Ulawa.[2]

The final activity associated with hostilities and 'non-co-operation' was the boycott. Traditionally this was the response to an unpopular leader and in the 'Marching Rule' movement it was used against the two types of European thought to be hostile. 'Marching Rule' leaders on Malaita said that labourers would not engage for planters unless they had a wage of $24 per month and, as Allen says, this was an effective boycott. But on Ulawa and San Cristobal there was no minimum wage stipulation. The leaders simply forbade their followers to engage.[3] The war and the 'Marching Rule' boycott ruined the small planter. By the early 1950s only those planters who had shown that they were prepared to treat Solomon Islanders in a humane and fair way managed to obtain workers.

The S.S.E.M. mission was boycotted and it has never recovered its former influence. Yet the boycott against other missionaries was selective: those who had treated the Melanesians like men were on the whole undisturbed by the 'Marching Rule' movement, the remainder were ignored.

Political and disciplinary functions were a mixture of traditional ideas and experience which had been gained about the European/ 'big man'. The new 'big men' gave the same kinds of executive directions as the D.O. had done, but they achieved far greater success.

District Officers had urged the natives to leave the bush and

---

[1] For a similar kind of situation see P. Worsley 1957b:120.

[2] W. G. Ivens 1927:5, mentions the eagle as a symbol of a 'big man' on Ulawa.

[3] Personal communication from Mr. Leong Him, of Honiara, former planter on Ulawa.

settle on the coast, but had had little success. Under 'Marching Rule' leadership thousands settled on the coast. The administration had urged the natives to build model villages with little success. Under 'Marching Rule' leadership hundreds of model villages were built.[1] The administration had urged the natives to build watchtowers during the early part of the war to keep watch on enemy shipping movements—the 'Marching Rule' leaders built watchtowers to sight friendly American ships. Under supervision of European officers of the Solomon Island Labour Corps the natives had built storehouses to help the Americans to store their supplies—under the supervision of the new 'big men' storehouses were built on the home islands to store American goods.

Traditionally a 'big man' could send out his dependants to work in his garden. The S.S.E.M. missionaries had done the same thing and their influence can be seen, together with Government influence, in the movement's agricultural programme. Executive directions on agricultural matters were passed through a number of officials whose titles indicated a relationship with the S.S.E.M. and Government. The 'Marching Rule' men who were called 'duties' had their counterparts (who had the same name) in the S.S.E.M. 'Duties' had been responsible for supervising work in the gardens. 'Farmer chiefs' were the same as the Melanesian agricultural assistants of the Government Agricultural Department.

The new 'big men' imposed discipline and solved disputes in the traditional manner of a 'big man' using the modern machinery of the European/'big man'. Offenders against the 'Marching Rule' norms were brought before 'courts', which were the same as the District Officer's court. Fines were imposed in the same way that the D.O. imposed fines. The communal work was more rigorous and the imposition of discipline more harsh than work or discipline had been, either under the traditional 'big man' or the District Officer.[2]

---

[1] C. H. Allen 1951:199 above, says that the 'Marching Rule' villages were a cross between the model villages which had been advocated by the administration and the U.S. army camps. My research has shown that the U.S. forces did not lay out their camps in neat lines. They were interspersed among the coconut trees to secure maximum camouflage against air attack.

[2] See H. W. Scheffler 1965:182, who says that each manager ('big man') on Choiseul island in the Solomons had to demonstrate his own worth before and while in 'office'. And see also R. H. Codrington 1891:47 who shows that the traditional Solomon Island 'big man' often used his powers harshly.

THE DECLINE OF 'MARCHING RULE'

By 1950 the Malaita leaders of the 'Marching Rule' movement indicated that they would be prepared to make peace with the Government if their demands were met. In September of 1950 they put these demands to the High Commissioner when he visited Auki. They wanted a Council for the whole island of Malaita and a flag. But more significantly they wanted to be able to place their own 'big men' on the council. And they wanted to be able to pay them tribute.[1] There was no mention any longer of higher wages or of the constitution of any widely representative body for the Protectorate.

The Government's view was that the powers which the 'Marching Rule' leaders wanted already existed on a sub-District basis on Malaita. A Regulation had been passed in 1947 providing for the establishment of local government on a sub-District basis on Malaita. But the 'Marching Rule' leaders remained obdurate, they wanted a council on an island basis.[2]

In January 1953 the High Commissioner for the Western Pacific attended the first meeting of the council at which the 'big men' were installed.[3] 'Marching Rule' was then finished on Malaita. The Malaita men made their peace separately with the Government, they made no demands on behalf of other Melanesians. And on the other islands 'Marching Rule' died as councils were established and the Melanesians were allowed to elect their own 'big men' to serve on them.

The Malaita men gained a council which on an island basis had exactly the same powers as the council which had existed on a sub-District basis. The only difference was that under the 1947 Regulations the sub-District committee was under the chairmanship of the headman while the new council was under the District Commissioner and a Solomon Islander President. He decided all policy matters, made appointments, drew up the budget, and left very little to the Melanesian members of the council.[4] Politically it cannot be said that the Malaita men gained very much and yet they made their peace with Government.

Economically the adherents of 'Marching Rule' gained nothing.

[1] A. M. Healey 1966:202, 203. And I have confirmed this in my own conversations with the administrative officer who was in charge of the District at the time.
[2] C. H. Allen 1951:*passim.*
[3] See Sir Robert Stanley's remarks, above:16.
[4] *District Commissioner Malaita's Annual Reports 1953–54.*

Much has been made of the fact that a demand was made for a minimum plantation wage of $24.[1] This demand was not met and by 1967 plantation wages had only risen to $16 per month and in the interim there had been a considerable rise in the cost of living. Wages were not increased, the 'cargo' did not come and yet the leaders made their peace. Socially, the adherents of 'Marching Rule' gained very little. They were no longer treated as 'rubbish men' but they were under no illusions that they had gained equality with Europeans. Discrimination still existed. But the Melanesians had been recognized as men.

The new 'big men' were treated as persons of importance and as the equal of Europeans by the administration. The early council members' only concern was with the status of the President. Salana Gaa's the 'Marching Rule' leader was the first President of the council. They voted him a salary of $4,000 a year which the D.C. turned down. At the same time they thought that employees of the council in the sub-Districts should work for 10s. a month. But that was a measure of the difference between 'big men' and ordinary men.

The council President refused to tour round the island on the same ship as D.C. Malaita in case his status should be in doubt. He was afraid that people would think that he was not the equal of the D.C. For the first time Melanesians travelled 'saloon' on Government ships, shared food with the Government officers, and were accommodated by Europeans in their own houses. 'Big men' were recognized as the equal of Europeans.[2]

Government had received a very severe shock from 'Marching Rule' and measures were taken to ensure that a 'new look' administration came into being as soon as possible. Commercial interests were no longer considered of paramount importance. Strict Regulations were laid down for the treatment of labourers. Administrative officers were instructed to form close contacts with the people. Native courts were constituted as soon as was practicable. Elderly officers were replaced by young administrative officers who, in addition to their administrative training, had undergone courses in social anthropology. An official instruction was issued ordering

[1] P. Worsley and C. S. Belshaw in their analysis of the movement have stressed the significance of this wage demand, believing that it confirms that members of the 'Marching Rule' movement suffered from a sense of economic deprivation.

[2] Personal communications from Mr. T. Russell and Mr. R. Davies who were both serving on Malaita at the time of 'Marching Rule'.

officers to delete any further reference to 'natives': the correct term was 'Solomon Islander'.

Considerable analysis has been undertaken into the origin of the name, 'Marching Rule'. A Solomon Islander when asked to say 'marching' does not say 'masinga' or 'masina': he pronounces the word correctly in the English manner. Mutation in pidgin English works from the English to the vernacular and not vice versa. The name 'Marching Rule' came from the opening phrase of the old S.S.E.M. hymn which was sung on the way to work in the mission gardens: 'We're marching along together . . .'.

The impact of the Second World War on the Solomon Islanders has been over-emphasized. No military action took place on Ulawa, Malaita, or San Cristobal. These islands had experienced the might of the technological age much more intimately during the reprisals that were taken by the Navy during the 'blackbirding' days. Guns and warships which the Solomon Islanders saw during the early Naval reprisals had not caused a cargo cult, their presence had not amazed Solomon Islanders. The Solomon Islanders had adopted an organizational solution to this military problem—they killed as many of the Europeans as they could and they felt that their leaders had won the contest.[1] As men the Solomon Islanders had felt that they were the equal of anyone.

Out of the thousands of natives who were convicted for political offences as a result of 'Marching Rule' only 12 per cent had come into close contact with the Americans through service in the Defence Force or Labour Corps.[2] In south San Cristobal none of the 'Marching Rule' members had served in the Defence Force or the Labour Corps and few had seen the Americans' amazing store of wealth.

The Americans were not 'big men' like the British. They never had any power over the Solomon Islanders. They were thought to be kind and generous. Americans gave away their possessions 'like children': they were thought to be foolish, since they did not ask for anything in return. Solomon Islanders acted as scouts for the Americans in the jungle, and they knew that they were better soldiers than the Americans. This military service in which the

---

[1] Personal communication from ex-Headman C. Baetalua of Bita'ama, North Malaita. W. T. Wawn 1893:213 said that the Islanders were so unimpressed by the retaliatory measures taken by the Royal Navy that they said warships were like 'old women'.

[2] 'Marching Rule' court records, District Office, Kira Kira.

leaders of the 'Marching Rule' movement were prominent had placed the Americans in the position of having an obligation which it was thought that they would repay. The obligation was to be repaid by bringing 'cargo'.

The only role to be played by the Americans in 'Marching Rule' was to bring the 'cargo'; and in terms of the Solomon Islanders' own experience it was quite reasonable that they should do this. But the Americans were not a vital part of the 'Marching Rule' ideology nor were their goods. In south San Cristobal there was no mention of the Americans—the Pope was expected to bring an army.[1] And at the time of the Korean War the Americans vanished from the scene. It was then thought that the Russians would bring the cargo.[2] But the Solomon Islanders knew that the Americans were not going to drive away the British: they had to come to terms with the British in their own way.

The problem of explaining European superiority and Melanesian inferiority had to take place within the confines of existing experience. A 'big man's' power was thought to be unlimited: success was a matter of a man who had the right attributes applying an organizational solution. A man's ability to control the multi-purpose organizational framework was empirically testable. Because of this the new 'big men' were recognized because they were identified with the traditional way of life and since they were known to have achieved success in European activities.

The traditional status system had been egalitarian—superior performance had gained superior status. Within the confines of their experience the Melanesians had no reason to doubt that their new 'big men' would not gain recognition if their performance was as good as that of the Europeans. This competitive atmosphere, with all the Melanesians trying their utmost to prove themselves as men, characterized the whole movement.

In 'Marching Rule' traditional notions about power and status remained unchanged. And the movement must be considered a success because the Europeans were forced to recognize indigenous concepts of status. They recognized that 'big men' were the equal of Europeans and that the ordinary natives were men.

[1] Tawarogha, above: pp. xviii, xxiv.
[2] 'Marching Rule' court records, District Office, Kira Kira.

VI

THE DOLIASI 'CUSTOM' MOVEMENT

THE administrative division of North Malaita is made up of To'abaita, Baegu'u, Baelilea, Fataleka, and Kwara'ae sub-Districts. The only common language is pidgin English. Native population in North Malaita is estimated by the administration at approximately 25,000.

There are no Europeans engaged in commerce in the area, though expatriate missionaries of the Melanesian and Roman Catholic mission live at Fuambu'u in Kwara'ae, Takwa and Kwailimbesi in Baelilea, and at Usu Usue and Araki in Baegu'u. The administrative headquarters of North Malaita is at Malu'u in the To'abaita sub-District.

North Malaita is rugged and mountainous, rising steeply from a narrow coastal strip to the interior, which in places is 4,000 ft. high. Cultivation of cash crops is confined to the coastal strip stretching some forty miles from Auki to Malu'u, varying between two and five miles in width.

Cultivation of cacao is not of much importance. In 1966 the whole island of Malaita produced only 10 tons of cacao. Copra production from North Malaita is estimated at 800 tons per annum; the majority of this comes from the north-west coast, since there is little cultivable land on the north-east coast. This small output of cash crops means that cash incomes are very low.

During the Second World War no military action took place on Malaita and the island was not visited by any large number of Americans or Japanese troops. A small Japanese signals party landed at Bita'ama in the To'abaita sub-District, but they were surprised by natives loyal to the administration and killed with little difficulty.

As a result of 'Marching Rule' large numbers of natives who formerly lived in the bush moved down to the newly established 'towns' on the coast where they have remained after the decline of 'Marching Rule'. Those natives who did not join the movement remained in the hills.

The majority of natives in North Malaita are subsistence agriculturists, growing all their own food and supplementing their diet of
taro and sweet potatoes with fish, coconuts and occasional meat
from wild pigs and possum.

MAP 4. North Malaita.

There are no native-owned stores in North Malaita and the only
capital goods possessed are four small 'cutter' boats used for fishing which are based on the Lau lagoon in north-east Malaita. These
boats are owned by native co-operatives. Itinerant Chinese traders
travel round North Malaita on their ships selling trade goods and
buying copra for cash on the beach.

THE LOCAL GOVERNMENT COUNCIL:
ITS LEGACY FROM 'MARCHING RULE'

Malaita council, the local government authority on the island, has 'headquarters' at Kwainefala in west Baelilea, Bita'ama in To'abaita, Matakwalao in Baelilea, Ataa in east Baegu'u, and Faumamanu in east Kwara'ae. Each of these sub-District 'head-quarters' has a court-house where the native court sits, and a school staffed by a council teacher. The sub-District 'headquarters' are in the charge of a clerk who is responsible for collection of taxes, issuing of licences and receipts, registration of births and deaths, and recording cases heard by the native court.

The President of the council gave feasts and, by virtue of his official position, fed his subordinate staff. From time to time the council gave feasts at their 'headquarters' at Aimela, near the administrative centre of Auki. These feasts were meant to mark the inauguration of new council programmes. Occasionally feasts were given by the council when the High Commissioner visited Malaita. During meetings of the council the President fed the members in the same way that a traditional 'big man' had given food to his followers.

Tax was paid to the President of the council in the same way that tribute had been paid to the traditional 'big man'. This money was thought of and referred to in conversation as the President's money. It was kept by the President in his 'treasury' at Aimela. And it was understood that this money would be used for the good of the people.

The President of the council was thought to have a special responsibility for the maintenance of the traditional way of life. He discharged this responsibility by helping the council to legislate on matters of 'custom'. By-laws, which were directly attributable to the President's influence, were passed, setting a minimum bride price, setting penalties for breach of special local customs, or even establishing a maximum price for groups of native dancers. Europeans were not thought to have an interest in the traditional Malaita customs and yet they were very powerful people. It was commonly thought that one of the President's tasks was to ensure that Europeans did not destroy the Malaita people's cultural heritage.

Following the success of the 'Marching Rule' movement, an essential status attribute for 'big men' was familiarity with the European way of life. The criterion was whether or not Europeans regarded the individual as an equal or not. When the President of the council went to Honiara he often stayed at Government House with the High Commissioner; in Auki he went frequently to the District Commissioner's house; and when on tour, he and Government D.O.s shared their food and slept in the same cabin on the ship.

The council President possessed exceptional organizational powers which were demonstrated in his initiation, organization, and execution of all council projects. Since there was no specialization in the council's activities, the same organizational structure performed multiple functions. In supplying this organizational framework the President set standards—standards that resulted in recognition of status when they were achieved by individuals working in the council area.

The President provided a synthesized cultural image of Malaita society. He had achieved successes in the European world as well as in traditional society. In effect, like the traditional 'big man', he was a symbol of the society's cultural integrity. Malaita council *was* the President in the same way that the D.O. *was* Government and the traditional 'big man' had *been* society. The President encapsulated the council and the council encapsulated the President. The ideology was traditional though the context was modern.

Servants of the council were referred to as the 'council's soldiers'. They wore uniforms, gave salutes to visiting dignitaries, and sometimes drilled at the sub-District 'headquarters'. These activities were not thought important by the administration though it was clear that they had a strong link with the 'Marching Rule' movement. In the sub-Districts there were 'prisons' which were under the control of the council. These prisons were for people who were sentenced by the native courts for offences against custom. The council performed an important part of the administration of justice on the island, a part which, in its operation, was often referred to in military terms.

The President of the council spent a great deal of time touring the island making speeches. In these speeches he urged the people to support the council, and he explained in detail what the functions of the council were, and how it intended to help the people. He went to Honiara to consult with senior Government officers and it was assumed that he had a great deal of power over the Europeans. As a mark of the President's importance, the District Commissioner frequently visited his meetings.

On economic matters the President advocated increased production of cash crops. He stressed that material prosperity and the well-being of the people were dependent on economic progress. Those who did not work hard and who took no interest in the cultivation of cash crops were not doing their share to help the island of Malaita. They were like 'rubbish men'. This was the message that the President emphasized.

The President gave the same kinds of executive directions that had been given by the traditional 'big man'. All communal projects were organized by the President: he arranged for the voluntary building of schools, for voluntary work done on the roads, and at the same time he was responsible for the upkeep of all the 'headquarters'. Since the administration could no longer order Solomon Islanders to work, the President's executive power was the only form of executive power which covered the whole island.

The President was responsible for discipline within the council organization. He dismissed men; he rewarded others for working hard. The President of the council was the ultimate local authority. Since the Local Government Ordinance of 1963 the District Commissioner only had the power to tender advice to the President; he could not do anything if the President declined to take his advice. Frequently the President was asked to arbitrate in land disputes between Malaita men. His role in these disputes was like that of the traditional 'big man'.

'Marching Rule' had been a success and the President of the council was a symbol of this success. He was the heir of the 'Marching Rule' movement, and also of the pre-war D.O. The role of the administration in the years after 'Marching Rule' became advisory. Because of this, and because the climate of opinion did not favour pre-war administrative attitudes, power was slowly transferred from the administrative officers to the local government council. As a result the President had more status than a D.O. and was considered the equal of the D.C.

One area in north-east Malaita had not been able to share in the success of 'Marching Rule'—the consequences of this omission are now examined.

THE SCENE

The geographical area where the Doliasi 'custom' movement took place is situated on the north-east coast of Malaita. It covers the linguistic area given by the Baegu'u, Baelilea, and Fataleka sub-Districts.

Bounded on land by the mountainous spine of the island running on a north-east to south-west axis, the coastline had fringing coral reefs with no suitable anchorage for small vessels. The land mass of the north-east coast plunges steeply into the sea making cultivation of gardens or village construction on the coast impossible. The majority of natives in North Malaita lived on the cultivable strip on the north-west coast.

Ideas on the nature and roles of central and local government were rudimentary, and the general sum of knowledge was far below that of coastal communities. When I asked what Government's work was they said: 'You always tell the people on the coast to plant coconuts or do something to make money, because when they have money they will make progress.' But they added a saving qualification: 'We can't make money here in the bush and that's why we are behind.'

Council, they thought, was a 'big man' like the D.C. And though I phrased my questions in a number of ways they were unable to see any real difference between the President of the council and the D.C. Within their horizon of experience this was a fair appreciation of what was happening on the coast. Government and the council were worried that, despite massive injections of staff and funds, Malaita was economically standing still. An all-out attempt was being made to stimulate production of cash crops and in this policy both the President of the council and the District Officers were saying the same kinds of things to the people on the coast. But none of these meetings was held in the bush of north-east Malaita.

Since the majority of Government and council touring was done by ship few council or Government officials visited the bush area on the north-east coast. The idea was that anyone who wanted to see an official went to a regular ship's anchorage and waited.

The area was small in population and had little economic potential: basic services were provided through regular patrols by police and medical personnel. But none of the 'big men' in Government or council visited the area.

The missions worked from their stations on the coast. They had no need to go into the bush. Bush people were pagan and had resisted repeated attempts to convert them to Christianity. When I first visited the bush area on the north-east coast in 1963 it was the first visit by a European for six years.

The bushmen were unable to make money. Land in the bush was unsuitable for coconuts or cacao. Bushmen showed a marked reluctance to engage as plantation labourers. And though they appreciated that by moving down to the coast they would be able to make money they preferred their life in the bush. Life in the bush had compensations—there was no malaria, no shortage of land to make gardens, and there were good opportunities for hunting.

European money was required for axes, knives, calico, cooking utensils, and salt. Bush people preferred to buy their salt rather than go down to the sea and bring back bamboo containers full of salt water, the traditional way that salt had been obtained. Although bush people were supposed to pay council tax they very seldom did, and their failure to do so was not followed by legal action. It was appreciated by Government and the council that the bush people could not earn money.

Surprisingly, material possessions such as knives and axes were plentiful. But these had been retained, mended, and sharpened long after they would have been thrown away on the coast. Calico was in short supply; there were few shotguns or rifles and no radios. None of the bushmen had a savings account. Only 5 per cent of the bush people were literate and in the fifteen months that I was in the area no one received a letter. For the older men a desire to have European money and goods had not been a sufficient attraction to break the habit of life in the bush. Out of a sample survey of 150 men, only two had spent their adult life working for money, 23 had worked on plantations for an average of two years each, and the remainder had lived all their lives in the bush.

The pattern of living for natives living on the coast was different from the pattern of living of natives in the bush. 'Bushmen' in pidgin English was a term of contempt; it implied that a man did not wash, could not swim and was afraid of the sea, never wore clean calico, was a pagan, and knew nothing of the European way of life.

Social intercourse between bush and coastal people had been virtually non-existent for some years prior to 1963. Out of 105 people I questioned in four villages only six had been down to the coast in the preceding twelve months. In the same period only two people had seen visitors from the coast. Intermarriage between bush people and coast people did not take place. In part this was because the bush people had not got the wealth to pay bride price, and in part because fathers on the coast thought that life in the bush was too hard and uncivilized for their daughters.

By 1964 the bush people had been earning small amounts of money by selling strings of shell wealth (Tafuliae) and pigs to people on the coast. Those who lived on the coast needed these things. Tafuliae were used in payment of bride price and there was a constant demand for pigs to give feasts. But these exchanges resulted in a gradual running down of the bush economy. The effects of this could be seen in the absence of feasts, and in the very low bride prices that were paid. European money was not an acceptable substitute for traditional wealth forms for these transactions.

Since the importance of a transaction was judged by the amount of wealth expended or attached to it this shortage of wealth affected the status of the bushmen. Their transactions became like those of 'rubbish men' who were unable to pay bride price or give a feast.

Collectively the bush people referred to themselves as 'rubbish men'. The social scene in the bush was one of complete apathy, with regret for the passing of more stirring times. Old men talked of fighting—their rifles had been taken away by D.O. Bell who was killed at Sinerangu—how they had killed people living on the coast in the old days. Young men were sceptical: 'We're just like pigs scratching for a living.' I estimated the total bush population at 2,500. The bush villages were small, containing only four or five houses. Few activities were undertaken in common with other villages. Life was dull for the young people; those who went away to work seldom returned.

The bush people had not taken part in 'Marching Rule'; they had remained in the bush, ignored by Government and the council. But they were unable to understand why they were inferior to the coastal people. They knew that many of the people living on the coast had been born and brought up in the bush. Indeed, the bush people had relatives on the coast who ignored them. The question of finding a solution to the problem of explaining their inferiority grew more urgent as time went by.

In January 1963 Malaita council celebrated the tenth anniversary of its foundation. The celebrations were held at Aimela, the council 'headquarters' near Auki. This function was attended by the High Commissioner, senior Government officers, and former

District Commissioners of Malaita. The old 'Marching Rule' leaders had been invited. Vouza and Salana Gaa'a sat on the presidential platform with the other 'big men'. Mariano Kelesi, the council President, was the man of the day. In his speech welcoming the High Commissioner he repeatedly paid tribute to 'those old "Marching Rule" leaders without whose efforts we should have made no progress, and I would not be in a position to welcome you here today, Sir'. The High Commissioner, in making his reply, had little choice other than to endorse the comments of the President.

This meeting provided the inspiration for the Doliasi 'custom' movement. In the crowd was Thomas Doliasi and, as he said afterwards, the things that were said by the 'big men' made him think very hard. He then realized how much the people owed to the 'Marching Rule' movement. The result of Doliasi's inspiration is now described and the description follows Allen's layout in order to emphasize the similarity between the Doliasi 'Custom' movement and 'Marching Rule'.[1]

During the year 1963 when the Government had just completed celebrations marking the tenth anniversary of the foundation of the Malaita council (and the finish of the 'Marching Rule' movement) there began in the sub-District of Baegu'u on the island of Malaita a 'Marching Rule' type cult known as the Doliasi 'Custom' movement.

It was believed that it had been originated by old 'Marching Rule' members and that it was spread through the hill villages of Baegu'u by a man named Doliasi and his principal henchman, one Liliga.

By 1964 it had spread throughout the bush area in the sub-Districts of Baegu'u, Baelilea, and Fataleka, and in the same year there were rumours that it had started on the 'weather' coast of Guadalcanal.[2] The movement reached its climax in 1965 and by 1966 it had totally vanished. In the three years of its existence it

---

[1] Traditional society, 'Marching Rule' society, and contemporary bush society in north-east Malaita form a kind of trilogy: a traditional warrior was the same as a 'soldier' or member of the 'Marching Rule' movement and a 'Custom Movement Warrior' (the name chosen by Doliasi to describe the rank and file in his movement); 'headquarters' in the 'Marching Rule' movement was the same as the traditional fortified hill village or 'headquarters' of Doliasi's 'Custom' movement.

[2] Personal communication from Mr. J. L. O. Tedder, District Commissioner Central District.

presented the Government with a serious problem, for, at a time when the Government was striving to further economic and political development it undermined the authority of the Malaita council and ignored the advice of Government officers.

The movement combined admirable and progressive objects with a studied system of non-co-operation and a deep-rooted belief in the efficacy of the traditional way of life. Had it not been for the patient good sense of other former 'Marching Rule' members in other parts of Malaita the council might have suffered a serious setback.

The essential characteristic which differentiated the 'Custom' movement from a mere cult was its organization. The founder of the 'Custom' movement, Doliasi, despatched letters and emissaries to all the hill villages in Baegu'u, Baelilea, and Fataleka with instructions to choose a 'ramo' or village chief. Many of those chosen were former S.I.D.F. men and ex-Government headmen. They met frequently to discuss matters of policy, though in the main all the decisions were taken by Doliasi. These 'ramos' were assisted by men known as 'warriors' who were responsible for minor executive matters: they made arrangements for meetings, sent letters and collected the tax that was levied by Doliasi on all members of the movement.

The 'ramos' and 'warriors' were also responsible for supervising the work that was undertaken in the large communal gardens that Doliasi had established. They stood guard on Doliasi's 'treasury' where valuables belonging to the movement were stored. They also acted as guides in the 'museum' at Doliasi's 'headquarters'.

In the middle of 1964 the movement began to the establishment of its own courts to deal with breaches of 'custom'. It was claimed that members of the court were submitting voluntarily to the jurisdiction of these courts and that since this was really only a process of arbitration the Government should not consider the courts illegal. However, the Government made it clear that matters being determined by these courts properly fell within the competence of the native courts. But the cult members ignored the native courts.

Doliasi began to codify native 'custom'. Literate members of the movement were engaged in writing down the names of all the trees, stones, and plants on Malaita lest they be forgotten. The information was collected in a number of very large exercise books. A small 'museum' was established. In this building were placed traditional artifacts, together with an explanatory note on their origin and method of manufacture. Numerous meetings were held by Doliasi at which he asked for details of distinctive local customs. These were also noted down in exercise books.

Doliasi went twice to the Malaita council 'headquarters' at Aimela and asked the councillors to allow him to put nine 'Customs Chiefs' on the council. These men were to ensure that all by-laws passed by the council were in conformity with the traditional customs on Malaita. It was explained to Doliasi that only men who had been duly elected for a constituency could serve on the council.

An important feature of the 'custom' movement was the 'headquarters'. Hill people who had lived for generations in scattered hamlets containing four or five houses suddenly uprooted themselves and came down to the coast to build 'custom headquarters'. These were built for the most part on eminently suitable sites. The people did not remain in the 'headquarters' as they had done when the 'Marching Rule' towns were built, they stayed at most for one or two weeks and then returned to their villages in the hills. In one of the 'headquarters' there were 'churches' named after all the missions represented in North Malaita. Yet none of the adherents of this movement was a Christian.

In the 'headquarters', as in the 'Marching Rule' 'towns', were built the 'custom houses'. Here were welcomed the officials of the movement; here were argued the 'customs' and the policy; the latest news and instructions were disseminated, the customs written down and tax collected; here, during the times when the 'headquarters' was inhabited in 1964 and 1965, the latest orders and moves of the council were discussed. To the ordinary native, to whom council had never meant very much, life suddenly became full of meaning. Never were shell ornaments worn with so much pride as new rumours spread through the meeting house of what the council was going to do for the bush people.

The leader discussed, planned, and promised his followers social services on the same scale as existed on the coast. 'Custom schools' were to be established for the children. Communal farms were to be established. And when these farms had been established a European would come and advise on agricultural matters. Finance was to be found for these schemes by a system of taxation. The traditional social system on Malaita had always provided for the aged and infirm. For many years the young people had gone off to the

towns and plantations and had left the old people to fend for themselves. Doliasi promised to create locally the conditions which the
young men had sought on other islands.

The 'cargo' belief of the 'Marching Rule' movement was not
present in the Doliasi 'Custom' movement. Doliasi was going to be
the saviour of the bush people. By following his instructions, by
making traditional artifacts, and providing garden produce for
sale in Honiara they would make money. These things would en-
able them to prove that they were not 'rubbish men'.

THE MAN, DOLIASI

Doliasi in 1963 was a man of about fifty years of age. He was
born in a Baelilea bush village on the mainland opposite the island
of Manaoba. He had lost his sight through illness while still a
young man. Thomas Doliasi was educated by the Marist Fathers
at their mission school at Takwa, North Malaita. After completing
his education he became a catechist for the Catholic Mission and
was reported to be very good at the job. During 'Marching Rule',
though not a leader of the movement, he served a term of imprisonment for a political offence. On leaving prison he severed his
ties with the mission and retired to his home village. He lived there
quietly and without attracting attention until 1963. In that period
it was reported that he made numerous trips to Honiara where
he sold traditional valuables to Malaita labourers for European
money.

Doliasi's principal henchman was a man named Liliga. He
played a very shadowy part in the movement. He was thought to
have been the architect of many of the economic schemes though he
was not regarded as a 'big man' by the followers of the movement.
Liliga, like Doliasi, was born in Baelilea, and like Doliasi, he was
educated at Takwa mission school. An intelligent pupil with a
marked scholastic aptitude, Liliga was sent to Fiji on completion
of his primary education for further studies, the intention being
that he might eventually become a priest. Liliga failed his exams
and after a year he returned to the Protectorate. He then purchased
a small boat with the aid of a loan from the Agricultural and Indus-
trial Loans Board and tried to earn a living by fishing and freighting copra to Honiara.

Feasts were given by Doliasi. When the 'headquarters' were
completed and when very large meetings were held Doliasi gave a

feast. At ordinary meetings which were attended by officials of the 'custom' movement Doliasi gave out 'rations'. These 'rations' were yams and sweet potatoes and occasionally some native cured tobacco.

When a hill village decided to join the 'Custom' movement they were required to pay a group 'subscription'. There was no fixed amount; the villagers were supposed to give as much as they could afford. In one village, where there were only twenty families, Naliwawao, 174 Tafuliae were given. In another village, where there was a shortage of wealth, young men went down to the coast to earn money to pay the 'subscription'. Each member was supposed to pay a monthly 'subscription' of five porpoise teeth, but in fact this was seldom paid. 'Subscriptions' were placed in a 'treasury' in Doliasi's 'headquarters'.

The 'subscriptions' could not be paid in European money since the bush people had no way to earn European money. But from time to time, when European money was needed to buy nails for the 'headquarters' or exercise books, Doliasi sent Liliga to Honiara to exchange the Tafuliae for money.

There were obvious similarities with the council's tax. The 'subscriptions' had also been a feature of the 'Marching Rule' movement. But the 'subscriptions' were placed in a 'treasury' which was like the council treasury. No one questioned Doliasi's handling of the money. It was assumed that he, like the council President, would use it for the good of the community.

The traditionalist section of the 'Custom' movement owed its popularity to the emphasis placed on tradition by 'Marching Rule' and a growing feeling among the older people in the bush that customs were dying away and that something must be done to preserve them. Doliasi's emphasis on preservation of Malaita culture made a tremendous impact on the bush people. In addition to the 'museum' (Doliasi probably got the inspiration for this idea from the British Solomons Training College in Honiara where there was a museum) and the work that was undertaken on recording traditional names and customs, young people were instructed about Malaita traditions in 'custom schools' at the 'headquarters'. They spent two or three weeks listening to old men telling stories and showing how traditional artifacts were made.

Members of the 'Custom' movement wore distinctive traditional clothing and ornaments. These were beaded armbands, turtle shell ear-rings, and nautilus shell ornaments.[1] Calico was still worn though some men adopted the traditional breech-clout and a few women wore grass skirts.

Doliasi's claims to have received recognition from Europeans and to be familiar with the European way of life were impressive. Doliasi said that he had been to Honiara on several occasions and that he had stayed with the High Commissioner while discussing his 'Custom' movement. This was believed by the bush people, though it was far from the truth. Yet, Doliasi had made attempts to discuss his 'Custom' movement with the High Commissioner. On one occasion, aided by one of his henchmen, he climbed over the wall at Government House. He was found walking about in the grounds by the High Commissioner and summarily dismissed. On another occasion he was apprehended by Government House guards in the process of climbing over the wall.

Several times Doliasi announced that he was going to Auki for discussions with the District Commissioner. At other times he would announce that the High Commissioner and the District Commissioner would visit his meetings. The announcement that the High Commissioner was to attend one of his meetings had an obvious historical link with the meeting held at Aimela in 1953 when the High Commissioner had agreed to the demands of the 'Marching Rule' leaders. Doliasi also claimed that the Government had offered to send him to America but that he had been too busy to go.

This claimed recognition by Europeans was in effect the same kind of recognition that a powerful traditional 'big man' gained when news of his power and prestige had spread to other islands. Recognition by other tribes had determined whether he, like the President of the council and the 'Marching Rule' leaders, should be thought of as a very 'big man'.

Doliasi possessed exceptional organizational powers which were demonstrated in his initiation, organization, and execution of all 'Custom' movement projects. There was no specialization and the same organizational structure performed multiple functions. In supplying this organizational framework Doliasi set standards, standards that were meant to result in recognition of status when they were achieved by members of the 'Custom' movement.

---

[1] Many ethnographic accounts describe Solomon Island artifacts as 'inlaid with mother-of-pearl'; this is not strictly correct, as artifacts were inlaid with nautilus shell.

ORGANIZATIONAL FEATURES

The 'Custom' movement's equivalent of the 'soldier' was the 'warrior'. These men attended high officials of the movement, dressed in their traditional ornaments. They supervised work in the gardens and performed guard duties. Several of these guards were always stationed on the paths leading down to the coast so that no one could approach the 'custom headquarters' unobserved. In a very friendly manner they barred the way and inquired the nature of the visitors' business—though they were never known to have refused permission for further progress into 'custom' territory.

Liliga was like the council's executive officer: responsible for payments, financial matters, and supervision of all the movement's paper work. The 'ramos', like council sub-District clerks, were responsible for local collection of subscriptions, recording of minutes of local 'custom' meetings, and keeping local 'custom' property in good repair. Many of these 'custom' officials carried traditional and modern weapons as they went about their business. From time to time they drilled at the 'custom headquarters'.

Doliasi's political activities were the same as those of the council President. He held meetings at his 'headquarters'. He travelled round Malaita explaining the work of his 'Custom' movement and asking for support, and he made trips to other islands. His trips to other islands were mainly concerned with giving speeches to Malaita labourers. He went frequently to Honiara and sometimes to Lever's Pacific Plantations H.Q. at Yandina in the Russell Islands.

Doliasi's political meetings contained no criticism of Government or Europeans. He did not deal with the economic supremacy of the Europeans, he simply stressed the distinctive features of Malaita culture and asked for assistance in preserving them. Political decisions were taken in the 'big man' tradition—all decisions were made by Doliasi; there was nothing democratic about the movement.

At the beginning it was interesting to speculate how Doliasi would answer possible jibes that the council President had Europeans within his jurisdiction. But Doliasi was not lacking in initiative. He paid several conspicuous visits to expatriate mission stations in the vicinity of north-east Malaita and then announced that the missionaries supported his movement. As proof of this he had churches built at his 'headquarters', representing the missions, which he said would be used by the missionaries when they came to attend his meetings.

Doliasi's political role had similarities with the political role of the traditional 'big man': he represented his people in talks with Government and the council. One example of this was his request to have nine 'Custom Chiefs' placed on the Malaita council.[1] On questioning Doliasi about this he admitted to me that he knew that the men could not possibly be elected but he wished to remind people what the 'Marching Rule' movement had stood for. Customs were passing away and nothing was being done about it. But it was only the customs of the Malaita people that Doliasi was interested in. Neither he nor any of his followers took the slightest notice of what went on in other islands.

I was asked repeatedly, as I toured in the bush, when the High Commissioner would come, whether I had come for advice from the 'big man' (Doliasi), and whether people in the 'big places' (Metropolitan countries) knew about the movement. Doliasi's political standing had become much higher than the standing of the council President in the bush.

There was no mention either of cargo or of aid from the Americans: but the economic section of the 'custom' programme was the heir of the cargo ideology of 'Marching Rule'. The economic section had as its declared object a desire to give the bush people an opportunity to make money. These money-making methods were entirely pragmatic, involving appreciation of the means/end relationship and acceptance of the fact that money could only be earned as a result of hard physical work. Money (like cargo) which was obtained was not to be shared out but was to be kept by Doliasi.

As in the 'Marching Rule' movement, work was undertaken in communal groups. The idea was that money would be earned through the sale of garden produce in Honiara, and also from the sale of artifacts, and harvesting of lawyer cane (which was used by the Chinese in Honiara in the manufacture of cane furniture). Transport to Honiara would be provided by Liliga with his boat.

The 'Custom' movement members were sent out to work like a

---

[1] These 'Custom Chiefs' had also been part of the 'Marching Rule' programme, above.

traditional 'big man's' dependants. But the kinds of activity were not in themselves either strange or invested with any special significance. What was distinctive was the communal nature of the undertakings, and the intensity of effort. Daily work in the gardens, or on other tasks, was done at a leisurely pace. 'Custom' activities involved sustained effort, and men frequently fainted from their exertions in the midday heat.

These activities were in a way the same kinds of things that were done on the coast. The President of the council had stressed the importance of money-making activities, and the coastal people followed his directions. Doliasi stressed the importance of money-making activities and the bush people followed his directions. But the 'Custom' movement members seemed concerned to put up a far better performance. I was asked if their gardens were not larger than the coastal people's and whether people on the coast worked as hard as they did.

The plans worked and large amounts of money were made. That this aspect of the 'Custom' movement was a success was very much to Doliasi's credit. Very large gardens had been planted, and the crops harvested and taken to Honiara where they were sold. Numerous artifacts including 'pan pipes', spears, clubs, rattles used in dancing, and small pieces of wood sculpture were also taken to Honiara and sold. This success continued for a year, and it was obvious from the frequency with which Liliga's boat left for Honiara that money was coming in. Visitors to the 'headquarters' were invited to inspect the 'treasury', where money and traditional wealth forms were kept. Certainly there was a large amount of wealth. Some reports put it as high as $20,000. Although I was not allowed to count the money, or shell wealth, I thought that a tenth of that figure might be correct.

In terms of symbolism, wealth, which was like the 'Marching Rule' 'cargo', had arrived. It was held by the 'big man' and formed part of his status attributes.

Doliasi's administrative complex was more impressive than that of the Malaita council. The Malaita council 'headquarters' was laid out in two orderly lines of buildings on either side of the road leading from Auki to Fuambu'u. For most of the year the 'headquarters' was empty. During meetings of the council it provided sleeping accommodation for members, a canteen, kitchens, and a hall for meetings. The President lived at the 'headquarters' in a small house which was some distance from the treasury. 'Head-quarters' is a term which was used to refer to a centre of 'Marching Rule' activities.

There were two large 'headquarters' in the 'Custom' movement. One H.Q. was at Fouloloia in west Baelilea and the other at Foubaekwa in east Baegu'u. Doliasi had his house built at Foulo-loia. This H.Q. contained 233 houses, a 'canteen', 'kitchens', a 'museum', a 'custom school' and a 'hall'. In addition there were churches: the 'Roman Catholic Church', the 'Seven Day Church' (Seventh-Day Adventist), and the 'Melanesian Mission Church'.

At the east Baegu'u H.Q. Foubaekwa, there was no 'treasury' or 'museum' and there were no churches. But there were all the other facilities including 189 houses. In the Districts, Doliasi also had a more impressive set-up than did the council.

At each of the 'Custom' villages, he had a 'custom house' built. Each of these local centres, of which there were between forty-five and fifty, also had a communal garden and several houses which were meant to be used by officials of the movement. These facilities were in fact only used when visitors from other parts came, carry-ing messages or collecting tax. But the facilities which existed in the 'Custom' villages were almost an exact replica of those provided by the council at their sub-District 'headquarters'.

All communal undertakings were organized by Doliasi: he ar-ranged for the building of the 'headquarters', for the establishment of 'schools', and for the day-to-day functioning of the 'Custom' organization.

Initially an attempt was made to set up 'Custom courts' and to fine members of the movement for breaches of 'custom'.[1] Govern-ment was concerned at this development and it was made very clear to Doliasi when he visited Auki that he faced serious charges if he continued this line; the idea of courts then dropped from the 'Cus-tom' programme. But Doliasi continued with his work of codifying native custom and he hoped that the council would take notice of this work and that it might eventually become part of the body of native custom that was being administered in the native courts.

Discipline in the movement was not as harsh as it had been in 'Marching Rule'. It was the same kind of discipline that was being used on the coast by the D.O.s and the council President. Adminis-trative commands were no longer backed by force. Doliasi's ulti-

[1] For a similar kind of development see M. Mead 1956:309, 310.

mate sanction was dismissal from the movement and all the benefits that membership implied. This sanction was the same as those
of the D.O. or the council President—they would warn people on
the coast that failure to co-operate would mean failure to make
progress. A final link with the judicial and disciplinary functions
of the council President and the traditional 'big man' could be
seen in Doliasi's frequent attempts to solve land disputes.

But Doliasi's claim to solve land disputes was not thought any
more convincing than the 'Marching Rule' leaders' claims had
been. It is a striking fact that Solomon Islanders do not trust each
other to make impartial decisions over land. It was for this reason
that the 'Marching Rule' leaders envisaged difficult cases going to
the D.O.[1] Of course, in traditional times there were few disputes
over land. It was only when the natives came down from the high
bush to the coast and started to cultivate cash crops that disputes
arose. The problem was thus associated with Europeans and their
way of life and not with the traditional powers of a 'big man'.

DECLINE OF THE 'CUSTOM' MOVEMENT

By mid-1965 the 'headquarters' were all in ruins. Piles of potatoes lay rotting in great heaps in the communal gardens. Large
rolls of lawyer cane and traditional artifacts were stored in the
'custom houses' with no prospect of being taken to Honiara and
sold.

The 'Custom' programme did not in itself fail. Economic aims
had been achieved: the steady exports to Honiara had shown that
Doliasi's plans were sensible, and bush people admitted that for the
first time they had been able to make money. The 'Custom' ideas
had been put into practice, and they had gained widespread support. Members of the movement were agreed that this aspect of the
'Custom' programme had been a success.

Enthusiasm had remained at a high level in the bush. The movement's organization had functioned efficiently. There had been no
change in the pattern of leadership, and there had been no repressive measures taken by the Government. There had been no coer-
cion, no court cases, and none of the members of the movement had
been put in gaol.

Doliasi had convinced the bush people that he was a 'big man'

---

[1] C. H. Allen 1951, above. Even in 1967 the natives are suspicious of Solomon
Island administrative officers adjudicating on land cases.

like the council President. He had set up an organizational frame-work which enabled the bush people to do the same kinds of things that people on the coast were doing. In this way the bush people gained confidence that their performance was that of men, and not 'rubbish men'.

People living on the coast had, at the start of the movement, refer-red to Doliasi as a 'big man' who was thought to be like a tradi-tional 'big man'. But when details of the movement became more widely known they called him a 'crazy man'. The declared objects of the movement (not the 'Churches' and 'Headquarters') were thought very sensible by people living on the coast. Money-making and preservation of customs were thought admirable. But the other aspects aroused ridicule.

Coastal people lost no opportunity to laugh at the bush people: they asked them if they were going to church, and if the 'crazy man' took the service. Was it true that the 'crazy man' was going to make them all go round naked like their ancestors?

Government's reaction to the movement was mixed. While (as in 'Marching Rule') many of the activities such as gardening and production of artifacts were admirable and deserving of support, there was doubt about the real aim of the movement. There was concern that Doliasi or Liliga might make off with the money, and the administration did not want to be embroiled in endless claims for the return of native wealth.

But it was also clear that the movement had drawn heavily on 'Marching Rule' and the Government did not want any revival of that unpleasant period. Additionally there was the attempt to institute courts, which was an unfortunate development. But the whole complex of activity was sure to be detrimental to the image to the council. However, Government decided to merely keep the movement under surveillance. District Officers were instructed to make it clear that the movement had no form of official support. Government also made its anxiety felt over the large sums of money that were changing hands.

Malaita council had no strong views on the 'Custom' movement. Members regarded Doliasi with complete indifference. However, the local council member in the bush area of north-east Malaita took active steps to try to convince the bush people that Doliasi did not have any support from the council. He stressed that the kinds of activity that were being undertaken by the movement would have a greater chance of success within the local government framework. When the 'Custom' movement had started, the bush people had represented Doliasi among themselves as a very 'big man'. He was thought to be much more powerful than the traditional 'big man'. Doliasi's status as a modern 'big man', like the council President, had been dependent on his claim to have received recognition from important Europeans and to his supposed familiarity with the European way of life. But none of the Europeans gave the support that he had promised his followers that they would give. Neither the High Commissioner nor the District Commissioner had attended his meetings, and administrative officers began to tour in the bush pointing out that Doliasi's claims to have been promised Government support were not true.

Gradually the bush people realized that Doliasi was not a 'big man', and they deserted the movement. The 'Custom' movement no longer had any validity, the kinds of things they did no longer had any meaning. The organizational framework could not make men.

However, Doliasi's enthusiasm was undiminished, though Liliga went back to his fishing and copra freighting. But Government had no need to fear that the bush people would ask for the return of their money and traditional wealth forms—they had been taking part in a process that for them was as old as time, the making of a 'big man'. The bush people's attempt to make a 'big man' had failed and the situation did not call for extensive analysis. They had to wait for another 'big man' who appeared to have the solution to their problems. By March 1967 there was news of a new cult in the bush of north-east Malaita.

This movement was almost an exact replica of 'Marching Rule', the only difference being that it took place among a pagan population and that there was no mention either of 'cargo' or of the Americans. 'Marching Rule' had shown that possession of 'cargo' was not necessarily a measurement of man in European terms since the movement had succeeded even though the 'cargo' had failed to arrive. The 'subscription' was retained in the Doliasi 'Custom' movement since this was held to have influenced the success of 'Marching Rule'. But a more sophisticated appreciation of the nature of European status accounted for the absence of 'cargo'. Other forms of European wealth had become part of the Melanesian way of life but were not invested with any special significance.

However, money which came from sale of cash crops was thought to be a European status attribute.

'Marching Rule' had succeeded and further cult activity had been unnecessary when the status of the Solomon Island 'big men' had been recognized by those at whom the movement was directed. The Doliasi movement failed and activity discontinued when the 'big man' was not recognized by those at whom the movement was directed.

The real significance of the Doliasi 'Custom' movement lies in the fact that activity was directed not only at Europeans, but towards progressive Solomon Islanders living on the coast of northeast Malaita. These Solomon Islanders, and not only the Europeans, were treating the bush people as 'rubbish men'. They had accentuated the bush people's sense of status deprivation. The movement confirms that the major issues in 'Marching Rule' were concerned with status, not racialism. These Solomon Islanders living on the coast were not wealthy in terms of European goods or money. The Doliasi 'Custom' movement did not arise from a sense of economic deprivation. Moreover, economic objectives of the movement were achieved and yet the movement failed. This movement does seem to confirm the conclusions that have been reached about 'Marching Rule'.

VII

CONTEMPORARY SOLOMON ISLAND SOCIETY

GOVERNMENT policy in the post-war period has been directed towards development of the infrastructure of the economy by concentrating on education, health, and communications. An attempt has also been made to diversify the economy by experimentation with new varieties of cash crops in the hope of breaking the traditional reliance on copra, which is notoriously subject to wide fluctuations in price. This policy has resulted in the creation of conditions which are favourable for development. But despite hopes for the timber industry and cacao, copra still remains the mainstay of the economy. A Copra Marketing Board, set up in 1948, manages to stabilize local prices despite fluctuations on the world market.

In the indigenous sector of the economy there have been a number of significant developments since the war. In pre-war days, copra production was almost entirely in the hands of the big expatriate Australian companies, Levers, W. R. Carpenter, Burns Philp, and Fairymead Sugar Co. Of these companies only Levers returned to the Solomons after the war. The number of expatriate smallholders has declined. The uncertainties of production and of the political future, a punitive copra and *ad valorem* export tax, and a lack of capital for replanting have been common factors responsible for this development, which has also resulted in a decreasing demand for plantation labourers.

The number of plantation workers has fallen from a peak of 6,000 in pre-war days to a total of 3,000 in 1967. This figure continues to dwindle annually. The bulk of the manpower in the islands is unskilled, and this has meant the loss of a major source of island income. Little money can be remitted to the home islands by those who work in the towns. Workers have to buy their own food. A careful check on Ulawa for example, where District ships are the only mail carriers, revealed that in a six-month period only

$126 was remitted to the island, which has a population of 1,200. But if there are fewer sources of income for the home islands there has at least been an increase in indigenous copra production. Pre-war Solomon Island copra production was only 4 per cent of the total exported from the Protectorate. By 1966 indigenous production accounted for 50 per cent of the total. But most of this copra was produced in the western District.

The old pre-war trade in trochus shell, ivory nut, crocodile skins and bêche-de-mer has vanished and with it another source of income for the home islands. In the light of this information on changes which have affected island incomes since the war, and with the aid of statistics for copra production, it is now possible to make a rough estimate of contemporary *per capita* cash incomes on the island of Malaita.

By 1967 cash earned through remittances from other islands was negligible. Money coming from sale of copra is the only real source of income for the people on the island of Malaita.

Copra Production by Solomon Islanders on Malaita 1958–66
(Figures in tons)[1]

1958	621
1959	915
1960	966
1961	1009
1962	1060
1963	1015
1964	1020
1965	971
1966	536*

*½ year

Percentage increase 1958–66 = 56 per cent
Monetary value for crop at £60 per ton in 1965 = £58,260.

Local government taxes for Malaita are compiled on the basis of registers containing the names of all adult men on Malaita who are liable to pay tax. Malaita has a population of 48,000 (almost half the population of the Protectorate). On the basis of £2 per man the amount required for tax in 1965 was £20,000. Thus the *per capita* income for Malaita in 1965 was:

[1] Compiled from figures supplied by the Department of Agriculture, B.S.I.P.

1965 Gross income	£58,260
1965 Net income (after tax)	£38,000
1965 Income *per capita*	17s.

There are few entrepreneurial enterprises managed by Solomon Islanders on Malaita. Neither profits from these small local businesses nor remittances from other islands can substantially alter these figures.

The village of Ahia on Ulawa is a former 'Marching Rule' stronghold and it can provide information which is typical of village life on Malaita or San Cristobal. The village contained, at the time the survey was carried out, fifty-three houses all of which had been constructed in local materials. Ahia had a population of 257 containing fifty-two adult men, and of this number six were working on other islands.[1] From figures supplied by the Chinese trader[2] who bought the villagers' copra (the only means of earning money) it was possible to compute an annual income after tax of 30s. *per capita*. This gave a village income of roughly $760.

Trade goods were obtained from the Chinaman, and in a twelve-month period he took in his ship's store $344 (this was the only store the village people had access to). This money had been spent on calico, axes, knives, tea, and a host of other small items. But these purchases were entirely accounted for by nineteen households. A further ten households estimated that they would make purchases from the Chinaman in the next twelve months.

Ahia villagers produced all their own food. They had no preference for European food though they did like sugar when they could get it, and tea. Kerosene used for lamps to light the long evenings was also popular. Small amounts of money earned from the sale of copra went in donations to the church. Some money was also buried in the ground in the old 'tambu' places where traditional forms of wealth had been buried. Day-to-day transactions in the village were carried out with traditional wealth forms. Payments for bride price or land were made with shell wealth. Other payments were made in garden produce. But European money was being saved though it took me a long time to discover what happened to this money. European money which had not been spent or

[1] Survey carried out August–December 1966.
[2] Personal communication from Mr. Richard Leong of the M/V *Hung Lee*, who also informed me that these figures were in no way unusual. See also above: xviii–xx.

buried was used to buy pigs, since in this way a man could gain status.[1]

European goods were popular but indigenous preferences were stronger and European money was in the main being used in the same way that traditional forms of wealth had been used. A desire to purchase pigs, or traditional forms of wealth, formed the greatest incentives to money-making activities.

But what effect on the village scene did men who had worked in urban areas have? When I visited Ahia in December 1966 I knew that two men who had played a part in the 1965 strike in Honiara had returned to the village, and I was anxious to find out how they had resettled. I found that they had made some copra and sold it to buy pigs.

Traditionally wealth-making activities formed part of the organizational framework which was provided by the 'big man'. Copra-making in contemporary Solomon Island society conforms to this pattern. All modern 'big men', Government and council alike, stress that men make copra—it is a concomitant of the new way of life. A man demonstrates his claim to manhood in the new society by making copra. Copra-making is a man's task, women are not involved.

The activity of making copra is the important thing. A man ate what he produced from his garden in traditional times or he used it for a feast—there was thus a certain standard of production set by the 'big men'. But in contemporary Solomon Island society men do not eat copra nor can it be used in a feast—the 'big men' simply say 'make copra'. Making this copra establishes a man's identity in the organizational framework provided by the new 'big man'. This is particularly noticeable on islands which have very exposed coastlines. It is impossible for ships to call regularly. In these areas copra which cannot be collected often becomes mildewed and unsaleable. But the men continue to make copra even though they know that it will not be collected.[2] They are establishing their identity.

In every village in the coastal areas men spend a little time each day 'making copra' even though there are few coconut trees and

---

[1] D. L. Oliver 1955:202, 203, shows that among the Siuai of Bougainville Australian money could only be used in a limited number of transactions, none of which were associated with the gaining of status.

[2] This is particularly noticeable on the 'weather' coast of San Cristobal.

no ships to collect the copra. I have never come across a coastal village where the people admitted that they made no copra. Since 1938 expatriate salaries in the Protectorate have risen by between 500 and 600 per cent. The cost of living, taking as an index 100 items commonly purchased by Solomon Islanders, has risen over 300 per cent. Belshaw gave a *per capita* figure of 9s. 3d. for the Solomons in 1938.[1] In examining the Solomon Island economy at the time of 'Marching Rule' he wrote:[2] 'Unless the Solomons can experience an economic revival of a democratic kind . . . bitterness will continually hamper the efforts of the administration, however well-meaning.'

There has been no economic revival of a democratic nature for Malaita or Ulawa, islands which between them account for half the population in the Protectorate. If Solomon Islanders living on these islands were expressing wants of an economic kind in 'Marching Rule' then it is clear that there has been little progress in providing the means of their satisfaction. And I can confirm from personal experience that bitterness is not hampering the work of the administration.

THE POLITICAL SCENE

The formal political structure of the Protectorate is divided into Central and local government on the basis of functions germane to each body in much the same way as responsibilities are devolved in the United Kingdom. In 1960 an Order-in-Council provided for the establishment of Legislative and Executive Councils with an official majority. Early Solomon Islander members of these councils were drawn from prominent men in all walks of life who represented the four administrative Districts of the Protectorate.

A further development took place in 1964 when, under an Order-in-Council of that year, Solomon Island members of Legislative Council were chosen by Electoral Colleges made up from the members of the local government councils. The 1967 Electoral Provisions Regulations provided for a further revision of the Constitution by increasing the number of Solomon Island members of the Legislative Council from eight to fourteen. An official majority is still maintained.

It has been a source of disappointment to the Government that

[1] C. S. Belshaw 1954:124, 125.   [2] C. S. Belshaw 1950a:128, 129.

these constitutional advances have been ahead of public demand. In practice, although the Legislative Council debates are widely reported through the media of press and radio, its activities have aroused little interest among Solomon Islanders. Political parties are not yet in existence because the Solomon Island members have no common platform.[1] Though Solomon Island members have gained considerable confidence in their ability to speak in the council the tendency has been for each member to act as a delegate thinking and speaking only in terms of what he can obtain for his home island.

Speeches by Solomon Island members of the Legislative Council have shown that there is no deep feeling for the Protectorate as a whole. The members do not think of the Protectorate as a single political entity. Malaita men are universally disliked by other Solomon Islanders and this can be seen from time to time in the Legislative Council. No Solomon Islander can speak for the islands as a whole. Mariano Kelesi, the President of the Malaita council, has tried to, and the common reaction by Solomon Islanders was: 'Who does that bloody Malaita man think he is?'

There has been very little criticism of the Government in the Legislative Council. Speeches of Solomon Islanders have been mainly confined to trivia. But they have repeatedly asked for assurances that the British Government will continue to develop the islands and that the Government will do its utmost to provide more expatriate staff. The Legislative Council debates, which reflect the views of elected Solomon Island leaders, show that the people are basically satisfied with their present system of government. They have no real desire for independence, nor even a desire to assume a greater degree of responsibility for their affairs.

But in the prevailing climate of world opinion, and in view of the 1960 U.N. Declaration on the abolition of colonialism, the British Government has no wish to stay in the islands any longer than is strictly necessary. A little political agitation would be a welcome sign that the Solomon Islanders are willing to take their place in the modern world.

On a local level Solomon Islanders have shown no interest in central Government politics. There has been no pressure for de-

---

[1] Since this was written, political parties, mainly the inspiration of European members of the Council, have been formed though I have little information on their activities.

volution of political power, for the creation of a ministerial system, or for the abolition of the official majority in the Legislative Council. Things that happen in the capital are remote and have little interest. Government for Solomon Islanders living in rural areas is still by 'big men'. The Legislative Council can influence their lives but it does so through the agency of 'big men' like the D.C. Thus the Solomon Islanders cannot understand how the existence of a Legislative Council really makes any difference to their way of life. Politics are still viewed in the context of the 'big man' relationship.

An experience I had while D.C. Eastern District illustrates this attitude. For several years the Government had planned to build an airstrip in the Santa Cruz group. The project was exhaustively debated in the Legislative Council in 1966 and the proceedings were publicized by press and radio (the broadcasts were heard and the news-sheets were read by the Santa Cruz people). The Legislative Council decided that there were insufficient funds for the project and that it should be deferred. This was supported by the Solomon Island members of the Legislative Council. But the Santa Cruz people held me personally responsible for the Government's failure to build the strip. Their attitude was that I was the Government: why did I not build the airstrip?

Since the enactment of the Local Government Ordinance in 1963, which devolved a great deal of responsibility onto the local councils, considerable expansion in local government activities has taken place. But local government in the Districts is regarded in the same way as the council. The council is the President, the President is a 'big man', and ordinary council members have no more status than that of a Government clerk. Local government council meetings show the operation of the traditional 'big man' relationship with ordinary men. There is little discussion, all the motions of the President are inevitably carried unanimously.

Political activities in contemporary Solomon Island society consist of meetings between the 'big man' and his followers on a traditional pattern. The actual content of discussion at these meetings is not important, the most important thing is the activity of holding the meeting. In performing this activity men establish their identity within the organizational framework provided by the political activities of the modern 'big man'. As in traditional meetings, the content of the meetings is often in the form of a lecture with few questions being asked. Such questions as are asked are only asked to clarify what the 'big man' has said.

The 'big man' explains what Government or the council is doing. This shows that in traditional terms he has the welfare of the people at heart. There is nothing democratic in the meetings: 'big men' tell their followers to make copra, to clean up their villages, or to build a wharf. Most 'big men' try to get a better response from the people by saying that the men on other islands are doing better, that they work harder, etc. All these kinds of things conform to the traditional pattern of a 'big man's' meetings.

Many Government officers have been amazed by the enthusiasm with which Melanesians regard the meetings held in a village after a day's touring. They have found that it does not matter what is said: one can talk about other islands, the price of copra or tell endless stories. But a meeting must be held.

There is only one European engaged in commerce on Malaita, there are no resident commercial expatriates on Ulawa or San Cristobal. (There were no resident commercial expatriates on these islands in pre-war and early post-war days.) Commercial trading in these islands is run entirely by Chinese: no other people have the commercial expertise which is required, nor are any willing to work the same excessive hours as the Chinese, on small profit margins.

However, the Chinese are universally disliked. Representations were made by Solomon Island members of the Legislative Council in the second session of the Council in 1966 to have all the Chinese deported from the Protectorate. This shows that Solomon Island members of the Council have the capacity for racial feeling and that they can express this feeling. But there is no contemporary record of any such feeling having been directed against Europeans.

Solomon Islanders say: 'We know you Europeans come to help us, but the Chinaman has only come to take our money and cheat us by paying low prices for our copra.'[1] Racialism in the contemporary Solomons shows the same pattern that was evident during 'Marching Rule': there are Chinese who are not engaged in commerce who are thought to have the welfare of the people at heart and who are popular.

[1] One of the characteristic features of the small trader who buys copra in the islands is the rigidity of his price. Fluctuations on the world market are very seldom reflected locally. On this point see J. S. G. Wilson 1965:*passim*.

Officers who have served in Africa inevitably tend to assume that the Melanesians may descend from the hills at any moment. But even allowing for this attitude, and attempts by police officers to create anxiety to assist 'empire building', no evidence of substantial anti-white feeling in the rural areas has been collected.[1]

But how do Solomon Islanders view their relationships with Europeans? They have now found out that all Europeans are not 'big men', yet these Europeans are tolerated because it is felt that they have come to the islands to help. But when occasion permits they pay more deference to their own 'big men' than to Europeans who are not thought to be so important. In a mixed gathering where there are modern 'big men' and not so important Europeans, Solomon Islanders regulate their conduct accordingly. They address the Melanesian 'big man' as 'Sir' and they rise when he enters the meeting. But they refer to the not so important European by his Christian name and remain seated when he enters the gathering.

It is accepted without unfavourable comment, though the point is taken, that Europeans have better houses, more money, and ample clothing. But the reasons for all this are also widely appreciated: European superiority is attributed to superior education and training, and Solomon Islanders encourage their children to work hard at school because they can see that Solomon Islanders who have been educated overseas have the same kinds of jobs as Europeans. Europeans visiting Solomon Island villages are accommodated in the best houses, at meetings they are given the best seats, and if they attend a feast they are given one of the largest portions. On ships Europeans have the best places. In a village football match a friend of mine (European) frequently played a fine game because no one was willing to take the ball from him.

Racial attitudes reflect the traditional relationship between 'big men' and ordinary men. Those who help Solomon Islanders, no matter what their personal circumstances or race, are thought to be friendly and are treated as such. Those who do not help are treated as enemies. Hostility is the relative coefficient of an expatriate's ability to pattern his performance in conformity with the traditional obligations of a 'big man'.

[1] Journals and magazines in the Pacific are normally sensitive to any outbreak of anti-white feeling on the part of the natives, but since the decline of 'Marching Rule' they have printed very little about the Solomons.

Elkin contended that 'Marching Rule' showed marked anti-white feeling which 'repressive measures, even if apparently successful, will only cause to simmer and eventually to boil over'.[1] If 'Marching Rule' had been anti-white, it is too much to suppose that the simple action of allowing the Melanesians to elect their own 'big men' to the council would have solved the problem. Evidence has been adduced on European superiority in contemporary Solomon Island society. But in the fourteen years since the decline of 'Marching Rule' there has been no revival whatever of anti-white feeling in the rural areas. One must conclude that racialism was never a dominant feature of 'Marching Rule'.

LIFE IN THE TOWNS

In March of 1965 while the Doliasi 'Custom' movement was expressing the grievances of the bush people of north-east Malaita, armed police were struggling with a full-scale riot in Honiara. Europeans' cars were stoned, tear-gas was used, and there were fears that essential services could not be maintained. The Melanesians in Honiara were agitating for higher wages.

The pattern of living of the modern urban wage earner is significantly different from that of the pre-war plantation labourer. Modern wage earners spend most of their lives working in the towns. Employees are no longer rationed. It is now impossible for them to find land near the towns to grow their own food—all the food they eat has to be bought from their wage earnings. Solomon Islanders sum up this development by saying: 'In the towns we live by money.'

In turn this residence pattern and inability to send money home, because wages are entirely used up in day-to-day living, has resulted in a weakening of kinship ties with those remaining on the home island. But the majority of urban dwellers find it impossible to dodge the obligation of feeding their friends and relatives when they visit the towns. Senior employees, as a class, almost completely sever their ties with their homes, often spending their vacations in the towns. Junior employees have a continual struggle to make ends meet.[2]

[1] A. P. Elkin 1953:109.
[2] In 1966 the B.S.I.P. Civil Servants Association produced figures in support of their claim for a salary increase which showed that the cost of keeping a man in Honiara prison was greater than the average wage of a junior clerk.

Concepts of status among Melanesian urban dwellers are completely Europeanized. Status is dependent on earnings, clothing, possession of a car or bicycle, and a white-collar job. There is no obligation to follow the traditional customs in the towns. Status comes from getting as close as possible to being a 'black European'.[1] The only kind of power is economic power. Organizational ability counts for little. Unlike in the rural areas, there is a complex division of labour; traditional forms of wealth have no function in the towns. Those who are unskilled come to the towns to see life and their ambition is to return home as soon as they have saved enough money. But the majority of Melanesian town-dwellers are skilled and articulate, men who earn relatively high wages in relation to the 'floating' population of labourers.

These successful town-dwellers do not think of themselves as being Melanesians. Young sophisticated urban Melanesians will go to the market to laugh at people from the bush. Others laugh when they see native dancing. Many urban dwellers will refuse to be seen in public with their relatives from the home islands. The sophisticated townspeople have entered into a kind of 'cultural no-man's-land'.[2]

Resentment is expressed about the dominant economic position of the Europeans in the towns. Melanesians resent the fact that they seem to work as long and as hard as the Europeans and yet the Europeans have far more money. Through the stories of houseboys, the urban Melanesians have intimate details of the European way of life. Housing for Melanesians in the urban areas is in short supply. Often they are forced to sleep five or six to a room. Many are unable to bring their wives to the towns or to support them if they do come. The situation is exacerbated at the higher levels where the trained and skilled Melanesians make far less money than their European counterparts.

Melanesians are discriminated against in the towns. They are generally not allowed to enter European clubs or bars.[3] Harsh reprisals are taken by the law when Melanesians sexually assault

---

[1] This jibe is frequently made by young educated Solomon Islanders in the towns. Many of them feel that more should be done to promote their own culture in the towns.

[2] B. Malinowski 1945:157–62.

[3] The Hotel Mendana does not allow Solomon Islanders into the European section of the hotel; the Guadalcanal Club, while professing an open house, has consistently managed to exclude Solomon Islanders.

white women. But the Melanesian section of the population that feels most strongly about discrimination is the permanent one which is made up of fairly senior people from all walks of life. Crime figures are high and the nature of the crimes which are committed in the urban areas reflects the urban tensions. Assault, sexual crimes, theft, and occasionally murder are all committed on a much higher *per capita* basis than in the rural areas. At present the major problem in the rural areas is the creation of centres and activities where black and white can meet and learn a little about each other.

Urban conditions are the almost exact opposite of rural conditions. Honiara contains, and has contained for a long time, all the features and attitudes that were thought to be part of 'Marching Rule'. In the towns there is economic deprivation and racial hatred. In the towns the Melanesian's gap between his wants and the means of their satisfaction is very wide. But the natives' resentment is not, and never has been, expressed in cult activity.

Resentment against the Europeans has been expressed in other ways. It has been expressed in strikes, in assaulting Europeans, in throwing stones at their cars, in attempts to rape white women. None of these forms of protest were used in the cults. The social structure of the towns is different from that of the rural areas and the concepts of power and status are different.

CONTEMPORARY ADMINISTRATIVE ACTIVITY

In each of the four administrative Districts of the Protectorate there is now a team of specialist officers. These normally include a doctor, together with agricultural, forestry, survey, and police officers. These officers constitute a team under the direction of the D.C. The District Commissioner's task is to co-ordinate the activities of these Departments to secure the maximum effect. Administrative officers are still primarily responsible for economic and political development, local government affairs, and Magistrate's court work, which they undertake as *ex-officio* Magistrates.

The complexities of modern administration have inevitably resulted in a great increase in the volume of paper work which in turn has limited the amount of time that officers can spend on tour.

Broadly speaking, all Departments can be classified as extension or controlling Departments, though some exercise both functions. Extension Departments are responsible for the implementation of a specific programme 'in the field'. Thus, the Agricultural Department is responsible for propagating sound methods of animal husbandry and for encouraging production of copra. Controlling Departments function to ensure that existing regulations are obeyed or to operate checks. Treasury Department, for example, makes payments under authority and the Police maintain law and order.

The work of controlling Departments in the Districts is comparatively simple. They operate on commonly known rules and principles which cause a minimum of inconvenience or surprise to the Melanesians. Breaches of the Penal Code are understood, the need for medical attention is appreciated and so on. But controlling Department officers are not thought of as 'big men'. They do not give orders. Controlling officers do not organize people. They have none of the traditional attributes of a 'big man' and they are thought to have little power.

Extension work is considerably more complicated, because, with the abolition of the former sanctions, Solomon Islanders are under no obligation to do what the extension officer advises. Two cardinal principles are involved with all extension work. The officer responsible for the programme must establish good relations with the people in his District. The idea behind this is that if the Melanesians regard him as a friend they are likely to follow his advice. Secondly, the administrative officers and the council President must throw their weight on the scales, since no extension programme can succeed without the active assistance of the 'big men'.

The Melanesian views the technical officer as no more than an employee of the 'big man'. A technical officer is only responsible for one project—say medical or agricultural—but the administrative officer and the council President cover all activities in the manner of a traditional 'big man'. And in the last analysis the Melanesians know that it is the administrative officer or the council President who has the power.

The administrative officer and the council President, like the traditional 'big men', are the only officers or men who have economic, political, and executive power. They gain their status in the traditional manner, with the added attribute that they must now be familiar with the modern way of life. They have the power to impose sanctions for disobedience, or to withhold money for development projects in the event of non-co-operation by the

Melanesians; and they represent the ultimate local authority on their islands.

However, although administrative officers and council Presidents can organize, they have been unable to change traditional ideas. Their role in propagating constitutional changes, and in attempting to achieve a significant increase in copra production has met with little success. The conclusion now being painfully reached in the Protectorate is that current extension work is not very successful. Further experimentation, utilizing sociological analysis into the Melanesian pattern of incentives in depth, community development, and audio-visual techniques, will be necessary if progress commensurate with the funds that are now being spent on development is to be made. Agricultural development on Malaita, using the most sophisticated extension techniques, has shown that there is no direct relationship between the number of extension workers employed and increases in production.

CONTEMPORARY MISSIONARY ACTIVITY

In the missionary field the main developments since 'Marching Rule' have been the almost total eclipse of the S.S.E.M., and the strengthening of the Roman Catholic and Melanesian missions. In addition there are now Solomon Island 'big men' in the missions. Solomon Islanders are Bishops in the Melanesian mission, and fully qualified priests in the Catholic mission. There is virtually no theological debate among Solomon Islanders over the merits of individual missions. The Catholics and Melanesian missions are popular because they exercise strong discipline over their members. They use power, they organize their members, and they have recognized indigenous status by creating Melanesian leaders in the missions.

Religion is not something that Solomon Islanders discuss, it is an activity, something that is done every day by going to church. By going to church and going through the activity individuals are able to establish their identity in the organizational framework of religious activities provided by the modern 'big men'/Church leaders. Further opportunities for identification are provided through communal church activities in the villages.[1] Individuals make copra to help the church fund or help to build a mission

[1] For an interesting illustration of the concepts of power and status in the religious background of village life, see N. Petersen 1966.

school. In their organizational aspects these activities have credibility and impact.[1] Churchmen in the Solomons have not found that Solomon Islanders are more religious in 1967 than they were in pre-war days, but they have found that church attendances are far higher.

CONTEMPORARY COMMERCIAL ACTIVITY

Neither European, Chinese, nor Melanesian entrepreneurs are recognized as 'big men' on Malaita, Ulawa, or San Cristobal. A successful businessman does not have the same status as a District Commissioner, a Bishop, or a council President though he may have a great deal more money than any of these individuals. The activities of businessmen do not involve other people: they do not give orders or commands, they do not organize, and, prima facie, their success means that they have turned their backs on the traditional way of life.

Joe Konihaka lives on Ugi Island in Eastern District, and has a net annual income from copra of about $16,000. But it is widely reported (and I have confirmed the fact) that he did not give his brother Willy $20 for a store licence. Thomas Titiulu is an outstanding farmer on Ulawa. On the basis of his past performance Titiulu was given a $4,000 loan by the Agricultural Loans Board. This loan was to finance new coconut plantings. But he does not divide his wealth among his relatives. Both these men have broken the 'web of kinship'. Neither Konihaka nor Titiulu is recognized as a 'big man', though they are both very wealthy. These men do not conform to the traditional 'big man' image. The average Melanesian knows that the effort to break the 'extended family' can be too expensive. The only way to achieve financial success without social stigma is to go to the towns. Only in the towns can traditional obligations be avoided.

CONTEMPORARY 'BIG MEN'

The position of Solomon Islander administrative officers in the Government is now examined. They show, in the ways in which they are regarded by Melanesians, that they have gained their status in the same way that the traditional 'big man' gained his status, and that they use their power in the same way. But, more important,

[1] K. O. L. Burridge 1960:260, 'A man becomes a man within terms of activities that are organized.'

these new 'big men' are not yet institutionalized. If they do not conform to the traditional 'big man' pattern then they lose their status even if they continue to hold their official positions.

There are three Solomon Islander administrative officers in the Protectorate's Civil Service. Silas Sitai from Santa Anna in Eastern District; Fred Osifelo from Guadalcanal; and Francis Talasasa from the Marovo lagoon in Western District. The first two are thought of as 'big men', Talasasa is not.

Talasasa was educated at Pawa School in Eastern District and then at Wellington University in New Zealand where he graduated with an arts degree in 1956. After a year's administrative training at Cambridge he took up his appointment in the Protectorate. His pattern of living had become completely Europeanized. But this was not the reason given for his failure to acquire the status of a 'big man'. Talasasa was thought to be weak: he did not have the personality of a 'big man'. North Malaita people said he was like the Americans: he wanted to play, wanted to go shooting pigeons, wanted to see traditional dances. He gave freely of his food and beer which was thought wrong—'big men' should eat apart from ordinary men. Solomon Islanders did not grant him high status nor did they pay much attention to what he said. They had examined his qualities and attributes, clinically and empirically, and found them wanting. It was frequently said by Melanesians that they would prefer a European D.O.

Silas Sitai, of Santa Anna in Eastern District, joined the Government as a trainee clerk in 1939. He had a very distinguished war record and eventually, after a year's administrative training in England in 1962, he was promoted to the rank of administrative officer. Sitai's way of life had always been Melanesian, but in his actions he patterned himself on the 'big men'.

In his personal relations with Melanesians he remained stern and aloof. He enjoyed using his authority. But Sitai had very considerable organizational ability which he was very fond of using. In addition, he continually urged the Government to better the conditions of Solomon Islanders. These things were in conformity with the traditional 'big man' image. Sitai is thought of as a 'big man' the equal of any European. As a measure of his status he was allowed by the people to hear native court cases involving land on his own island: Talasasa's attempts to do the same thing had resulted in complaints being made to the High Commissioner.

The Hon. J. Campbell, President of the San Cristobal council, is the son of F. M. Campbell who was the first Commandant of Police in the Solomons. His mother was a Malaita woman. Campbell was educated privately by his father who brought tutors to San Cristobal from Australia and New Zealand. For some years after his father's death Campbell's attitude was ambivalent—he had the status of a European and yet he had a strong leaning towards his people. But slowly he began to conform to the traditional pattern of a 'big man'.

Given to frequent bouts of heavy drinking, Campbell began to declare that he was just a 'poor bloody native'. He became President of the San Cristobal council. And in running his own plantation and the council he showed that he had very considerable powers as an organizer. In operation Campbell's role had a strong resemblance to the traditional role of the 'big man'. If a feast was held in a village near his home he gave more pigs and garden produce than any other man. Punctilious in his observance of native custom, he gave large feasts in memory of his mother after her death. In many cases he settled disputes over land, and young men sought his permission to marry.

Campbell's lifelong friend has been Geoffrey Kuper of Santa Anna. Kuper's father was a German trader who settled on Santa Anna and his mother was the daughter of a local chief. Kuper is a man of remarkable talents. He qualified as the first Solomon Islander native medical practitioner before the war, served as a coast-watcher during the war, earning a B.E.M., became Master of the Melanesian mission's ship the *Southern Cross*, was appointed to the Advisory Council, and then in 1960 gave up all his appointments and retired as a comparatively young man to Santa Anna.

A few years ago Kuper entered local government politics, and served as the member for Santa Anna on the San Cristobal council. Although superior in education and training to Campbell, he has never rivalled him for the Presidency of the council. This is attributable to two factors. Kuper's organizational powers are not as strong as Campbell's, and he has never identified himself with the Melanesians. Kuper refers to the local people as 'natives', to himself as a European, and refuses to uphold the traditional way of life. Kuper has not got the attributes of a traditional 'big man'. He is not thought of as a 'big man', though he is relatively wealthy in terms of European possessions. But Geoffrey Kuper's father was thought of as a very 'big man' and people on the island of Santa Anna are fond of contrasting the behaviour of father and son. The Anglican Bishop, Leonard Alufurai, O.B.E., of the Melanesian mission, is a widely travelled and educated man whose home village is Adigege, in the Kwara'ae sub-District of Malaita. As a keen educationalist and a nominated member of the Legislative Council, Alufurai has identified himself with Melanesian interests. And in performing his spiritual role he has been sensitive to the strength of custom.

Bishop Alufurai has the powers of a traditional 'big man'. He excommunicates (this is quite frequently done). He imposes discipline and fines on his flock. His instructions are obeyed since they are believed to be backed by spiritual sanctions. Indeed the Bishop has more power than a D.C. In a recent case a couple asked the D.C. if it was legally possible for them to marry since they were not sure whether or not they were too closely related. Permission was granted. Other people appealed to the Bishop on grounds that the marriage infringed custom, and the Bishop forbade the marriage. The marriage did not take place.

Alufurai has considerable organizational powers. Like Government and council 'big men' he *is* the church, and donations which are given to him are thought of in the same way as Government taxes, that is, as tribute to a 'big man'.

VIII

COMPARATIVE ANALYSIS

IN this chapter comparative analysis of the movements which have been examined is undertaken. Movements are referred to by their date of origin, e.g. 'Vailala Madness': 1919, 'Marching Rule': 1944, Doliasi 'Custom' movement: 1963. Comparative analysis is concerned with three questions: (a) Was the nature of European contact, and the effect that Europeans had on indigenous society, the same in 1919 and 1944? (b) In terms of their respective organizational structures did the relationship of the movements of 1919, 1944, and 1963, to their traditional backgrounds indicate that the movements were in conformity with existing indigenous experience? (c) Did concepts regarding the nature of power and status change?

In terms of their existing experience the Papuans and the Melanesians both recognized individual European Magistrates and District Officers as 'big men'. They did this because both these kinds of European Government officer had the attributes of a traditional 'big man'. And they used their power in the same way that the traditional 'big man' had used his power.

European contact, both in Papua and the Solomons, destroyed the power and status of the traditional 'big man'. Moreover, the natives found that no matter what they did the European treated them as 'rubbish men'. And in both traditional Solomon Island society and Elema society 'rubbish men' were not really thought of as men; they had no rights, no status, and no power.

Among the Elema the 'big man' had initiated, organized, and executed economic projects. He possessed exclusive religious knowledge which enabled him to perform rituals on behalf of his people; he imposed discipline, upheld the traditional way of life and gave executive directions.

But the Magistrate, who also did these things, showed that he had much more extensive power than the Elema 'big man'. He initiated, organized, and executed economic projects; he possessed exclusive religious knowledge, and this could be seen from the successes that he obtained; he imposed discipline, upheld traditional customs, and gave executive directions.

But the Magistrate refused to recognize the integrity of the indigenous culture and he treated all the Elema as if they were 'rubbish men'. The traditional 'big man' had been in control of the organizational framework, the Magistrate took over control of the organizational framework. Magistrates could be seen by the Elema as more powerful versions of the traditional 'big man'.

In the Solomons the traditional 'big man' had controlled the multi-purpose organizational framework. He made war and peace, upheld traditional customs, gave executive directions and feasts, and imposed discipline.

But the District Officer, who also did these things, showed that he had much more extensive power than the 'big man'. He gained control of the multi-purpose framework. He made war and peace, upheld traditional customs, gave executive directions and feasts, and imposed discipline. District Officers could be seen by the Melanesians as more powerful versions of the traditional 'big man'. But he refused to recognize the integrity of indigenous culture. He treated all the Solomon Islanders as if they were 'rubbish men'.

In both Papua and the Solomons the Europeans seized control of the indigenous society's organizational framework, and the effects of this action were similar in both territories. The organizational framework still existed, but it no longer had any validity. It could not make men while the Europeans refused to recognize indigenous concepts of status. It was impossible to escape the Europeans. They could not be resisted. And the problems that they posed could not be avoided.

'CARGO'

'Cargo' beliefs were only present in the 1919 and 1944 movements, there was no idea of cargo in the 1963 movement. 'Cargo' in 1919 and 1944 consisted of large quantities of food, the kinds of food that had been associated with the Magistrate and the District Officer. Food in traditional Elema society and in traditional Solomon Island society had been associated with status.

Ideas about the kinds of goods that were thought to be in 'cargo' remained static because indigenous ideas on the nature of status remained static. For example, among the Elema, the Germans were expected to bring the same kind of 'cargo' in 1939 that the dead had been expected to bring in 1919. And in the Solomons the Russians were expected to bring the same kind of 'cargo' in 1952 that the Americans had been expected to bring in 1946.[1]

'Cargo' was not an elastic concept accurately reflecting the material wants of the indigenes. This can be seen from the fact that in some areas affected by the 1944 movement there was no 'cargo' belief, although there was a demand for European goods. And in 1963 there was no 'cargo' belief among people with very few European possessions. Material needs in the areas that were affected by the movements had grown. As time went by a wider range of European goods were desired. This desire was not reflected in the content of 'cargo'. In some areas affected by the 1944 movement the status of a 'big man' had not been associated with the kinds of goods that were contained in 'cargo'—these areas had no 'cargo' belief. The success of the 1944 movement had shown that 'cargo' was not necessary for recognition of status—there was no 'cargo' belief in 1963.

Yet the demand for European goods and traditional forms of wealth had grown steadily between 1919 and 1963. European money, corrugated iron for houses, cooking utensils, medicines, and traditional shell wealth were not a part of 'cargo'. Nor did pigs ever form a part of 'cargo'. But Europeans had none of these things, their status rested on other attributes which were in conformity with the traditional status attributes of a 'big man'. The content of 'cargo' was a logical deduction from European status attributes seen in the light of traditional theory.

In 1919 the method used to obtain 'cargo' was in conformity with traditional religious experience. This method was based on deductions which had been made about European behaviour. Theory was traditional and within the confines of existing knowledge. The method was eclectic (based on deductions made about missionary, administrative, and traditional Elema rituals) and within the confines of experience. Given the knowledge at their disposal, and in relation to the traditional belief system, the 1919 attempt to obtain 'cargo' was entirely pragmatic and sensible. It did not represent a radical departure from traditional rituals and ways of achieving results.

There was no 'cargo' ritual in 1944. The activities of the 1944 movement were solely concerned with demonstrating that the new

[1] This deduction stems from personal investigation.

'big men' had the same power and status as the Europeans. But the method of obtaining the 'cargo' was still traditional. Cargo stemmed from the establishment of reciprocal relationships with the Americans. The leaders of the 1944 movement were thought to have entered into a reciprocal relationship with the Americans. They had helped them in the war and they knew that the Americans were grateful: in return the Americans would discharge their obligation by bringing 'cargo'.[1] When the Russians were expected to bring the 'cargo' in 1952 the Solomon Islanders expected to have to pay for it by giving the Russians land for a base.[2] The theory was entirely pragmatic and sensible, and did not represent a radical departure from traditional beliefs.

What kind of men were to bring 'cargo'? The 1919 movement was strongly based on the traditional belief system and the dead were thought of as the only people who could bring 'cargo'. This was quite logical. By 1939 the traditional belief system of the Papuans had been replaced by Christianity. When a 'cargo' movement broke out among the Elema in 1939 the Germans were expected to bring the 'cargo'.[3] This was also a logical development since 'cargo' was no longer thought of in religious context.

In 1944 the traditional religious belief system in the Solomons had been replaced by Christianity, and the Americans were logically thought of as the purveyors of 'cargo'. The last Americans left the Solomons in 1948 and obviously could no longer bring 'cargo'. Americans were replaced in 1949 by the Russians who were thought to be friendly to black people.

The kinds of men who were expected to bring 'cargo' were chosen logically in the light of information available at the time. Ideas which were associated with the method by which 'cargo' was to be obtained were not static: they changed and adapted to new circumstances just as in traditional times rituals and organizational solutions had been adapted to change. But the nature of 'cargo' was static because traditional aims and objectives had been static.

Seen in the light of the then existing system of preferences and values, possession of the kinds of 'cargo' that were expected to come in the 1919 and 1944 movements would not have resulted in

[1] Personal communication from Mr. Salana Gaa'a.
[2] Information given by members of the San Cristobal local government council.
[3] H. A. Brown MSS.

the creation of a Utopia: it would merely have given the 'big men' a certain kind of equality with the Europeans—equality in the sense of possessing status-giving goods. The content of 'cargo' did not point to the existence of any desire on the part of the natives to create a completely new environment. It pointed to a continuing and inflexible desire to maintain existing values and ideas.

LEADERSHIP

What were the attributes of the movements' leaders in comparison with the traditional attributes of a 'big man'? Did the new leaders claim new attributes or were their attributes in conformity with traditional experience? Traditionally 'big men' in Papua and the Solomons gained their status through possession of exclusive knowledge and because they possessed exceptional organizational ability. They knew the correct rituals and organizational procedures. 'Big men' had communal economic expertise, and an acknowledged obligation to uphold the traditional way of life. The possession of superior wealth in the form of garden produce was in some areas important because the 'big man' was expected to give feasts and to feed his followers.

In 1919 the attributes claimed by the leaders were the same as the attributes that had been necessary for a traditional 'big man'. Apa-Hevehe had been produced by the 'big man' to show his control over the sea monsters, and his ability to ensure garden fertility through his control of the spirits of the dead; the symbol of the European Magistrate's power was a ship which showed his ability to control sea monsters, and cargo, which showed his ability to obtain benefits from the dead. The new Papuan leaders in 1919 claimed to demonstrate a traditional attribute of a 'big man' in controlling the spirits of the dead, using the new method of the Europeans. The new leaders also claimed to possess exclusive religious knowledge. Attributes in theory were traditional, though the kinds of knowledge associated with these attributes were modern. New leaders demonstrated organizational ability, and their desire to maintain the traditional way of life. No new attributes were claimed by the leaders; the way in which possession of attributes was demonstrated was new, but the semantic implications were still traditional.

The attributes claimed by the leaders in the 1914 movement were the same kinds of attributes that had been claimed by the traditional 'big man'. The claims of the 1944 leaders were involved with two things: ability to control the multi-purpose organizational framework, and possession of wealth.

Demonstrating their control of the multi-purpose organizational framework the new leaders engaged in economic, war, executive, and judicial activities. The activities were new in structure and appearance, but the semantic implications were still traditional. Status, that had traditionally come from possession of wealth, was achieved through 'subscriptions'. And in those areas where status had traditionally been dependent on the ability to command large-scale food supplies, cargo was expected. No new attributes were claimed by the 1944 leaders, though the ways in which they showed that they possessed the traditional attributes of a 'big man' were new and were the result of deductions made about Europeans.

In 1963 the attributes that were claimed by Doliasi were still those of a traditional 'big man'. This claim was involved with two things: ability to control the multi-purpose organizational framework and possession of wealth. Doliasi demonstrated his control of the multi-purpose organizational framework through operation of a semi-military movement, an engagement in economic activities, and a programme which was designed to uphold the traditional way of life. The status that a traditional 'big man' had gained through possession of wealth was claimed because Doliasi received 'subscriptions' which were like the tribute paid to a traditional 'big man'. Doliasi did not claim any new attributes, though the ways in which he showed that he possessed the traditional attributes of a 'big man' were new and were the result of deductions made about Europeans.

The attributes claimed by the 1944 and 1963 leaders suggest that the movements form part of a traditional pattern of Melanesian and Papuan leadership. Attributes claimed by the modern 'big men' in contemporary Solomon Island society form part of this pattern.

The attributes thought to be possessed by the leaders of the 1919, 1944, and 1963 movements were the same as those thought to be possessed by the Europeans at the time of the movements. Since in traditional society superior performance had resulted in recognition of status, the leaders of the movements attempted to show that they possessed the same power and status as the Europeans. If they demonstrated the same ability as the Europeans then, in terms of their existing experience, they should acquire the appropriate status. A characteristic feature of many revolutionary religious or millenary movements has been the emergence of a single charismatic leader whose popularity has continued despite the non-fulfilment of his policies.[1] Has this feature been present in the movements that have been examined in this study?

Traditional leadership in the Solomons and Papua was oligarchical. Within any particular social grouping there were a number of 'big men' with coterminous authority and none of these men was considered as a paramount leader. The 'big men' were not chiefs, retention of status was dependent on satisfactory performance.

In 1919 and 1944 there were a number of leaders and none of these leaders achieved supremacy: in 1963 Doliasi was the only leader. But claims to leadership were in traditional times empirically evaluated. Was this process present in these movements?

Leaders connected with the 1919 and 1963 movements lost their leadership status very soon after it became obvious that they could not produce results. They were then considered no different from ordinary men and they are no longer thought of as 'big men'.

The plural aspects of leadership in the movements and the ways in which the leaders lost their status were in conformity with the traditional pattern of leadership in the Solomons. The pattern of leadership in these movements, in its plural aspects, is also in conformity with the contemporary pattern of leadership in the Solomons.

Did the leadership role in the movements represent a radical departure from the traditional leadership role of the 'big man'? In traditional Elema society the 'big man's' role was economic, political, ritual, judicial, and representative. During the 1919 movement the leaders' role was the same as that of the traditional 'big men': they did not attempt to exercise any new functions. In traditional Solomon Island society the 'big man's' role was concerned with war, economic, political, judicial, and representative functions. During the 1944 movement the leaders' roles were the same as those of the traditional 'big men'; they did not attempt to exercise any new functions. The pattern in the 1963 movement was similar.

The leaders in the 1919, 1944 and 1963 movements were simply more powerful versions of the traditional 'big man'. A characteristic feature of the traditional leadership pattern was the inability of

[1] See N. Cohn 1957 and R. A. Knox 1950:*passim.*

the 'big men' to initiate new policies,[1] designed to obtain new results, as distinct from the initiation of new activities designed to obtain traditional results.

The role of ordinary men was the same in 1919, 1944, and 1963 movements as it had been in traditional society. And the role of ordinary men in these movements was the same as the role of ordinary men in contemporary Solomon Island society: ordinary men accepted the discipline imposed by the 'big man' and followed his direction. In doing this they were able to establish their manhood within the organizational framework that he provided. Success was a matter of working hard, following the traditional norms and obeying the 'big man'.

The object of the movements does not appear to have been to claim that all Papuans and Solomon Islanders were entitled to the same status as Europeans, but only that existing concepts of status be recognized by the Europeans. Europeans were to recognize 'big men' as their equals and were to recognize that the natives were men. The European and the native 'big men' were to continue to have more status than ordinary men. This interpretation blends in with the contemporary conditions in the Solomon Islands where indigenous sets of status have been recognized. The average Solomon Islander knows that the Europeans have superior status. But indigenous sets of status did not, in traditional times, give ordinary men the same status as 'big men': that is why in terms of their existing experience Solomon Islanders do not now regard European superiority as being unjust or a matter for agitation.[2]

Concepts of status and power are different in the urban areas and there, of course, the situation is not the same as in the rural areas which were affected by the 1944 and 1963 movements.

---

[1] P. Lawrence 1964:11 mentions this point in discussing Melanesian leadership.

[2] Lawrence and Burridge, whose accounts are the best that we have, have assumed that all those men who engage in 'cargo cult' activity are striving for the kind of status possessed by Europeans. In relation to the Solomons this kind of idea would be incapable of explaining past 'Marching Rule' developments. Similarly these authors, in company with many others, have no explanation for the absence of 'cargo cults' from the urban areas.

IX

THE NATURE OF 'CARGO' CULTS

A VERY great deal has been written about 'cargo' cults and it is not possible, within the framework of this inquiry, to examine each theory in detail. The present analysis aims to examine, briefly, theories which have been put forward to explain the 1919 and 1944 movements. This approach inevitably necessitates the omission of several kinds of existing theory.

Theories which have dealt with cargo cult phenomena in terms of concepts such as 'nativistic', 'acculturative', 'vitalistic', or 'revitalistic' are not examined. Such theories would, at best, only be capable of providing a partial explanation of the movements that have been examined. But they cannot reveal what is fundamental in cult activity since this kind of theory is, by definition, merely descriptive.[1]

Evidence which has been adduced suggests that it may not be necessary to seek an explanation in psychological terms. Existing theories of this nature cannot, in any case, provide a satisfactory explanation for the movements that have been examined. The psychological theories which have been advanced to explain the 1919 and 1944 movements are virtually untestable. They seem to indicate that all hope of reaching a deeper level of understanding about the nature of the movements has been abandoned.[2]

These psychological theories have been put forward without any really detailed analysis of the affected societies before, during, or after the movements. They have been justified because it is held that the morphology of the movements has exhibited similarities with religious, millenary or chiliastic movements in other cultural areas. But when examined over a period of time, as in this study, the purposive nature of the movements does seem to become more

[1] A. Wallace 1956:264–81 and R. Linton 1943:230–40. And see M. Smith's comment 1959:12.
[2] There can be no advance in knowledge about these movements when they are termed: 'escapist' (Linton), 'projection into phantasy world' (Berndt), 'phantasy substitute for political action' (Mair), 'irrationality' (Firth), and 'automania' (Williams).

clear.[1] And for this reason no attempt will be made to explain the movements which have been examined in terms of individual psychology.

THEORIES ABOUT 'PROPHETS'

The 'prophet' is now a familiar figure in literature dealing with Melanesian cargo movements. His role has been depicted in mystic, millenarian, apocalyptic, or religious terms in relation to the movements. Intensive analysis of the 'prophet' as a man has taken place since it has been assumed that it is possible to isolate and identify empirically describable qualities that are possessed by these individuals. On this basis 'prophets' can be categorized into three main groups: (i) institutional 'prophets' of the orgiastic or visionary type, (ii) the emotionally powerful type of leader who may in time become a millenary or revolutionary leader, and (iii) the 'prophet' as a moral or intellectual leader.[2]

Examination of the 1919, 1944, and 1963 movements has shown no substantial evidence of the existence of orgiastic 'prophets'. Mysticism which has stemmed from the inspiration of the 'prophet' is thought by some anthropologists to be part of religious tradition or simply clever showmanship.[3] But the visionary's inspiration is not really susceptible to reason because of the special relationship that he has entered into with a divine power.[4] However, the actions of the leaders, which have been examined in this thesis, have not been part of a religious tradition throughout the period from 1919 till 1967. The claims of the leaders were susceptible to reason, and the actions of the leaders were evaluated empirically. None of the leaders claimed any special relationship with a divine power, in the sense that they felt that they were revealing divine knowledge.

The actions of the leaders in the 1919, 1944, and 1963 movements do seem to have been part of an organizational tradition. The movements centred round the 'big men': they contained society and society contained 'big men'—all relationships with divine power (and this is only relevant in the 1919 movement) were really incidental to the major issues.

---

[1] Cf. P. Lawrence's schema 1964, which illustrates the purposive ideological development of the movements.
[2] D. Emmet 1959:313–23.   [3] J. Inglis 1957:252, 253.
[4] R. A. Knox 1950:554.

What of the emotionally powerful leader? None of the movements that have been examined have really shown any revolutionary or millenary aspects. This kind of theory suggests, to some extent, that the charisma of the 'prophet' is responsible for the movements. But the number of leaders in each of the movements, and the societies' ability to produce a second wave of leaders when the first wave were imprisoned or discredited, show that the movements were not dominated by individuals with rare gifts.

Charismatic leaders are rare individuals. Knox has said that all millenary movements outlive the non-fulfilment of their policies. But this was not the case with the movements that have been examined in this study. Leaders were dismissed when their policies did not succeed. And the movements have disappeared when they failed: in 1919 the movement failed and it was succeeded in 1939 by a totally different kind of movement, and this pattern was repeated with the failure of the 1963 movement. Movements and leaders have been logically evaluated. And this process appears to have been dictated by reason rather than emotion.[1]

What is the relevance of the idea of the 'Prophet' as an intellectual or moral leader? This kind of theory does cover some of the issues which have been examined. But it can only offer a partial description. 'Moral and intellectual' is too abstract and simplistic a description for what the leader meant to the people. It really gives no idea of the real basis of power nor of why the leaders have acted as they have done.

Examination of the 'prophet' as a man is a suspect form of analysis. Concentration on the personal qualities of the 'prophet' has often been at the expense of appreciating the nature of the relationship between the man and his followers. These theories tend to concentrate on the man and not on the social relationships: *the 'prophet' is* a bearer of charisma, *the 'prophet' is* a breaker with tradition, etc.

By concentrating on the abnormal, the exotic, and the relationship with other religious and millenary movements, opportunities are lost. The activities of the 'prophet' are not related to the network of persisting social relationships: it often seems to be.

[1] R. A. Knox 1950:585, 'more generally characteristic of ultra-supernaturalism is a distrust of our human thought processes'. The rejection of leaders was not in conformity with the millenary pattern.

assumed that the 'prophet' was an entirely new phenomenon.[1] It has been maintained that in a 'closed' society religion provided the only means of innovation.[2] But there was really no mandate in traditional religious technology for changes of a revolutionary or millenary nature. The limit of innovation was determined and set by the then existing concepts of status and value and the organizational framework of the society.

Three points of importance do emerge from this body of theory about the 'prophet': the 'prophet' is thought to possess considerable organizational powers, his relationship with the deities may be viewed in traditional context, and his message can be conceived as part of the traditional pattern of innovation. Therefore, while parts of the existing body of theory may offer some explanation, none of the theories adequately describes the overall pattern of leadership between 1919 and 1967.

The kinds of things that 'prophets' have actually said can be divided into three categories: religious formulae and spells, individual comments, and commands given to followers. Spells only concern the 1919 movement; the 1944 and 1963 movements did not rely on religious tradition. The claim in the 'Vailala Madness' to speak in alien tongues, and to speak to the spirits of the dead through the medium of a flag-pole, was in conformity with traditional religious experience because this indicated that the leader possessed exclusive religious knowledge.

The 'prophet' succeeds because he says things that the people have hoped to hear. He gives an indication of being able to solve problems which are urgent.[3] A further theory maintains that the 'prophet' may act as a kind of safety-valve.[4] But this sort of theory gives little indication that the 'prophet' is any more than a catalyst. Some anthropologists have maintained that the imposition of discipline and the fusing together of elements of society do show that the 'prophet' cannot be regarded as a mere catalyst.[5] The organizational pattern and the discipline were so readily accepted by the ordinary members of society that the 'prophet' must have been acting in a recognizable role. His actions were not, as Stanner

---

[1] Lawrence's 1964 study contains these defects. Throughout his study Lawrence never succeeds in answering the question of *why* Yali was recognized as a leader. Instead of concentrating on social relationships Lawrence emphasizes Yali as a man, his personal qualities, reactions, and so on.

[2] R. Firth 1967:159.   [3] W. E. H. Stanner 1958:22.
[4] P. Worsley 1957b:256.   [5] R. Firth 1967:161.

has suggested, part of a pattern of the inexplicable credulity of leader and led.[1]

There has been relatively little discussion about the relationship between the 'prophet' and the duration and existence of the cults. Lawrence has shown a relationship between the existence of the cults and the existence of leadership. It seems to be generally agreed that where there is no leader there can be no cult.

Concentration on what the 'prophet' says is a suspect form of analysis. A man's beliefs are not evidential: 'Our insight into these cults will grow to the extent in which we abandon the effort to base interpretations on the primacy and efficacy of belief. Belief can be stimulated from any number of motives which are beyond our sure knowledge.'[2] This kind of approach may often fall into the error of attempting to explain ritual by belief.

The major defect in existing theories regarding the nature of cult leadership is that they are capable of only partial explanation. None of these theories can adequately describe the developments that took place between 1919 and 1967. Those theories, which have concentrated on millenary, mystical, and semi-religious or revolutionary aspects of the 'prophet's' role, are unable to account for the development in form and content of the leadership role in the 1944 and 1963 movements, a coherent pattern of development, which ranges from the emotionalism of the 'Vailala Madness' to the pragmatism of the Doliasi movement.

In Lawrence's penetrating and sympathetic study of Yali, the Madang cult leader, he remarks (without appearing to attach any significance to the comment) that Yali was regarded by the Melanesians as a more powerful version of the traditional 'big man'.[3] It seems more profitable in the present circumstances to continue on this line. The term 'prophet' gives a misleading impression of the nature of leadership in the movements. The basis of power for the leaders of the movements that have been examined lay in the nature of their relationship with the people and not with any divine power.

THEORIES OF A POLITICAL NATURE

It has been suggested that one inference that can be drawn from cargo cults is that the 'forces of political organization, initiative and

---

[1] W. E. H. Stanner 1958:*passim*.   [2] W. E. H. Stanner 1958:25.
[3] P. Lawrence 1964:v.n.254.

authority exist in the new system to a degree hitherto unsuspected'.[1] Some theories have suggested that the cults are to some degree nationalistic or that they may be thought of, even if they are unsophisticated, as forms of nascent or emergent nationalism.[2] Lawrence, in defining embryo nationalism, said that the term referred to an indigenous growth expressing militant opposition to European rule, and designed to hold together a permanent combination of hitherto autonomous political units.[3] Such theories imply that the cults have given rise to a completely new form of political organization. They also imply that the natives have nationalistic aspirations in the European sense of the term. But they do not, of course, account for the particular form taken by the movements.

The movements which have been examined were political in so far as they were responsible for the maintenance of social order.[4] But they did not give rise to new political units. The political process was one of intensification within an existing organizational structure—the process of maintaining social order underwent no change.

This contention seems to be validated by the political history of the Solomons after 'Marching Rule'. No new political units or pressures for political change have developed. Theories which have seen 'Marching Rule' as an example of nascent nationalism can only be held valid if they have supporting data drawn from the subsequent political history of the affected area.

There is no evidence to suggest that the 'Marching Rule' leaders on various islands in the Solomons felt that they had a common cause. There were no visible nationalist aspirations in the Doliasi movement. These theories, perhaps, pay too little attention to the fact that the movements were meant to force the Europeans to co-operate, not abdicate.

Little factual evidence has been offered in support of these rather intuitive and sophisticated interpretations. They appear to rest to a large degree on speculation that the existence of antipathy towards Europeans provides evidence that nationalism may take root; the movements may be viewed as attempts to gain power, and

---

[1] R. Firth 1951.
[2] J. Guiart 1951a and 1951c and P. Worsley 1957b:254-6.
[3] P. Lawrence 1964:257, 258.
[4] See Introduction to *African Political Systems*, 1940.

thus as being political.[1] But Melanesian political notions are also bound up with notions of status and ideas about social organization.[2] Events in the Solomons since the decline of 'Marching Rule' have shown that the movement was not primarily a form of nascent nationalism. But in any case this kind of theory cannot describe the development of the movements examined in this study over a period of time.[3] They tell nothing about Melanesian society which might serve to distinguish it from many other societies in which political movements have occurred through the ages. These kinds of explanation use the conceptual tools of the historian rather than those of the anthropologist.

The societies which were affected by cult activity in this study suffered from *anomie*, the breaking down of social ties, and a gradual growth in disintegrative tendencies. Melanesian political activity is the antithesis of *anomie*; it provides and depends on a 'big man', in effect a mechanism for enforcing group solidarity.

What the native of any country, and the representative of any culture is ultimately, even if unconsciously, interested in is self-assertion and self-expression. He may want some of the advantages of civilized technique, and some of the results of civilized knowledge, but he will inevitably want to make use of them in a rhythm of his life and in a society he has inherited even if it is a modified society.[4]

A substantial body of theory maintains that the movements were anti-European. It is maintained that in some cases Europeanism is rejected. If anti-European elements were not visible in the early stages of many of the cult movements, they rapidly became a feature of the cults in their later development.[5]

Factors commonly responsible for this anti-European feeling are thought to have been a sense of economic deprivation, or a desire to get rid of European manifestations of secular authority.[6]

Rejection of Europeanism is thought to be implicit in the adoption of traditional or 'nativistic' activities. But this is only a partial explanation of what actually happened. Traditionalism had always been present in these societies; the cults only resulted in emphasis being placed on existing ideas and values. 'Marching Rule' envisaged difficult court cases going to the D.O. and farms being run

---

[1] J. Inglis 1957:254, 255.   [2] B. Malinowski 1922:510, 513, 514.
[3] P. Worsley 1957b:255 maintained that these political forms would only continue in the more remote and backward areas.
[4] R. Thurnwald 1936:357.   [5] P. Worsley 1957b:24, 54.
[6] J. Guiart 1951b:175.

by Europeans. And other evidence adduced about these movements indicates that they were primarily directed at securing European co-operation.

It is necessary to distinguish between hostility expressed by the cult members and ethnic intolerance, which is claimed as a function of the movements. During the 'Vailala Madness' the Rev. Pryce-Jones became more popular as time went by.[1] In 'Marching Rule' many Roman Catholic and Melanesian mission Europeans experienced no hostility. European planters and S.S.E.M. missionaries were rejected. Yet white American troops were expected to bring cargo.

The facts do not seem to support the view that Europeanism was rejected or that there was a strong foundation of ethnic intolerance. A more fruitful line of inquiry lies in examining the basis for expressions of hostility. Lawrence has shown in his study of Madang cargo cults that the inclusion of rifles in cargo is a function of relationships between Europeans and Melanesians at a particular point in time. When relationships were good and it seemed that the Europeans would co-operate, then rifles were included in the cargo.[2] The political history of the Solomons since 'Marching Rule' shows that the idea that the 1944 movement rejected Europeanism cannot really be sustained by the facts.

Many investigators in Melanesia have reported an absence of Melanesian racial discrimination against Europeans.[3] Evidence adduced in this study has indicated that hostility is a function of relationships between movement members and a group of persons. It is not concerned with whether a group or class of persons will co-operate. Hostility was related to the amount of force thought necessary to compel a group or class or individual to recognize indigenous sets of status.

Theories which deal with rejection of Europeanism and anti-Europeanism are unable to deal with the developments that took place between 1919 and 1967. At best they can only offer a partial description for particular events.

THEORIES ABOUT 'CARGO'

A group of theories suggest that 'cargo' had intrinsic or social value. 'Cargo' was made up of objects and materials which were

---

[1] Pryce-Jones MSS.   [2] P. Lawrence 1964:233.
[3] M. K. E. Read 1947:passim.

capable of social use. Such theories hold that 'cargo', or the kinds of goods that made up 'cargo', had become an economic necessity for the natives.[1] Extreme versions of this kind of theory hold that 'cargo cults' have arisen because of native envy of European possessions.[2]

The actual 'triggering off' of the cults is thought to have been due to contact with American military forces during the war. This contact increased the Melanesian's sense of economic deprivation, compared with the Europeans, to unbearable limits.[3] P. Worsley has maintained that there is a relationship between the outbreak of the cults and the general economic situation. When prices and wages are low, cults tend to break out.

'Cargo' has normally been taken to include tobacco, axes, knives, calico, rice, meat, etc.[4] In the movements that have been examined there has been little evidence to suggest that the natives had developed a preference for European food.

All those who took part in the 1919 and 1944 movements were subsistence agriculturists. There is no evidence to suggest that they were suffering from food shortages. Tobacco was grown by the natives themselves, in the Solomons, and in the rural areas European brands of tobacco did not become really popular until well into the 1950s.[5] There is also no real evidence to support a claim that European kinds of food had become an economic necessity.

Axes, knives, and fish-hooks, do not appear to have been a necessity either. The movements died down in 1919 and 1944 without the natives having gained any additional axes or knives. Evidence has been adduced on the economic position on Malaita and Ulawa in 1967. The natives' ability to obtain the kinds of goods that were represented in 'cargo' is no greater in 1967 than it was in 1944. Yet there is no great demand for 'cargo', or for the kinds of goods contained in 'cargo', in contemporary Solomon Island society.

Pre-war Solomon Islanders' dress was scanty in the extreme, being only a breech clout for men and a grass skirt for women. It cannot be said that calico was an economic necessity in 1944. But a demand for European kinds of clothing has grown steadily since

---

[1] P. Lawrence 1964:232.   [2] J. Inglis 1957:253, 254.
[3] C. S. Belshaw 1950a:*passim.*
[4] P. Worsley 1959b:94, 115, 117, 212–19.
[5] Personal communications from several pre-war residents.

the war. This demand was not reflected in the Doliasi movement. There seems to be little logic in the idea that 'cargo' had become an economic necessity for the natives.

The idea that American troops accentuated the natives' sense of relative deprivation needs examination. In September 1965 a party of 23 officers and N.C.O.s of the U.S. Army established a base at Mohawk bay, Reef Islands, in the eastern Solomons. Their task was to track satellites passing overhead. Within a short period of time the Americans had established friendly relations with the 450 people of Ngadeli village nearby.

The village of Ngadeli is in the most economically depressed area in the Solomons. The people have no coconut groves, and no regular means of earning money. And in the Reef Islands on one island, Nupani, the population reaches 844 per square mile.[1]

Several of the men from Ngadeli village went to work for the Americans. They received high wages and liberal supplies of tobacco and beer from the Americans' 'PX'. The tracking station was extremely impressive: air-conditioned quarters had been built, electric light was on 24 hours a day, and cinema shows were given for the village people every evening. Very large naval ships came from Fiji bringing supplies. Senior officers came on tours of inspection by amphibious aircraft. I knew that a large number of old 'Marching Rule' members were living in Ngadeli village. What would they do, and say, when the Americans left?

The Americans left in August 1966. Shortly afterwards I heard rumours that they would return to establish a big base at Mohawk bay, because the war in Vietnam was going badly.[2] But there was no mention of 'cargo'. When I visited Ngadeli at Christmas 1966, all rumour of the Americans' return had died away. The material possessions of the Americans had not sparked off a 'cargo cult'.

The gap between the Melanesians' wants and the means of their satisfaction is at its widest in the towns. But there has never been a 'cargo cult' in a town. None of the economic deprivation theories seem to be able to account for this. Nor can they explain why the cults have not broken out in all the most economically depressed areas. This tends to weaken the heuristic validity of this kind of theory.

[1] The Government has plans to resettle these people in more fertile areas of the Solomons. I estimated that the Ngadeli villagers had an annual *per capita* income of 2s.

[2] See R. Firth 1967:141–62 on rumour in the Solomons.

Theories which see 'cargo cults' as a result of an indigenous relative sense of economic deprivation appear to rely, prima facie, on the assumption that the Melanesian pattern of wants has a marked similarity with the European pattern of wants. But this idea must be examined against the kinds of wealth that were contained in 'cargo' and what is known about indigenous concepts of wealth, power, and status. If 'cargo' had represented a general licence to order from Heaven it should, given the then existing indigenous concepts of wealth, have produced a very different bill of fare. 'Cargo' contained no pigs or traditional wealth forms. Analysis which has been undertaken into indigenous concepts of wealth, in the Solomons and in Papua, has shown that the kinds of goods contained in 'cargo' were bound up with indigenous notions of status.

It is observed that 'cargo' contained goods which were thought to be required by the natives, and that wages and material possessions of the natives were minimal. It is then concluded that there was a shortage of European wealth. From this observation comes the postulate that there must have been some demand-like agency to rectify the situation—termed a need. The need is then made responsible for the observation from which it is derived. The 'need' is both a summary of the observed regular mode of behaviour, and a machine invented to account for it.[1]

This kind of theory is presented as a deductive theory, while it is really inductive. Reduced to its elements this kind of theory only produces a provisional explanation; provisional in the sense that further evidence must be adduced to prove the hypothesis.[2]

Theories which have dealt with the symbolic value of 'cargo' are in broad agreement with evidence that has been adduced. Europeans were thought by the natives to have acted immorally, because they withheld 'cargo'. 'Cargo' was not only access to goods, but access to goods within a particular moral relationship.[3]

The content of 'cargo' has been seen as a symbol of the relationships between Europeans and Melanesians. When these relationships have been thought unsatisfactory then the 'cargo' will contain rifles.[4] Possession of 'cargo' will confirm the Melanesians' status as men.

Stanner has maintained that the Melanesian transaction with the

---

[1] S. F. Nadel 1951:198, and see P. Worsley's treatment of 'Marching Rule' 1957b:*passim*.

[2] K. R. Popper 1961:131.   [3] K. O. L. Burridge 1960:67.

[4] P. Lawrence 1964:233.

spirits is a one-sided transaction. This is because institutions and modes of behaviour determine 'in life' values, but because this cannot be done for 'cargo', 'for life' aspects have been stressed.[1] The cults die because they attempt to overvalue 'cargo' socially, social value being the use which cargo has in the everyday life of the society. 'Cargo' is a meaningful unity, and not a vast miscellany of objects.

As Stanner has pointed out, no arrangements are made to divide the 'cargo'. It must be considered as a unitary symbol. The basic defect in this kind of theory, which holds that 'cargo' had symbolic value, lies in its inability to reconcile a unitarian and apparently indivisible symbol with a cult society where each member would have wanted a portion or share.[2] This is the result of viewing the cults in egalitarian terms. It seems to be assumed in these theories that all Melanesians have the same status and the same aspirations. The cults are thought to be directed towards securing equality with the Europeans for all Solomon Islanders or Papuans. But when it is appreciated that 'cargo' was to accrue to the leader as a symbol of his status there is not the same difficulty in dealing with cargo as a unitary symbol.

It has been noted that the presence of rifles in the 'cargo' denotes hostility. But, unfortunately, this lead has not been followed by examining the other goods in 'cargo'—what kind of relationship does their inclusion point to? Why should axes and food be more symbolic than ships and radios?

If possession of 'cargo' is necessary to indicate the existence of satisfactory relationships between Europeans and Melanesians, and if the withholding of 'cargo' was thought to be immoral, then there should have been a continuing demand for 'cargo'. But 'cargo' did not arrive in 1944 in the Solomons: Melanesians do not consider that they are now morally equal to the Europeans, and yet there was no demand for 'cargo' in the 1963 movement.

Elema 'cargo' myths from 1919 to 1939 showed considerable plasticity, they underwent modification to suit changed circumstances.[3] There was no tendency to ossification. The myths provided moral justification for actions which were taken and they were

[1] W. E. H. Stanner 1958:2, 3.
[2] There is no evidence to suggest that any arrangements were made for the division of the cargo—K. O. L. Burridge 1960:42, and W. E. H. Stanner 1958:24.
[3] See also P. Lawrence 1964:240.

regarded as a sole repository of truth.[1] These ideas blend in with the theory that believes that in societies with simple technologies, myths (like the cargo myth) are the only means of dealing with large-scale innovation.[2] The genesis of myth is recognized as a mechanism for providing directives to action in Melanesia.[3] The 'cargo' myth genesis in the 'Vailala Madness' was in conformity with the then current religious technology and was thus within the confines of experience.

As the traditional belief system was replaced by Christianity, and as notions regarding the nature of European power and status became more sophisticated, myths vanished from everyday life. The cargo myth also vanished. There was no 'cargo' myth in 1944 or 1963. In 1944 the idea of the Americans bringing the 'cargo' was pragmatic and based on actual experience.

The development of the movements from 1919 to 1963 showed a movement from religion to pragmatism, from myth to self-help. In 1963 myth no longer had any function to perform since the basis of European (and Melanesian) power and status was known. Men who traditionally interpreted myths were replaced by men who claimed familiarity with the European way of life. But both these kinds of men were still 'big men'.

Throughout the period which has been examined myth, when in existence, has performed its traditional role. Theories which have held that there has been a separate and distinct cargo myth which has millenary aspects are incapable of describing the events of 1944 and 1963.

There is no evidence to suggest a cult of cargo. Rituals associated with these movements were designed to acquire recognition of existing indigenous concepts of status, not cargo alone. Within the confines of then existing experience, the kinds of goods which were represented by cargo were only a means to an end. Nor can the events of 1919, 1944, or 1963, be termed a cult. There were no new beliefs, and the actions that were taken did not convey any new meanings. The concept of the 'cargo cult' is, in the context of this study, misleading.

In general it is maintained that it is not the 'cargo cult' theories themselves which are erroneous, but the facts on which these

---

[1] K. O. L. Burridge 1960:249–54.   [2] R. Firth 1967:159.
[3] K. O. L. Burridge 1954a:241.

theories have been founded. Much of the information on which existing theory has been based is very thin.[1] Theories which were put forward at the height of the post-war wave of movements have not been validated by later surveys or additional evidence. The particular social or cultural theory within which an explanation is sought determines the way in which the problem is posed, and the way in which deductions are drawn. This is no less true of 'cargo cult' theories. A major defect of many existing theories is that they stand as tentative hypotheses and not proven deductions.[2] The important thing is not the finding of a theory, but the ways in which the theory has been tested.[3] And unfortunately many of the existing theories have not been tested over a period of time.

[1] P. Lawrence 1964:1.   [2] W. E. H. Stanner 1953:63.
[3] K. R. Popper 1961:135.

X

CONCLUSIONS

SOME of the explanations that have been given for 'cargo cults' have been broadly based:

It seems to me fairly obvious to assume that cargo cults tend to arise as a resultant of several factors in operation together; a markedly uneven relation between a system of wants and the means of their satisfaction; a very limited technical knowledge of how to improve conditions; specific blocks or barriers to that improvement by poverty of natural resources or opposed political interests. What constitutes a cult is a systematized series of operations to secure the means of satisfaction by non-technical methods. Yet the implications of technical methods may, as I have shown, approach cult behaviour if they are used more to give immaterial satisfaction.[1]

This kind of theory does not really tell us very much about 'cargo cults'. It does not indicate that there is anything distinctive about 'cargo cults' or the societies in which these movements have arisen which could serve to distinguish them from political and economic-based movements which have arisen in underdeveloped territories in other parts of the world.

The attempt here must simply be to provide an explanation which can satisfy curiosity.[2] An explanation which can attempt to show that the 'cargo' movements have been distinctive because Melanesian and Papuan cultural and belief systems have been unique. This explanation should be involved with two things: a factual explanation of the various movements which can be arrived at deductively, and a theoretical explanation which can contain the facts. A factual account should, considered in its entirety, suggest the theory. The theory should be no more than a minimum intellectual framework which contains, but does not 'explain', the facts.

---

[1] R. Firth 1967:158.   [2] S. F. Nadel 1951:202.

FACTUAL EXPLANATION

The origins of the movements examined go back to the time when the Melanesians and Papuans saw their first white men.[1] Europeans posed a problem—who were they, were they spirits or men? As time went by the natives learnt that the Europeans were men. Within terms of their existing experience the Europeans were categorized by the natives as 'big men', because of the attributes they possessed, and the ways in which they acted.

These European 'big men' seem to have differed in two respects from the traditional 'big men'. Their actions and attributes gave them much more power and status than the traditional 'big men', but they refused to assume the traditional responsibilities that a 'big man' had towards his people. Europeans did not treat the natives as men: they did not eat with them or enter into reciprocal relationships, they did not uphold all the traditional customs, and they made far greater demands on the time of the people than the traditional 'big men' had done. In every field of activity where the natives and the white men met the Europeans were superior. Natives were unable to establish their manhood in relationships with Europeans.

European contact completely destroyed the power and status of the traditional 'big man'. 'Big men' had been symbols of their society's cultural integrity. They had guarded and sustained the indigenous culture and had, so to speak, carried it on their shoulders. When they went there was little left. Ordinary men lost the ability to establish their manhood in the organizational framework that the 'big men' had provided. The natives were unable to establish their manhood in the organizational framework provided by the Europeans. They were also unable to escape the Europeans' influence.

These factors seem to have been responsible for the origin of the movements, but what factors were responsible for actually 'triggering off' the movements? In 1919 the administration's agricultural experiments in the Gulf of Papua had increased European intervention in the lives of the Elema. In 1944 European administrative pressure on Malaita people increased as a result of the war. These movements appear to have been precipitated by a sudden increase in European contact.

The origin of the 1963 movement had its roots in the actions of the Solomon Islanders. The effect of the coastal people's attitude

[1] K. O. L. Burridge 1960:246.

to the bush people was the same as the effect that Europeans had had in 1919 and 1944. In 1963 the movement was the result of a long process of maturation.

Areas which were affected by the movements had experienced a greater degree of European contact than other areas where the movements did not break out. For example, movements did not break out in Santa Cruz or on Bougainville, where there had been little contact between the Melanesians and the Europeans. Movements also did not affect areas which had been exposed to a very great deal of European contact. There was no cargo movement on Gela or in the Russell Islands in the Solomons.

It appears that European contact has only been germane to the problem of explaining why the movements broke out 'here' instead of 'there', when contact was with island societies with a particular structure and belief system. Where the indigenous authoritarian and organizational system had not had 'big men', then the Europeans may not have been categorized in this way.

Where this happened the Europeans did not appear to be more powerful versions of the traditional leaders. This meant that there was no conflict between the actions and attributes of the Europeans and the actions and attributes of the traditional leaders. In turn the indigenous concepts of manhood continued to have validity since the standards and methods for achieving manhood remained traditional. In this sense movements did not break out in the towns because native urban social structure and values were Europeanized —they did not conflict with traditional values and ideas on social organization.

However, in some areas there was also no conflict because the European/'big men' treated the natives as if they were men. In this instance the European was able to discharge all the obligations of a traditional 'big man'. The 'Vailala Madness' probably had no appeal in Orokolo village because the L.M.S. missionaries had assumed the responsibilities of a 'big man'. But why should some areas in Papua and Melanesia which have experienced movements be different from other areas which have not? There is a possible explanation.

The societies where the movements broke out had, in the period before the white men came, distinctive environmental and structural features which distinguished them from other areas where movements have not broken out. These features were a function of the number of people in the societies, the location and topography of the areas where they lived, and the existence of an almost continuous state of warfare.

Historically, in any independent village the number of people who lived in the village and considered themselves as an independent entity was very small, seldom more than 200. Continuous warfare, which was a feature of their lives, meant that the natives seldom combined to form larger political associations. The formation of larger political associations would have required a cessation of hostilities and would inevitably have resulted in the creation of an institutionalized political system. Two factors may have counted against this development.

The peculiar nature of these societies demanded that warfare had to continue because the activities associated with warfare were responsible for validating indigenous concepts of status and power. Warfare proved manhood. And, like gardening, warfare was thought to be a good and necessary activity. Secondly, topography of the country lent itself to the formation of small independent units. Each group lived in an easily fortified area. They were economically self-sufficient, and infanticide was practised to ensure that the population of the group did not outrun resources.[1]

In turn these circumstances were responsible for the flexible nature of leadership. Due to the continuous state of warfare, mortality rates among the leaders were high. Since replacements had to be found quickly, this may have led to the institutionalization of the attributes of leadership. Attributes and qualities were institutionalized because men with the necessary attributes and qualities had to be chosen quickly to replace those who had fallen in battle or died as a result of illness. Continual warfare militated against the creation of hereditary systems of leadership.[2]

The white man's peace was the first peace that these islands had known. It was this peace, and the actions of Europeans, which forced the formation of larger political units. These units were

[1] Results of personal inquiry on Malaita and San Cristobal. J. Holmes MSS. mentions that a state of continuous warfare existed among the Elema before the white men came.

[2] This early Melanesian leadership seems to have had much in common with the earliest Germanic and Anglo-Saxon leadership. Early Germanic leaders were chosen by popular consent as war-leaders and leadership only became hereditary when larger political associations were formed and there was no longer continuous warfare. G. B. Adams 1965:1–43.

made by the white men, they were Districts and island groupings. These political associations, which were made by the white man, have continued. It is a striking thing that there has never been any attempt, in any of the areas affected by the 1944 movement, to alter the political boundaries. There has been no quarrel with the arbitrary political boundaries of the white men.

Political boundaries always seem to have followed the limits of the 'big man's' power. There are now no 'big men' who hold sway over island groups. Perhaps that is why larger units have not been formed by the indigenes since the white men came. This development was helped because the white man's political system was like the indigenous political system—or it appeared to be like it. The white man's system was not hereditary—District Officers came and went in much the same profusion as traditional 'big men', who were killed in war activities. And the attributes possessed by the white men conformed to the traditional institutionalized attributes of a 'big man'. In this way the peculiar ideas and values surrounding traditional social organization in these areas may have been perpetuated.

In the areas where the movements broke out there was no institutionalized political system. Everything depended on the impermanent authority of the 'big man'. The peculiar nature of this traditional social organization and the peculiar nature of British Colonial administration were bedfellows—European contact maintained the 'big man' system and its values. In Sir Henry Maine's terms the societies where the movements broke out were distinguished from the societies where the movements did not break out by the fact that they had not moved from status to contract.[1] The maintenance of social order was dependent on status, the status of the 'big man'. And the 'big man's' status was dependent on his ability to achieve results.

The movements were spontaneous reactions against status deprivation. They were attempts to force Europeans (and Melanesians in the 1963 movement) to recognize indigenous concepts of status. In traditional society the Elema and the Solomon Islanders had recognized two kinds of status, the status of ordinary men and the status of 'big men'. The movements appear to have concentrated on forcing the Europeans to recognize these two kinds of status. Additional objectives of the movements appear to have been

[1] H. S. Maine 1931:138-41.

concerned with the kinds of European that the natives had distinguished. Europeans who were thought to be semi-friendly were to be forced to co-operate. Those who were thought to be unfriendly or hostile were to be boycotted or driven away by force of arms.

Concepts of power and status had remained static—even though the presence of Europeans had forced critical examination of traditional ideas and values—and in conformity with traditional institutionalized values. There were no new aims or objectives, only new ways of achieving traditional objectives. Political objectives were also static. The spheres of influence of the movements' leaders corresponded to the political boundaries which had been created by the white men.

Certain individuals from time to time may have made revolutionary statements but these cannot be considered as evidential. Consideration of the overall pattern of the movements, which involves appreciating the relationship between ritual and belief, does seem to show that the affected societies were only concerned with taking action which was designed to achieve recognition of indigenous concepts of status.

The 'extraordinary' features of the movements represented a carryover of pre-existing styles of ritual and organizational behaviour[1] combined with deductions which had been made about the nature of European power and status. Both in Papua and the Solomons traditional epistemological assumptions about ritual and organization remained static. This traditional knowledge, added to the deductions made about Europeans, accounted for the morphology of the movements.

Physical characteristics of the 1919 movement were also a carryover from pre-existing styles of ceremonial behaviour. In 1944 and 1963 there was no sign of any special physiological features; this is attributable to the disappearance of the traditional religious system. The physical effort which was put into cult activities was designed to show that the members could act like men—they felt that they had to try very hard.

In 1919 traditional ideas and religious beliefs were combined with ideas gained from experience of European behaviour to secure maximum effect. Epistemological assumptions about the nature of power and status remained unchanged. Ritual, or the method of demonstrating power and status, showed a blend of old and new.

[1] W. E. H. Stanner 1953:65.

There were no new theories or ideas, only new rituals and activities which were designed to achieve traditional results.

In the 1944 movement traditional organizational ideas were combined with ideas gained through experience of European behaviour to secure maximum effect. Epistemological assumptions about the nature of power and status remained unchanged but organizational activities, or the method of gaining status and demonstrating power, showed a blend of old and new. There were no new ideas about the nature of power or status, only new activities which were designed to achieve traditional results.

The 1963 movement modified traditional techniques in the light of experience gained from Europeans and Melanesian behaviour. But epistemological assumptions about the nature of power and status were still traditional. Organizational activities, or the method of gaining status and demonstrating power, showed a blend of old and new. As in 1919 and 1944, there were no new ideas or theories, only new activities which were designed to achieve traditional results.

In the Gulf Division of Papua movements continued to break out until a few years ago. The later Elema movements have shown the same pattern as those of the Solomons. They still had the same organizational and structural features as the 1919 movement, but they were more pragmatic, with fewer 'extraordinary' features; the 'cargo' belief disappeared.[1] In the Solomons, the only movement which has broken out since the decline of the 1944 movement, affecting the islands which have been examined, has been the 1963 movement.

Indigenous concepts of status were recognized by the Europeans in the Solomons in 1953. Movements have not reappeared in areas where indigenous status was recognized. In the Gulf Division indigenous concepts of status were not recognized by the Europeans in 1919 and the movements continued. The status of the bush people in north-east Malaita was not recognized by the coastal Melanesians in 1963 and activity continues.

Periodicity cannot be linked with political or economic issues. Economic objectives were not achieved in 1944 though they were achieved in 1963. In the Solomons and in Papua there has been a

[1] Personal communication from Mr. J. K. McCarthy, Director of the Department of District Administration, Port Moresby. Movements among the Elema ceased a few years ago. It was at this time that the first Elema were recognized as people of importance by the Europeans.

continuing indigenous syndrome of economic and political deprivation. Nor can it be said that the geographical patterning of the
movements has corresponded with the most economically and
politically depressed areas. Periodicity does seem to have been
related to the kind of European contact experienced by the natives.
Where European contact has been continuous and direct, this may
have emphasized the indigenous sense of inferiority and hastened
the outbreak of cult activity.

A factor which may also have influenced periodicity is the existence of leadership. In the early days of European contact, when
indigenous notions about Europeans were unsophisticated, it was
relatively easy for new leaders to convince their followers that they
were familiar with European technological processes. A higher
standard of education and technical competence is now required
from the leaders. This may have had a limiting effect in some areas
where other conditions are ripe for a movement.

The leaders were chosen because they appeared to have the
attributes which were considered necessary to solve the problems
which had been created by contact with the Europeans. In traditional society the 'big man' had presented a synthesized cultural
image of the society he lived in; the new leaders presented a synthesized cultural image of their contemporary society which had
absorbed European ideas and techniques.

In all the movements the new 'big men' gained their status in
conformity with traditional epistemological assumptions about the
nature of a 'big man's' status and the ways in which he used his
power. The theory behind the use of power was traditional. But it
was overlaid with experience which had been gained as a result of
European contact. The new 'big men' expressed social concepts
and ambitions, they expressed the cultural integrity of their
societies. But they did all these things in a traditional manner and
their status did not rest on an ability to reveal divine knowledge.
'Big men' *were* society, not 'prophets'.

New problems in traditional Elema society had called for ritual
solutions, new problems in traditional Solomon Island society had
called for organizational solutions. The only person in native experience who was capable of implementing these solutions was the
'big man'. And 'big men' could only be recognized when they
appeared to possess the traditional institutionalized power and
status attributes.

The new leaders were only able to evoke a response from their followers in so far as they were able to pattern their performance on that of the traditional 'big man'. Their successes and failures were evaluated in the same manner. New leaders gained their power in a traditional manner—they also lost power in a traditional manner when it was evident that they were no longer able to achieve results. The most striking feature about the new 'big men' was the intensity of their operations. This feature was the result of a desire to put up a much better performance than that of the Europeans. If this was done, then the Europeans would be forced to recognize the validity of their operations, and the morality of their claims to status.

Why did the movements end? In the 1919 movement (a) the cargo did not come, (b) leaders were imprisoned and repressive action was taken by the Government, and (c) the Europeans continued to treat the Elema as 'rubbish men'. In 1944, (a) the cargo did not come; (b) leaders were imprisoned and repressive action was taken by the Government; and (c) Europeans recognized indigenous concepts of status. In 1963, (a) there was no cargo but all the declared objects of the movement were achieved, which in effect was the same as if cargo had arrived; (b) the leader was not imprisoned, and no repressive measures were taken by the Government; and (c) the Melanesians continued to treat the bush people as 'rubbish men'. In the areas affected by the 1919 and 1963 movements activity continued.

This comparison shows that the only factor which has determined the decline of the movements has been whether or not indigenous concepts of status have been recognized. Indigenous concepts of status were recognized in 1944 and the movement came to a dramatic halt. But in 1919 and 1963 it was gradually realized that the movements were not a success. Activity declined awaiting the emergence of another 'big man' who could find the right ritual or organizational solution to the problems posed by the Europeans.

Disappearance of distinctive morphological features may profitably be distinguished from the phasing-out of the enabling conditions. Imprisonment of the leaders or failure of their policies in areas where indigenous concepts of status have not been recognized has merely resulted in the disappearance of distinctive morphological features associated with a particular individual's attempt at a ritual or organizational solution. This has meant that the ideological basis for the movement has remained temporarily out of sight. 'Temporarily', because in these instances activity has continued as soon as a new leader comes forward who appeared to possess the necessary attributes for success.

Government action may only have been responsible, in the main, for assisting the natives to evaluate the claims of a new 'big man' quickly or over a long period of time. This process would seem to depend on the nature and intensity of the Government's repressive measures.

The inference that can be drawn from the development of these movements over a period of time is that success, and disappearance of the ideological basis of the movements, or failure of a particular organizational or ritual solution and the continuing existence of the movements' ideological basis, is linked with the recognition or non-recognition of indigenous concepts of status by those at whom the movements were directed.

THEORY

Two kinds of social change can be distinguished. These are cultural change and structural change. The process of cultural change has been real and continuous. Analysis of structural change is really involved with explanations for non-change.

Cultural change took place mainly on the grounds of convenience, in some cases because of European pressure. Steel tools and cooking utensils of the Europeans were more robust and utilitarian than their indigenous equivalents. European clothing was more comfortable, European weapons were more efficient in hunting, and so on. These kinds of cultural change were dictated by convenience. Their adoption did not collide with the indigenous system of values or with traditional social organization. This kind of change was continuous and it took place throughout the period which has been examined, causing no resistance or resentment. As a result the natives were given a new set of preferences, but these were still determined by traditional values.

When the natives were presented with a choice between European utilitarian goods and indigenous status-giving goods they chose status rather than comfort. In this way men bought pigs instead of calico or radios. They preferred to give feasts rather than buy kerosene to light the long dark evenings. The natives were pressed to become Christians. This did not result in a great deal of conflict because Christianity was interpreted in terms of indigenous values and beliefs. The Government insisted on new methods of hygiene and housebuilding, and new criminal offences were created. This development did not result in conflict because it did not collide with traditional notions of status and power.

The multi-purpose organizational structure which was intimately linked with institutionalized notions about status and power remained relatively unaffected by European contact. Traditionally the multi-purpose organizational framework was the only relationship that affected all the members of society. There was virtually no structural change because the Europeans simply replaced the 'big men' who had had control of the framework. Europeans took over the control of the multi-purpose organizational framework.

This in turn meant that indigenous attempts to establish manhood would continue to be phrased in a traditional manner, because the organizational structure and institutionalized values had survived. Attempts to establish manhood in the traditional manner failed—the system could have no validity while the Europeans continued to ignore indigenous concepts of status.

In the towns built by the Europeans there was no multi-purpose organizational framework because European executive functions were specialized. The natives in the towns adopted European values and the peculiar needs and ambitions of urban Solomon Island society were phrased in European terms.

In traditional society the structure can be described as integrated, social, stressed, and articulate.[1] Integrated because the functioning of the multi-purpose organizational framework gave existence, impact, and credibility to a set of known rules for the determination of individual status; social, because within the complex of organizational relationships it was morally possible for an individual to increase his status; stressed because the fissiparous centrifugal tendencies given by kinship and other segmentary groupings were counteracted by the centripetal integrative force supplied through existence of a 'big man'; articulate, because notions about the society's cultural integrity could be expressed through the 'big man' who was in himself a synthesized cultural image.

It seems that in traditional society ordinary men relied, for the

[1] A form of description adapted from D. F. Pocock 1961:111, 112.

determination of their individual status, on the existence of two polar status concepts, the 'big man' and the 'rubbish man'. By looking at either of these individuals a man could determine where he stood. He could see that his performance was better than that of a 'rubbish man' but not as good as the performance of a 'big man'. The existence of these two kinds of polar status concept gave ordinary men a form of individual status calibration. This system had validity because concepts of status and power had become static through institutionalization.

When the Europeans had control of the multi-purpose organizational framework the system no longer worked, though its structural integrity was preserved. Ordinary men could no longer calibrate their own individual status against that of the 'big man'. The only standard they could evaluate their performance against was the standard of the 'rubbish men'. Indigenous society then became disintegrated, unsocial, unstressed, and inarticulate. Disintegrated because traditional methods of achieving status no longer had any validity; unsocial because no matter how hard they tried individuals were unable to gain status; unstressed because centrifugal tendencies given by the kinship and other segmentary groupings were not balanced by any centripetal force since there was no traditional 'big man'; inarticulate, because notions about the society's cultural integrity could not be expressed through the medium of the European/'big man'.

In this way all the actions and events connected with the movements that have been examined were evaluated within the natives' existing horizon of experience. The process of change exhibited by these movements has been continuous, carrying forward the past and yet in some ways breaking with it to form something new.[1]

[1] K. O. L. Burridge 1960:41.

EPILOGUE

It is not the possessor of many things whom you will rightly call happy. The name of the happy man is claimed more justly by him who has learnt the art wisely to use what the Gods give, and who can endure the hardships of poverty, who dreads disgrace as something worse than death.[1]

The events of 1919 in the Gulf Division, Papua, were neither 'extraordinary' nor can they be described as 'madness'. Nor can the events of 1944 or 1963 be thought of as 'irrational'. All these events were purposive and logical in the light of indigenous knowledge. These movements show the strength and integrity of indigenous cultures in Papua and Melanesia, and that traditional values and ways of doing things have to some extent survived the impact of European culture. But they have been restrained movements on the whole when one considers the native talent for bloodshed revealed by their history and the part played by the natives during the war. Perhaps the one new policy initiated by the 'big men' has been one of peaceful co-existence.

Many of the unique features of these movements have possibly been obscured by attempts that have been made to treat 'cargo cults' in the same context as religious and millenary movements that have occurred in other areas. Although in relation to these other movements the 'cargo cults' may have had a few common features they have grown out of different cultures and different belief systems.

Sir Hubert Murray suggested that while experience of Colonial administration in Africa could be helpful, the peculiar circumstances of Papua called for a different kind of administration which could cater for the unique features of Papuan society. Modern theories on 'cargo' movements show that the echoes of that dispute in 1919 between Williams, the anthropologist whose theories told him how the facts should be interpreted, and Murray, the administrator who believed in experience, sympathy, and imagination, may still be with us.

---

[1] Horace, *Odes*, IV. viii. 45.

BIBLIOGRAPHY

A.A.	*American Anthropologist.*
A.O.	*Australian Outlook.*
B.J.S.	*British Journal of Sociology.*
B.S.I.P.	British Solomon Islands Protectorate.
H.J.	*Hibbert Journal.*
I.R.M.	*International Review of Missions.*
J.O.A.O.	*Journal of Administration Overseas.*
J.P.S.	*Journal of the Polynesian Society.*
J.R.A.I.	*Journal of the Royal Anthropological Institute.*
J.R.L.I.	*Journal of the Rhodes-Livingstone Institute.*
J.R.S.A.	*Journal of the Royal Society of Arts.*
M.I.T.	Massachusetts Institute of Technology.
M.M.O.	Missions Mariste d'Océanie.
M.N.C.	*Le Monde non Chrétienne.*
P.A.	*Pacific Affairs.*
P.A.R.	*Papuan Annual Report.*
P.I.M.	*Pacific Islands Monthly.*
P.O.I.C.	Pacific Order-in-Council 1893.
S.W.J.A.	*Southwestern Journal of Anthropology.*
T.P.N.G.	Territory of Papua and New Guinea.
W.P.H.C.	Western Pacific High Commission.

ABEL, C. E. (1907) *Savage Life in New Guinea* (London).

ADAMS, G. B. (1965) *Constitutional History of England* (London).

ALLEN, C. H. (1951) 'The Marching Rule. A Nativistic Cult of the British Solomon Islands', *Corona*, Vol. 3, No. 3, pp. 93–100.

BARBER, B. (1941) 'Acculturation and Messianic Movements', *American Sociological Review*, Vol. VI.

BARROW, G. L. (1951) 'The Story of Jon Frum', *Corona*, Vol. 3, No. 10.

BARROW, G. L. (1952) *Outlying Interlude*, unpublished MSS., Rhodes House library, Oxford.

BAUER, P. T. and YAMEY, B. S. (1957) *Economics of Underdeveloped Territories* (London).

BEATTIE, J. B. (1961) 'Cultural Contact and Social Change', *B.J.S.*, Vol. 12.

BEATTIE, J. B. (1964) *Other Cultures* (London).

BEAVER, W. N. (1920) *Unexplored New Guinea* (London).

BEIDELMAN, T. (1964) 'Pig (Guluwe): An Essay on Ngulu Sexual Symbolism', *S.W.J.A.*, Vol. 20, p. 359.

BELSHAW, C. S. (1947) 'Native Politics in the Solomon Islands', *P.A.*, Vol. 20, No. 2, pp. 187–93.

BELSHAW, C. S. (1948) 'The Postwar Solomon Islands', *Far Eastern Survey*, Vol. 27, No. 8, pp. 95–8.

BELSHAW, S. C. (1950a) *Island Administration in the South West Pacific* (London).

BELSHAW, C. S. (1950b) 'The Significance of Modern Cults in Melanesian Development', *A.O.*, Vol. 4, No. 2, pp. 116–25.

BELSHAW, C. S. (1951) 'Recent History of Mekeo Society', *Oceania*, Vol. 22, pp. 1–23.

BELSHAW, C. S. (1954) *Changing Melanesia* (Melbourne).

BELSHAW, C. S. (1957) *The Great Village* (London).

BERNDT, R. M. (1952) 'A Cargo Cult Movement in the East Central Highlands of New Guinea', *Oceania*, Vol. 23, Nos. 1–3, pp. 40–65, 137–58.

BERNDT, R. M. (1954) 'Reaction to Contact in the Eastern Highlands of New Guinea', *Oceania*, Vol. 24, Nos. 3–4, pp. 190–228, 255–75.

BERNDT, R. M. (1962) *Excess and Restraint: Social Control Among a New Guinea Mountain People* (Chicago).

BETTELHEIM, G. (1955) *Symbolic Wounds* (New York).

BETTELHEIM and JANOWITZ (1950) *Dynamics of Prejudice* (New York).

BEVAN, T. (1890) *Toil, Travel and Discovery in British New Guinea* (Sydney).

BLACKWOOD, B. (1935) *Both Sides of Buka Passage*, O.U.P.

BOGESI, G. (1948) 'Santa Ysabel, Solomon Islands', *Oceania*, Vol. 18, Nos. 3–4, pp. 208–32, 327–57.

BOSANQUET, B. (1920) *The Philosophical Theory of the State* (London).

B.S.I.P. (1897–1937, 1948–1966) Annual Reports.

BROWN, H. A. (n.d.) Unpublished papers at the L.M.S. H.Q. library in London.

BRUHL-LÉVY (1928) *The Soul of the Primitive* (London).

BURRIDGE, K. O. L. (1954a) 'Cargo Cult Activity in Tangu', *Oceania*, Vol. 24, No. 4.

BURRIDGE, K. O. L. (1954b) 'Racial Tension in Manam', *South Pacific*, Vol. 7, No. 15, pp. 932–8.

BURRIDGE, K. O. L. (1960) *Mambu* (London).

BURRIDGE, K. O. L. (1962) 'The Cargo Cult', *Discovery*, February.

BURROWS, W. (1950) 'The Background to Marching Rule', *P.I.M.*, 22.

BURTON, J. W. (1949) *Modern Missions in the South Pacific* (Washington).

BUTCHER, B. (1963) *We Lived with the Headhunters* (London).

CATO, A. C. (1947) 'A New Religious Cult in Fiji', *Oceania*, Vol. 18, No. 2, pp. 146–56.

CAULTON, S. G. (1950) 'The Marching Rule Delusion', *P.I.M.*, 21, I.

CENTRAL OFFICE OF INFORMATION (1966) *Among Those Present* (London).

CHALMERS, J. (1902) *Pioneering in New Guinea* (London).

CHINNERY, W. P., and HADDON, A. C. (1917) 'Five New Religious Cults, in British New Guinea', *H.J.*, Vol. 15, No. 3, pp. 448–63.

COCHRANE, D. G. (1968) Review of J. S. G. Wilson's 'Economic Survey of the New Hebrides', *Economica*, May.

COCKERELL-PEPYS, J. L. (1963) 'Small Scale Business Enterprise on Malaita', S.P.C. paper, February.

CODRINGTON, R. H. (1891) *The Melanesians: Studies in Their Anthropology and Folklore* (Oxford).

COHN, N. (1891) *The Pursuit of the Millennium* (London).

COOMBS, F., and FOX, C. E. (1915) 'Isles of Enchantment', *J.R.A.I.*, Vol. 45.

DAUNCEY, H. M. (1913) *Papuan Pictures* (London).

DAVENPORT, W., and COKER, W. (1967) 'The Moro Movement of Guadalcanal', *J.P.S.*, Vol. 76, No. 2, pp. 123–75.

DEACON, A. B. (1934) *Malekula, A Vanishing People in the New Hebrides* (London).

DE GRATZIA, A. (1963) *The Political Community: A Study of Anomie* (Chicago).

DIAMOND, S. (1960) *Plato and the Definition of the Primitive*, essays in honour of Paul Radin (New York).

DOVEY, J. W. (1950) *The Gospel in the South Pacific*, World Dominion Press.

DUMONT, L. (1960) 'World Renunciation in Indian Religion', *Contributions to Indian Sociology*, No. IV.

DUPEYRAT, A. (1948) *Papuan Conquest* (Melbourne).

DURKHEIM, É. (1915) *The Elementary Forms of the Religious Life: A Study in Religious Sociology*, trans. by J. W. Swain (London).

ELIADE, M. (1958) *Patterns in Comparative Religion*, trans. R. Shade (London).

ELIADE, M. (1955) *The Myth of the Eternal Return*, trans. W. R. Traslz (London).

ELIADE, M. (1964a) *Myth and Reality* (London).

ELIADE, M. (1964b) *Shamanism: Archaic Techniques of Ecstasy* (London).

ELKIN, A. P. (1953) *Social Anthropology in Melanesia* (London).

EMMET, D. (1959) 'Prophets and Their Societies', *J.R.A.I.*, Vol. 89, Part I, pp. 13–23.

EVANS-PRITCHARD, E. E. (1937) *Witchcraft, Oracles and Magic Among the Azande* (London).

EVANS-PRITCHARD, E. E. (1940) *The Nuer* (London).

EVANS-PRITCHARD, E. E. (1951) *Social Anthropology* (London).

EVANS-PRITCHARD, E. E. (1954) *The Institutions of Primitive Society*.

EYERDAM, W. J. (1953) *Natural History* (London).

FELDT, E. (1946) *The Coastwatchers* (Melbourne).

FINDLAY, J. N. (1958) *Hegel: A Re-examination* (London).

FIRTH, R. (1929) *Economics of the New Zealand Maori* (London).

FIRTH, R. (1940) 'The Analysis of Mana: An Empirical Approach', *J.P.S.*, Vol. 49, pp. 483–510.

FIRTH, R. (1948) 'Religious Belief and Personal Adjustment', *J.R.A.I.*, Vol. 78.

FIRTH, R. (1951) *Elements of Social Organisation* (London).

FIRTH, R. (1953) 'Social Changes in the Western Pacific', *J.R.S.A.*, Vol. 101, No. 4909, pp. 803–19.

FIRTH, R. (1954) *The Institutions of Primitive Society* (London).

FIRTH, R. (1955) 'The Theory of "Cargo Cults": A Note on Tikopia', *Man*, Vol. 55, No. 142, pp. 130–2.

FIRTH, R. (1964) *Essays on Social Organisation and Values* (London).

FIRTH, R. (1967) *Tikopia Ritual and Belief* (London).

FLEISCHMAN, E. (1964) *La Philosophie Politique de Hegel, sous forme d'un commentaire de Fondements de la Philosophie du Droit* (Paris).

FLINT, L. A. (1920) 'Northern Division, Iowa District, Report of an A.R.M.', *P.A.R.*

FORTES, M. (1936) 'Culture Contact as a Dynamic Process', *Africa*, Vol. 9, No. 1, pp. 24–55.

FORTES, M. (1962) 'Ritual and Office in Tribal Society', *Essays on the Ritual of Social Relations*, ed. Gluckman (Manchester).

FORTES, M., and EVANS-PRITCHARD, E. E. (1940) *African Political Systems* (London).

FORTUNE, T. (1963) *Sorcerers of Dobu* (London).

176   BIBLIOGRAPHY

FOSTER, M. B. (1935) *The Political Philosophy of Plato and Hegel* (London).
FOX, C. E. (1924) *Threshold of the Pacific* (London).
FOX, C. E. (1958) *Lord of the Southern Isles* (London).
FOX, C. E. (1964) *Kakamora* (London).
FRERICHS, A. C. (1947) 'The Vailala Madness', *Lutheran Missionary*, May, No. 5.
FRIEDRICH, C. J. (1963) *Man and His Govt.: An Empirical Theory of Politics* (New York).
FÜLÖP-MILLER, R. (1935) *Leaders, Dreamers and Rebels*, trans. by E. and C. Paul (London).
GARDINER, P. (1959) *Theories of History* (London).
GLUCKMAN, M. (1962) *Essays on the Ritual of Social Relations* (Manchester).
GOODE, W. J. (1951) *Religion Among the Primitives* (Glencoe).
GRATTAN, C. H. (1963) *The Southwest Pacific Since 1900* (New York).
GROVES, W. C. (1936) *Native Education and Culture Contact in New Guinea* (London).
GREEN, T. H. (1895) *Lectures on the Principles of Political Obligation* (London).
GUIART, J. (1951a) 'Cargo Cults and Political Evolution in Melanesia', *South Pacific*, Vol. 5, No. 7, pp. 128–9.
GUIART, J. (1951b) 'John Frum Movement in Tanna', *Oceania*, Vol. 22, No. 3, pp. 165–75.
GUIART, J. (1951c) 'Forerunners of Melanesian Nationalism', *Oceania*, Vol. 22, No. 2, pp. 81–90.
GUIART, J. (1952a) 'Report of the Native Situation in the North of Ambrym (NH)', *South Pacific*, Vol. 5, No. 12, pp. 256–67.
GUIART, J. (1952b) 'The Co-operative Called the Malekula Native Company: A Borderline Type of Cargo Cult', *South Pacific*, Vol. 6 No. 6, pp. 429–32.
GUIART, J. (1956a) 'Culture Contact and the Jon Frum Movementi n Tanna, New Hebrides', *S.W.J.A.*, Vol. 9, No. 1, pp. 105–16.
GUIART, J. (1956b) 'Grands et petits hommes de la montagne, Espiritu Santo (N.H.)', Institut Français d'Océanie, New Caledonia.
GUPPY, H. B. (1887) *The Solomon Islands and Their Natives* (London).
HADDON, A. C. (1920) 'Migrations of Culture in British New Guinea', *J.R.A.I.*, Vol. 50.
HADDON, A. C. (1935) 'Sabai, A New Cult', *Report of the Cambridge Expedition to the Torres Straits*, I (London).
HANNEMAN, E. F. (1948) 'Le culte du cargo en Nouvelle Guinée', *M.N.C.*, Vol. 8.
HEALEY, A. M. (1966) 'Administration in the British Solomon Islands Protectorate', *J.O.A.O.*, Vol. 5, No. 3, July, pp. 194–204.

HERSKOWITS, M. J. (1938) *Acculturation* (New York).
HERSKOWITS, M. J. (1948) *Man and His Works* (New York).
HERTZ, R. (1960) *Death and the Right Hand*, English translation by R. and C. Needham (Aberdeen).
HIDES, J. G. (1935) *Through Wildest Papua* (London).
HIDES, J. G. (1938) *Savages in Serge* (Sydney).
HOGBIN, H. I. (1936) 'Mana', *Oceania*, Vol. 6, No. 3.
HOGBIN, H. I. (1939a) 'Social Advancement in Guadalcanal, Solomon Islands', *Oceania*, Vol. 8, No. 3.
HOGBIN, H. I. (1939b) *Experiments in Civilisation* (London).
HOGBIN, H. I. (1944) 'Native Councils and Native Courts in the Solomon Islands', *Oceania*, Vol. 11, No. 4.
HOGBIN, H. I. (1951) *Transformation Scene* (London).
HOGBIN, H. I. (1958) *Social Change* (London).
HOLMES, J. (1902a) 'Initiation Ceremonies of the Natives of the Papuan Gulf', *J.R.A.I.*, Vol. 32, pp. 418–25.
HOLMES, J. (1902b) 'Notes on the Religious Ideas of the Elema Tribe of the Papuan Gulf', *J.R.A.I.*, Vol. 32, pp. 426–31.
HOLMES, J. (1903) 'Notes on the Elema Tribe of the Papuan Gulf', *J.R.A.I.*, Vol. 33, pp. 125–34.
HOLMES, J. (1905) 'Introductory Notes to the Study of Totemism of the Elema Tribe of the Papuan Gulf', *Man*, Vol. 5.
HOLMES, J. (1908) 'Introductory Notes on Toys and Games of Elema, Papuan Gulf', *J.R.A.I.*, Vol. 38, pp. 280–8.
HOLMES, J. (1923) *By Canoe to Cannibal Land* (London).
HOLMES, J. (1924) *In Primitive New Guinea* (London).
HOLMES, J. (n.d.) Unpublished papers at the L.M.S. H.Q. library, London.
HOLMES, J. (1926) *Way Back in Papua* (London).
HOLTKER, G. (1946) 'A New Cult is Born', *P.I.M.*, Vol. 17, No. 4.
HOPKIN, A. I. (1928) *The Isles of King Solomon* (London).
HORTON, D. C. (1965) *The Happy Isles* (London).
HORTON, R. (1960) 'A Definition of Religion and its Uses', *J.R.A.I.*, Vol. 90, Part I, pp. 201–5.
HUGHES, B. (1959) *King Among Cannibals* (London).
HUMPHRIES, W. R. (1925–6) 'The Ehalo Ceremony', *Papuan Report*.
INGLIS, J. (1957) 'Cargo Cults and the Problems of Explanation', *Oceania*, Vol. 27, No. 4, pp. 249–63.
INGLIS, J. (1959) 'Interpretation of Cargo Cults: Comments', *Oceania*, Vol. 30, No. 2, pp. 155–8.
INGLIS, J. (1961) Review of Burridge, K. O. L.: 'Mambu, Melanesian Millennium, *J.P.S.*, Vol. 70.
INSELMAN, R. (1946) 'Cargo Cults Are Not Caused by Missions', *P.I.M.*, Vol. 16, No. 2.

IVENS, W. G. (1914) 'Native Stories From Ulawa', *J.R.A.I.*, Vol. 44.

IVENS, W. G. (1927) *Melanesians of the South East Solomon Islands* (London).

JACOBI, J. (1959) *Complex Archetype in the Psychology of C. G. Jung* (London).

JARVIE, I. C. (1964) *The Revolution in Anthropology* (London).

JONES-PRYCE (n.d.) Unpublished papers, L.M.S. H.Q. library, London.

JUNG, C. G. (1959) *Flying Saucers* (London).

KAUFFMAN, W. (1960) *The Owl and the Nightingale* (London).

KEESING, F. M. (1942) *The South Seas in the Modern World* (London).

KELMAN, J. H. (1906) *The Story of Chalmers in New Guinea* (London).

KESBY, J. D. (1963) 'British Missionaries in the South-West Pacific 1842–1900; Their Evaluations and Policies with Regard to the Indigenous Peoples'. Unpublished B. Litt. thesis (Oxford).

KHUMH, F. C. (1952) 'Messianic Movements in Western New Guinea', *I.R.M.*, Vol. 41, p. 162.

KING, C. (1912–13) 'The Baigona Cult', *P.A.R.*

KNIBBS, S. G. C. (1929) *The Savage Solomons As They Were and Are* (London).

KNOX, MGR. R. A. (1950) *Enthusiasm*, O.U.P.

KRIEGER, H. W. (1943) *Island Peoples of the Western Pacific: Micronesia and Polynesia* (Washington).

KROEF, J. M. VAN DER (1952) 'The Messiah in Indonesia and Melanesia', *Scientific Monthly*, Vol. 75, pp. 161–5.

LANAUZE, J. A. (1963) *Six Great Australians* (Sydney).

LANDTMAN, G. (1927) *The Kiwai Papuans* (London).

LAWRENCE, P. (1954) 'Cargo Cult and Religious Beliefs Among the Garia', *International Archives of Anthropology*, Vol. 47.

LAWRENCE, P. (1955) 'The Madang District Cargo Cult', *South Pacific*, Vol. 8, No. 1.

LAWRENCE, P. (1964) *Road B'long Cargo* (Manchester).

LEACH, E. (1964) 'Anthropological Aspects of Language: Animal Categories and Verbal Abuse', in *New Directions in the Study of Language*, ed. E. Lenneberg, M.I.T.

LEACH, E. (1966) *Rethinking Anthropology* (London).

LEESON, I. (1952) 'Bibliography of Cargo Cults and Other Nativistic Movements in the South Pacific', *S.P.C. technical paper No. 30.*

LEGGE, J. D. (1956) *Australian Colonial Policy* (London).

LEGISLATIVE COUNCIL (1960–1966) *Debates*, Govt. Printer, Honiara, B.S.I.P.

LENNOX, C. (1905) *James Chalmers of New Guinea* (London).

LETT, L. (1942) *The Papuan Achievement* (Melbourne).

LETT, L. (1949) *Sir Hubert Murray of Papua* (London).

LETT, M. (1955) 'Vailala Madness, Wave of Religious Fanaticism that Swept Papua in 1919', *P.I.M.*, Vol. 6, No. 5.

LÉVI-STRAUSS, C. (1949) *Les Structures Élémentaires de la Parenté.*

LÉVI-STRAUSS, C. (1958) *Anthropologie Structurale* (Paris).

LÉVI-STRAUSS, C. (1966) *The Savage Mind* (London).

LIENHARDT, G. (1962) *Divinity and Experience, The Religion of the Dinka* (Oxford).

LIENHARDT, G. (1964) *Social Anthropology* (London).

LIENHARDT, G. (1965) 'Plato and the Vailala Madness', B.B.C. 3rd Programme Talk, March.

LINK, L. M. (1915) *Chalmers the Peace Scout* (London).

LINTON, R. (1943) 'Nativistic Movements', *A.A.*, Vol. 45, No. 1, pp. 230–40.

LONDON MISSIONARY SOCIETY (1906–1922) Annual Reports.

LOVETT, R. (1920) *Tamate. The Life and Adventures of a Christian Hero* (London).

LOWIE, R. H. (1925) *Primitive Religion* (London).

LUKE, SIR HARRY (1945) *From a South Seas Diary, 1938–42* (London).

LUKE, SIR HARRY (1962) *Islands of the South Pacific* (London).

MACKAY, COLONEL K. (1909) *Across Papua* (London).

MACQUARIE, H. (1945) *Vouza and the Solomon Islands* (London).

MAHER, R. F. (1958) 'The Tommy Kabu Movement of the Purari Delta', *Oceania*, Vol. 29, No. 2, pp. 75–90.

MAHER, R. F. (1961) *New Men of Papua*, Madison, Wisconsin.

MAINE, SIR H. S. (1931) *Ancient Law* (London).

MAIR, L. P. (1948) *Australia in New Guinea* (London).

MAIR, L. P. (1958) 'The Pursuit of the Millennium in Melanesia', *B.J.S.*, Vol. 9.

MAIR, L. P. (1959) 'Independent Religious Movements in Three Continents', *Comparative Studies in Sociology and History*, Vol. I.

MAITLAND, F. W. (1911) *Constitutional History of England* (London).

MALINOWSKI, B. (1922) *Argonauts of the Western Pacific* (London).

MALINOWSKI, B. (1926) *Myth in Primitive Psychology* (London).

MALINOWSKI, B. (1935) *Coral Gardens* (London).

MALINOWSKI, B. (1946) *Dynamics of Culture Change. An Enquiry into Race Relations in Africa* (New Haven).

MANDER, L. A. (1954) *Some Dependent Peoples of the South Pacific* (New York).

MARCUSE, H. (1941) *Reason and the Rise of Social Revolution: Hegel and the Rise of Social Theory* (London).

MARTIN, P. H. (1956) 'Modern Cults in Melanesia', unpublished B. Litt. thesis on cargo cults, Oxford University.

MAUSS, M. (1967) *The Gift* (New York).

McCauley, J. P. (1960) 'We Are Men—What Are You?', *Quadrant*, Vol. 15.

McKeown, R. (1954) 'Dialectic in Political Thought and Action', *Ethics*, Vol. 65, No. 1, pp. 1–33.

Mead, M. (1942) *Growing Up in New Guinea* (New York).

Mead, M. (1956) *New Lives for Old* (London).

Miller, J. G. (1948) 'Naked cults in Central West Santo', *J.P.S.*, Vol. 57, No. 4.

Monckton, C. A. W. (1922) *The Last Days in New Guinea* (London).

Monckton, C. A. W. (1934) *New Guinea Recollections* (London).

Monckton, C. A. W. (1936a) *Experiences of a New Guinea R.M.* (New York).

Monckton, C. A. W. (1936b) *Further Adventures of a New Guinea R.M.* (London).

Montauban, P. (1948) 'Le Grand Rêve Buka', *M.M.O.*

Mooney, J. (1892) 'The Ghost Dance Religion and the Sioux Outbreak of 1890', 14th Annual Report of the Bureau of Ethnology to the Secretary of the Smithsonian Institute.

Morrell, W. P. (1960) *Britain in the Pacific Islands* (Oxford).

Mure, G. R. G. (1940) *An Introduction to Hegel*, O.U.P.

Murray, G. G. A. (1900) *Liberalism and the Empire* (London).

Murray, G. G. A. (1934) *The Cult of Violence* (London).

Murray, G. G. A. (1944) *Humanism*, one of three B.B.C. Talks.

Murray, G. G. A. (1955) *A Comparison of the Aims of the Anti-Slavery Movement* (London).

Murray, G. H. (1919–20) Reports on the 'Vailala Madness', *P.A.R.*

Murray, J. H. P. (1912) *Papua or British New Guinea* (London).

Murray, J. H. P. (1925) *Papua of Today; Or an Australian Colony in the Making* (London).

Nadel, S. F. (1951) *The Foundations of Social Anthropology* (London).

Nadel, S. F. (1957) *The Theory of Social Structure* (London).

Nairne, W. P. (1913) *Greatheart of Papua* (London).

Needham, R. (1960) 'The Left Hand of the Mugwe: An Analytical Note on the Structure of Meru Symbolism', *Africa*, Vol. 30, No. 1, pp. 20–33.

Oelricks, A. E. (1911–12) Annual Report on the Affairs of the Kumasi Division, *P.A.R.*

Oliver, D. L. (1955) *A Solomon Island Society* (Camb., Mass.).

O'Reilly, P. (1947) 'Les Chrétiennes Mélanésiennes et la Guerre', *Neue Zeitschrift für Missionswissenschaft*, 3rd year, No. 2, pp. 106–17.

O'Reilly, P. (1948) 'Malaita (Îles Salomon), un exemple de revendications indigènes', *M.M.O.*, 2nd year, No. 15, pp. 149–52.

O'Reilly, P. (1949) 'Prophétisme aux Jon Frum à Tanna (1940–47)', *M.N.C.*, No. 10, pp. 192–208.

O'REILLY, P. (1950) 'Jon Frum is New Hebridean Cargo Cult', *P.I.M.*, Vol. 20, No. 6.

O'REILLY, P., and SÉDÈS, J. M. (1949) *Jaunes, Noirs et Blancs* (Paris).

PAPUAN ANNUAL REPORTS 1906–7 onwards, Govt. Printer, Port Moresby.

PATON, W. F. (1952) 'The Native Situation in the North of Ambrym', *South Pacific*, Vol. 6, No. 5.

PETERSEN, N. (1966) 'The Church Council of South Mala: A Legitimised Form of Marching Rule', *Oceania*, Vol. 36, No. 3.

PLAMENATZ, J. (1963) *Man and Society* (London).

POCOCK, D. F. (1961) *Social Anthropology* (London).

POPPER, K. R. (1961) *The Poverty of Historicism* (London).

POS, H. (1950) 'The Revolt of Mansren', *A.A.*, Vol. 52, No. 4, p. 251.

RABAUL TIMES 27th August 1926, and 22nd March 1929.

RADCLIFFE-BROWN, A. R. (1952) *Structure and Function in Primitive Society* (London).

READ, M. K. E. (1947) 'Effects of the Pacific War in the Markham Valley, New Guinea', *Oceania*, Vol. 18, No. 2.

READ, M. K. E. (1952) 'Missionary Activities and Social Change in the Central Highlands of Papua and New Guinea', *South Pacific*, Vol. 5, No. 2.

READ, M. K. E. (1959) 'Leadership and Consensus in a New Guinea Society', *A.A.*, Vol. 61, pp. 425–36.

REASON, J. (1942) *Tales from Chalmers* (London).

REID, T. W. (1960) *A Man Like Bati* (London).

RENTOUL, A. (1949) 'Jon Frum: Origins of the New Hebridean Movement', *P.I.M.*, Vol. 19, No. 6.

RIVERS, W. H. R. (1914) *History of Melanesian Society* (London).

RIVERS, W. H. R. (1922) *Essays on the Depopulation of Melanesia*.

ROBSON, W. M. (1887) *James Chalmers, Missionary and Explorer of Rarotonga and New Guinea* (London).

RUSSELL, T. (1950) 'The Fataleka of Malaita', *Oceania*, Vol. 21, No. 1, pp. 1–13.

Report of the Commissioner to enquire into circumstances in which murderous attacks took place in 1927 on Govt. officials on Guadalcanal and Malaita. Command 3248, H.M.S.O.

SABINE, G. (1963) *A History of Political Theory* (London).

SAHLINS, M. D. (1964) 'Poor man, Rich man, Big Man, Chief', *Ethnology*, October, Vol. 3, No. 4.

SALISBURY, R. F. (1962) *From Stone to Steel* (Melbourne).

SALMOND, SIR J. (1957) *Jurisprudence or the Theory of Law* (London).

SARGENT, W. (1957) *The Battle for the Mind* (London).

SCHAPERA, I. (1953) 'Some Comments on Comparative Method in Social Anthropology, *A.A.*, Vol. 55.

SCHEFFLER, H. W. (1965) *Choiseul Island Social Structure* (Los Angeles).

SELIGMAN, C. G. (1910) *The Melanesians of British New Guinea* (London).

SETON, W. (1909) *Chalmers of New Guinea* (London).

SMITH, M. W. (1959) 'Toward a Classification of Cult Movement', *Man*, Vol. 59, No. 2, pp. 8–12.

SOUTH PACIFIC COMMISSION 1952 'The Purari Delta—Background and Progress of Community Development', technical paper No. 35 (Sydney).

STANLEY, SIR ROBERT (1956) 'Political Progress in the B.S.I.P.', unpublished Govt. paper, Honiara.

STANNER, W. E. H. (1953) *The South Seas in Transition* (London).

STANNER, W. E. H. (1958) 'On the Interpretation of Cargo Cults', *Oceania*, Vol. 29, pp. 1–25.

SUNDKLER, B. G. M. (1964) *Bantu Prophets in South Africa* (London).

TAYLOR, C. R. H. (1951) *A Pacific Bibliography* (Wellington).

TEULSCHER, N. J. (1948) 'Some Mission Problems in Post-War Indonesia', *I.R.M.*, Vol. 37.

THOMPSON, W. H. H. (1940–1) 'Native Disturbances in Mekeo District', *P.A.R.*

THRUPP, S. (1962) 'Millennial dreams in action', essays in comparative study, ed. by S. L. Thrupp (*Comp. Studies in Soc. and Hist.*, Supp. 1.2, The Hague).

THURNWALD, R. 'Price of the White Man's Peace', *P.A.*, Vol. 9, No. 3, pp. 347–57.

WALLACE, A. F. C. (1956) 'Revitalisation Movements', *A.A.*, Vol. 58, pp. 264–81.

WARD, J. M. (1948) *British Policy in the South Pacific* (Sydney).

WAWN, W. T. (1893) *The South Sea Islanders* (London).

WEBER, M. (1947a) *Theory of Social and Economic Organisation* (London).

WEBER, M. (1947b) *The Methodology of the Social Sciences*.

WEDGWOOD, C. H. (1927) 'Death and Social Status in Melanesia', *J.R.A.I.*, Vol. 57, pp. 377–97.

WILLIAMS, F. E. (1919–20) 'The Vailala Madness and the Destruction of Native Ceremonies in the Gulf Division', *Papuan Anthropological Reports*, No. 4.

WILLIAMS, F. E. (1928) *Orokaiva Magic*.

WILLIAMS, F. E. (1932) 'Trading Voyages from the Gulf of Papua', *Oceania*, Vol. 3, No. 2, pp. 139–66.

WILLIAMS, F. E. (1934) 'The Vailala Madness in Retrospect', *Essays presented to C. G. Seligman*, pp. 369–79.

WILLIAMS, F. E. (1939a) 'Seclusion and Age Grouping in the Gulf of Papua', *Oceania*, Vol. 9, No. 4.

WILLIAMS, F. E. (1939b) 'The Creed of a Government Anthropologist', *Presidential Address, Australian and New Zealand Association for the Advancement of Science*.

WILLIAMS, F. E. (1940) *Drama of Orokolo* (Oxford).
WILSON, J. S. G. (1965) *An Economic Survey of the New Hebrides* (London).
WOODFORD, C. M. (1890) *A Naturalist Among the Headhunters* (London).
WORSLEY, P. M. (1957a) 'Millenarian Movements in Melanesia', *J.R.L.I.*, Vol. 21, pp. 18–31.
WORSLEY, P. M. (1957b) *The Trumpet Shall Sound: A Study of Cargo Cults in Melanesia.*
W.P.H.C. (1937) *Public Services Reorganisation Report*, Govt. printer (Sydney).
W.P.H.C. (1938) Press Release, Public Relations Office, Suva, 31st July.
W.P.H.C. (1962) Education White Paper.
W.P.H.C. (1964) White Paper on Agriculture and Fisheries.
W.P.H.C. (1966) Communications White Paper.
W.P.H.C. (1967) White Paper on the Proposed Revision of the Constitution.
WRIGHT, L. W. S. (1940) 'The Vele Magic of the South Solomons', *J.R.A.I.*, Vol. 70.
WUTH, C. T. (1919) Northern Division Report, *P.A.R.*

INDEX